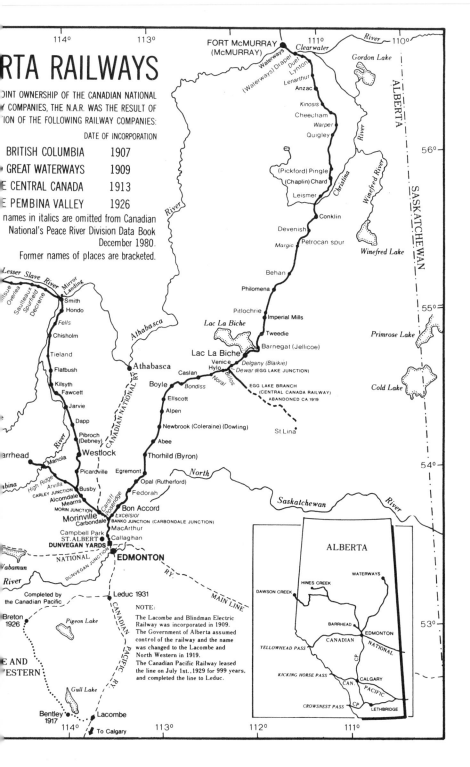

Ribbons of Steel

The Story of the Northern Alberta Railways

Ena Schneider

Detselig Enterprises Limited
Calgary, Alberta

© 1989, 2002 by
Ena Schneider

with the assistance of
Maurice Mahood and **Clarence Comrie**

Canadian Cataloguing in Publication Data
Schneider, Ena.
   Ribbons of steel

   Includes index.
   ISBN 1-55059-239-4

   1. Northern Alberta Railways – History.
2. Railroads – Alberta – History.   I. Title.
HE2810.N67S36   1989   385'.097123   C89-091209-2

Detselig Enterprises Ltd.
210, 1220 Kensington Road NW
Calgary, Alberta T2N 3P5

www.temerondetselig.com
email: temeron@telusplanet.net
phone: (403) 283-0900; fax: (403)283-6947   Front cover by Harry Savage

Printed in Canada   SAN 115-0324   ISBN 1-55059-239-4

Dedication

- To Maurice D.B. Mahood whose dearest wish was to see the Northern Alberta Railways story in print. He did not live to see his ambition realized, but left an accumulation of material from his proposed book and two partners who shared his vision. Although this is not the book he had envisioned, I hope it is one of which he would have been proud.

- To R.D. Clarence Comrie, the catalyst for this project. Without his assistance, enthusiasm and unwavering support it might have fallen by the wayside. Besides being generous with his time and advice, he provided an enviable collection of photographs, a wealth of archival material, experience and knowledge gained during a forty-five year railway career.

Contents

Part Four
NAR and the Depression: 1930-1939

Part Five
The War Years: 1940-1945

Part Six
The Final Years: 1946-1980

Foreword

The 920 mile network of railways north of Edmonton, stretching into the northernmost recesses of Alberta and long known as Northern Alberta Railways, formed, at one stage, one of eight provincially owned railway systems which existed at one time or another in the ten provinces of Canada.

The process of provincial government initiative in railway building in Canada began in the four Atlantic provinces between the 1850s and the 1880s – prior to the entry of each entity into Confederation – and continued well into the twentieth century. Quebec owned and operated its own railway system for a brief but colorful period in the 1870s and 1880s. Ontario, Alberta and British Columbia followed with development railways after the turn of the twentieth century; Manitoba and Saskatchewan alone avoided the challenges of provincial ownership. *Ribbons of Steel* describes the last of these provincial enterprises to be undertaken.

It is a complex yet fascinating story, using as a background the people and economic needs of countless hinterland communities, many of whose names commemorate pioneer settlers and railwaymen. Ena Schneider's approach to this work is, in my opinion, the embodiment of Thomas Carlyle's observation that history is the essence of innumerable biographies. Its emphasis is upon the personalities involved, rather than the minutiae of operations and technology.

The dominant figure at the inception of the story, John Duncan McArthur, a pioneer entrepreneur, brought railways to northern Alberta. He was accompanied, and followed by countless other individuals; many of more modest accomplishments but with colorful names such as "Cowboy" Barker, "Pinky" Fleming, "Smiler" Hadley and "Protestant Bill" Preston.

In a word, the text is based on that single, vital ingredient of any narrative of societal accomplishment: people. The author's zest for this aspect of the story and her thorough approach to the task is evidenced by the innumerable mini-biographies which the text incorporates as well as by the variety of sources listed in the notes. The result demonstrates that despite its relatively large size, the NAR was a "family-type" operation in the social sense. Obeying that concept, children often routinely followed their parents into its service.

Though I travelled on the NAR as far back as the 1950s, I knew only one of its major personalities, the late Ken Perry – a former CPR officer – who was the line's general manager until his sudden death in 1977. Even that casual acquaintance with the NAR made me conscious of a unity of purpose among its personnel which was more commonly met with on much smaller lines. That the author, as an NAR employee, was a part of the story lends a dimension of authenticity and credibility to this account, making it as much a "memoir" of the community which it served as a general history of a major Canadian railway.

Omer Lavallee
Emeritus Corporate Historian and
Archivist, Canadian Pacific Limited

Detselig Enterprises Ltd. appreciates the financial
assistance for its 1989 publishing program from

Alberta Foundation for the Literary Arts
Canada Council
Department of Communications
Alberta Culture.

Acknowledgements

A debt of gratitude is due to all those organizations and individuals who helped in various ways with this book. I am particularly indebted to Mary Mahoney-Robson, who volunteered many evenings and a vacation to edit the manuscript. Her assistance, patience and encouragement have been invaluable. The final format is the result of the untiring efforts of Editor Leslie Chapman to produce a class one product and her pleasant disposition has been much appreciated.

A special thank you to Harry Savage, an Alberta artist, photographer and professor with the Faculty of Extension, University of Alberta, who found the time to produce the cover of this book while preparing for a major exhibition of his paintings in Edmonton.

Thanks is also due Geoff Lester and his skillful staff at the Department of Geography, University of Alberta, who provided the detailed map for the endpapers.

My appreciation is also due Clarence Comrie, Omer Lavallee, Bill Donlevy, Gordon Waite, Otto Michetti, George Stephenson, Jim Pitts, and Al Smith who all proofread the work, and gave valuable advice. A special word of thanks is due Omer Lavallee who provided the foreword, Gordon Waite who gave access to his unpublished writings on NAR, Gerald Whiteman for the use of his papers and Jim Williams for his ED & BC Railway thesis.

CN Rail and CP Rail showed their confidence in a tangible manner by their commitment to purchase copies of this book. For their encouragement and assistance, thanks is extended to the staff at CP Rail Corporate Archives in Montreal and CN Rail staff in Edmonton, particularly Ross Walker, Senior Vice-President, Western Canada; Bo Jensen, Administrative Services; Paul Hawirko, Manager, Employee Relations Services; and Ed Boychuk, Supervisor, Pensions and Employee Benefits. Paul A. Foug, Mary Watson, Mike Maccagno, Lon Marsh, and Joe Pereira have all supplied useful and much appreciated information.

Regrettably, Glen Barker and Bill Smith, who provided first-hand accounts of the early railways, did not live to see the project completed. Their memories were something to be desired by those half their ages.

Acknowledgement must be made of the generous cooperation of the staff at the numerous archives and museums where I did research, particularly the Edmonton Public School Archives-Museum for the use of photographic facilities.

My gratitude is also due Helmut, my husband, who has endured piles of papers, photographs and books throughout the house, and now plans to have a huge bonfire.

The list could go on but the most important tribute must be paid to the railroaders and their families who shared their time, memories and photographs. They were an inspiration and this is their story.

E.S.

Introduction

This book salutes the dedicated men and women of the Northern Alberta Railways Company. Many of them were colorful and interesting characters who endured untold hardships to build and operate a network of rail lines spreading over northern Alberta and British Columbia. These men and women made the NAR, once Canada's third largest railway, one that has earned its place in the history of Canada.

The rail network scattered across the north comprised several small railroads until 1929 when Canadian National and Canadian Pacific Railways jointly acquired the railroads and molded them into one, the Northern Alberta Railways Company. John Duncan McArthur, an Ontario-born farm boy who became a lumberman, railroad contractor and millionaire, built the original railways. In northern Alberta and northeastern British Columbia, J.D. McArthur brought to reality the dream of railways. In the process, he lost the rail lines and a fortune, but he left a lasting legacy.

Working on the northern railways snaking their way through the vast unknown northland was not for the faint of heart. In the early days, conditions were atrocious and demanded a special breed of men. The workers on the railway came from many different backgrounds. Their reasons for being in Alberta were as diverse as their nationalities.

A few came looking for adventure. The idea of opening up the West appealed to them and they relished the thought of the vast wilderness and its isolation. Some had been blackballed on American railroads for various reasons, often trade union activities, and knew only railroading. To them Canada was a haven. Others came from central and western Europe. They left their homelands to travel to a land where the prospects for the future looked brighter. They were willing to work hard to make a decent life for themselves and their families. To most, the language and culture were formidable barriers they would overcome; but here there were opportunities denied them in their own countries. They accepted and adjusted to the harsh climate and tough lifestyle. Blacks came from the southern part of the United States searching for freedom from discrimination. Immigrants from the British Isles came out to "The Colonies," looking for jobs and a better life.

This rough and undeveloped land left very little room for class distinction. The crews who built and operated the railway were a cosmopolitan lot. Men born in Canada, worked alongside Englishmen, Italians, Swedes, Ukrainians, Poles, Americans, Irishmen, and Scotsmen. At the outset there were prejudices to overcome, but in time a closeness developed among these railroaders. As a result, members of different families married and thus strengthened the railroad family bonds.

Railroaders' wives needed the courage, determination and stamina that enabled pioneer women to endure the hardships and loneliness they had to face. Assistant station agents and telegraph operators moved constantly. Often their wives and children went with them and frequently home was a hotel room or tent. In many cases, the families of track maintenance men lived isolated from the rest of the world in bunk cars in the bush. Bridge and building workers could be away for months at a time, and those in the running trades and communications were subject to call at any time. Their spouses learned to cope with whatever family crises arose, and did so admirably.

There was a certain amount of squabbling and quarrelling in railroad communities, but when disaster befell a colleague's family the others were supportive, caring and compassionate. This family feeling continued throughout the lifetime of these northern railways. It was often disadvantageous as in the case of a derailment when the rest of the crew tried to cover up for the one at fault, so that he would not be disciplined by management or taken out of service. Many a station agent's wife saved her husband's job by taking over his duties if he was sick or took solace in the bottle. [General Rule G, which prohibits drinking by railroad employees, is used as a club by railway companies to make railroads safer. Discipline is meted out by the Brown system. Sixty demerits on the record of a railroader means it is time to get the walking shoes out and start job hunting.]

But, when happy events occurred in a railroad community all took joy in the sharing. It was common for another family to take in the children when a household split up. Not everyone could cope with the harshness of the land or the isolation, particularly during the 1930s, and railroaders saw much heartache and depression. A quality they had in common was kindness of spirit; dollars were in short supply, but friendship was in plenty. Entertainment was self-made, and the railroad had its share of practical jokers.

Recognizing the closeness akin to that of a family among Northern Alberta Railways employees, the railway's General Manager, Jim Pitts, honored surviving employees and pensioners who had been employed by the railway at the time of its incorporation in 1929. At an afternoon tea on 16 September 1979, as part of the NAR's fiftieth anniversary celebrations, these veterans shared the feeling that each had made a contribution to the building and operation of a railway which had opened up vast areas of western Canada.

Less than a year later, at a meeting of the Northern Alberta Railways board, an agreement was ratified by the parent lines for the acquisition by CN Rail of CP Rail's fifty percent share of NAR. The NAR system and staff were successfully absorbed into the CN Rail network in 1981. The days of northern Alberta's frontier railway operating as a separate entity came to an end, but the friendships cemented by the years among its employees continues.

Through these pages, you will walk between two steel rails, hand in hand with railroaders, and experience their trials and successes as the fledgling railways grow into a modern transportation system. I think you will agree Northern Alberta Railways Company was indeed no ordinary railroad and its people a breed apart.

Locomotive No. 7. Heavy canvas hung at entrance to open cab.
Photo: Courtesy of R.D.C. Comrie

Part One

*The Edmonton, Dunvegan & British
Columbia Railway: 1910-1919*

John Duncan McArthur
railway contractor, 1854-1927.
Photo: Courtesy of Miss Mary Watson

1

Being in the West is no Accident

"It's coming! It's coming! The railway is finally coming!" What excitement this news generated. In settlements scattered across the Peace River country in western Canada the general store was a buzz with anticipation. Settlers rushed home to tell the good news to their families who had endured much in this harsh, unforgiving northland.

News travelled by "moccasin telegraph" to the Peace River country in 1912. Rumors of railways building into the north had been reaching the ears of settlers for years, but they remained rumors and no railway was built. Finally work had begun on a railway into northern Alberta – a railway settlers believed would bring them prosperity. They could now look to the future with hope and perhaps supplement their meager resources with employment on the railway.

This was the era of "paper" railways. When the Edmonton, Dunvegan and British Columbia Railway [ED & BC] was chartered

in 1907 by a group of speculators, there was nothing to suggest that it was any different from the many others that remained the dreams of imaginative promoters. It too was a railway on paper until John Duncan McArthur, a speculator with vision and determination, brought the dream to reality. A pioneer railway contractor and lumberman from Winnipeg, Manitoba, McArthur took up the challenge of constructing railways through the vast, untouched northland of Alberta. The ED & BC was the first of three railways he eventually built in Alberta.

The ED & BC might have gone the route of many other such enterprises had the government of Alberta not yielded to public pressure in June 1912, and provided aid through guaranteed bonds.[1] McArthur was a staunch Liberal whose contributions helped keep the party's coffers filled. Among his friends were Sir Wilfrid Laurier, Liberal prime minister of Canada from 1896-1911, the Hon. Clifford Sifton, minister of the Interior from 1896-1905, and the Hon. Arthur L. Sifton, premier of Alberta's Liberal government.[2] He expected and received the Alberta government's support. In return, he opened up an empire of agricultural land in the Peace River country, timber resources in northern Alberta and the way to the mineral wealth of the Fort McMurray area.

Born and raised on a farm in the vicinity of Lancaster, Ontario, McArthur was not highly educated and often read the newspaper aloud to facilitate his reading.[3] Despite the lack of formal education the big, energetic man had an instinct for financial affairs along with the mental determination of his Scottish ancestors. In the words of his friend, Reverend R.G. MacBeth, "McArthur did not find a way ready-made, but he made one through life."[4]

At 25 years of age, along with brothers Arthur and Duncan, McArthur moved west to Winnipeg, the city that became the home of the J.D. McArthur Company.[5] Arthur engaged in some lumbering north of Winnipeg, but died young. Duncan, who remained a bachelor, was active as a sub-contractor on many of J.D.'s construction projects and was described by his cousin Stanley McCuaig as "a genial soul, much admired by his relatives, but he had nothing of the driving power of J.D."[6]

J.D. McArthur's interest in railways began with a work gang on the Canadian Pacific Railway and soon he progressed to handling small sub-contracts.[7] As his experience grew he gained importance as a railway contractor and obtained larger contracts with the major railways, arriving in Edmonton with the Canadian Northern in 1905.[8] The following year, besides handling other contracts, he began construction on the 250 miles of the Grand Trunk Pacific Railway between Superior Junction, Ontario, and Winnipeg, Manitoba. The contract, obtained by underbidding stiff competition, was completed successfully and McArthur made a substantial profit.[9]

He was a man who admired hard work and took pride in advancing ambitious employees. He once said, "The most satisfaction that I have had in my life in appointing men, was picking them out of the job, if I could see that they had some qualifications about them."[10] Nevertheless, he disliked being in the public eye. During the building of the ED & BC, Dr. John K. McLennan, vice-president of the railway, was often McArthur's representative at functions.

Stanley McCuaig worked for J.D.'s company for several summers while attending Queen's University. After graduating in 1913, and prior to coming to Edmonton to study law, he worked for a year as a paymaster on the Hudson Bay Railway, on which McArthur had a contract. McCuaig recalls:

> I had dinner with J.D. and Mrs. McArthur on the last Sunday I spent in Winnipeg, and he told me about his plans to build a railway into the Peace River country. He

had also been carrying on negotiations with the then Premier of Alberta, Hon. A.L. Sifton, to build the Alberta and Great Waterways Railway, which was to run from Edmonton to Fort McMurray.

J.D. had made a great deal of money out of his business ventures. On that Sunday afternoon I ventured to suggest that he and his wife should retire and enjoy life. He looked at me and said, 'I couldn't remain idle. The Peace River country is the last great West. Thousands of people are moving in there and it is ready for railway development. The finest farm land in the West is located in the Grande Prairie area.[11]

Although at an age when most men are contemplating retirement, McArthur was embarking on another railway building project. Besides his involvement with building railways, he had lumbering concerns and a number of other business interests scattered across Canada, from Ontario to British Columbia. When the railway construction between Superior Junction and Winnipeg was completed, the contractor was left with equipment standing idle and a number of experienced men available.[12] About this time the charter of the Edmonton, Dunvegan and British Columbia Railway captured his interest and he became the builder of the first railway to tap the rich agricultural Peace River country. It would cost him almost his entire fortune, then estimated to be around $26 million.[13]

By the time the government of Alberta announced that it had chosen the J.D.

McArthur Company to build the ED & BC, the firm was also busy with a construction contract on the Hudson Bay Railway.[14] McArthur lost no time in setting about obtaining land for townsites and right-of-way for his railway. At this time the West was beginning to open up and real estate was at a premium in Alberta. Having no intention of paying inflated prices for right-of-way and land, he entrusted Alex C. Galbraith, who later became superintendent, and Dr. McLennan with handling the task as discreetly as possible. McLennan enlisted the assistance of H.A. George to buy the required land in the Peace River area on a commission basis.[15] George's knowledge of the district and its inhabitants was second to none. He had been a Hudson's Bay factor, homesteaded and operated several businesses in the vicinity.

In March 1912, an advance party of four men organized by Thomas McNicol, an old friend of McArthur, set out for the Spirit River region ostensibly in search of homestead land. The rest of the group consisted of Hugh Macintyre, Alexander Morrison, and Donald Campbell, all residents of Pipestone, Manitoba. Outfitted by Duncan McArthur, the men travelled to the Grande Prairie area over the gruelling Edson Trail.

In his diary Macintyre writes,

My impressions of the two McArthurs from a very superficial acquaintance are not too well formed but I should say that J.D. is a man with a prophetic vision – a man who thinks in millions – while Duncan occupies the less exalted but very useful position as boss of the outfit – the man who sees the work done. It takes a good man to plan and scheme a railroad and it also takes a good man to control a bunch of 700 or 800 railroaders.

As instructed McNicol deftly sidestepped questions from the local Royal North West Mounted Police regarding their business in the area. Macintyre writes, "Mr. Patterson, the mayor of the town [then called Grande Prairie City], was anxious to know if we were the J.D. McArthur outfit – but he also was made no wiser." [16]

Dunvegan, with its sheer cliffs rising in splendor above the Peace River, was out of the question. Instead, it was decided the Spirit River area was more suitable and from there a railway could easily be extended to the Pouce Coupe area and beyond. On 24 April 1912, at the land office in Grande Prairie City, each man filed on a quarter section in the vicinity of the Spirit River Settlement. Then they travelled over the Edson Trail and shortly afterwards signed abandonment documents. This section was later purchased by J.D. McArthur at $3 an acre.[17] Some of the land was used as a divisional point, and the Spirit River townsite. The rest became a model farm.

To achieve his goals, McArthur often enlisted the assistance of friends and relatives. Surrounded by the familiar faces of those he trusted, especially in the top positions, he continued to work even though World War I caused financial reverses from which he never recovered. Although he lost the railways he loved, he continued to be interested in the development of the Peace River area.

J.D. McArthur died from pernicious anemia on 10 January 1927.[18] In keeping with his reserved nature he had requested a small private funeral, but his friends would not allow it. Kay Baylis recalls, "The church was just packed with old men."[19] His friends had come to pay their last respects. Canada had lost one of its least known pioneer railway builders – a contractor who had gambled and lost when he decided to open up northern Alberta and British Columbia with railways. The mists of time may obscure the achievements of this railway giant, but he changed the course of history in western Canada.

2

From Dream to Reality

The Edmonton, Dunvegan and British Columbia Railway was incorporated by Dominion Statutes 1907, Chapter 85, and assented to, March 22. Its provisional directors were James B. MacDonald of Winnipeg, John A. Sandgreen of Edmonton, Clive Pringle of Ottawa, and Donald McLeod and Thomas G. Galligher of Spokane, Washington.[1] The railway was to run from near Edmonton "by the most feasible route, to a point at or near the town of Dunvegan."[2] From there it was to continue via the Peace River Valley, westerly to the Parsnip River, in British Columbia, and then toward the town of Fort George.[3] Not one mile of track was laid until J.D. McArthur assumed control of the charter.

In 1911, McArthur hired Henry Dimsdale to undertake preliminary surveys along the route of the proposed railway.[4] Dimsdale was an adventurous and able Canadian whose zest for adventure and mathematical ability had led him into civil engineering. He came to know the Peace River country well as he tramped it on foot. A medium sized man, he was a tireless and fast walker who was always ahead of the others in his party.[5] Over the years he pursued other careers briefly, but always returned to railway construction. The hamlet of Dimsdale, nine miles west of Grande Prairie, bears his name.

The glowing accounts of the richness of the Peace River area received from Dimsdale and others first attracted McArthur. Their explorations convinced him that the country was worthy of development. He wrote, "In 1911, financial conditions were fairly easy, labor was plentiful and it seemed an opportune time to undertake such an enterprise."[6] McArthur commenced negotiations with the government of Alberta and the Grand Trunk Pacific Railway, that planned to build 100 miles of rail through the same territory. As a result, the Grand Trunk Pacific agreed to waive its right to the Dominion government subsidy. By May 1911, J.D. McArthur had applied to the Dominion government for a subsidy to build 350 miles of the ED & BC main line. It is widely believed that he did not receive this.

Without fanfare, control of the charter of the ED & BC passed into the hands of J.D. McArthur that fall. He lured Thomas Turnbull, with his expertise, from the Canadian Northern and appointed him chief engineer.[7] Turnbull had a distinguished career in railway surveying all across Canada. Beside the large bulk of McArthur, Turnbull's five foot four inch frame looked dwarfed, as they pored over Dominion Land Office maps of the area the new railway was to run through.

Pending financing of the railway company, McArthur advanced the monies required to undertake the preliminary surveys. By March 1912, he announced that two survey parties were at work. Each party had 15 to 18 men.[8] The first party handled preliminary mapping of the route. The second party followed some distance behind doing more detailed work. The surveyors discovered glaring inaccuracies in the Dominion government maps.[9]

Plans and bond guarantees at $20 thousand per mile were approved by the Alberta government in the spring of 1912, amid the objections of the opposition party. McArthur's contract guaranteed 350 miles and stipulated that 100 miles of track were to be completed by the end of the year.[10]

Jack G. Culshaw was a member of this survey crew shown watering horses on "move day" in 1912.
Photo: Provincial Archives of Alberta, A6923

In January 1912, the veteran contractor purchased 140 acres of land from John Watson Brown, a Winnipeg real estate agent, as a site for his Edmonton railway terminal. Originally part of the George Gagnon farm, this land was located in the area known as the Bronx.[11] The property, facing onto the St. Albert Trail, was then about six miles northwest of the heart of the city of Edmonton and was named Dunvegan Yards.

Glen Barker, a big man who stood six foot three in his socks, was one of the men who helped build the railway through bush and muskeg into the Peace River country. He recalled, "I was a gangling 19-year-old in Iowa. My brother, Mark [you'll remember that he topped me by more than an inch], a big Swede and I decided there wasn't much around Iowa for us. We headed for Canada where there were, so we heard, a lot of opportunities for young, willing workmen."[12]

They got a job with a contractor at Olds, Alberta, cutting ties for the Canadian Pacific Railway. When they were fired for lack of skill in a dodge to pay them off with less money than they had coming, they headed north to Edmonton. On the ED & BC a gang was putting in poles for a telephone line and Barker was hired by the railway in the spring of 1912:

> We lived in a boarding house. There were six men including the powder monkey [the man who used dynamite]. There was no boss. A.C. Galbraith came out every morning to inspect our work. Our tools were crowbars, a post hole auger and long handled shovels. We used a crowbar to dig the holes in the frozen ground when the weather got colder. We had a powder monkey to load the holes and blow them. Track-laying was from one to five miles ahead of us. Came fall and the pole line work was shutting down for the winter. I was lucky and got taken on as an engine watchman at Dunvegan Yards. That was 1 October [1912]. Eighteen days later I began firing a locomotive.
>
> On 18 April 1916, I moved over to the right side of the cab. I was a "hogger" [a locomotive engineer] wheeling along over a track built on top of a muskeg sponge. But I felt real good about it. I was up there with fellows like 'Chappie' Brown, 'Jinks' Frizzell, 'Big Mike' Morgan, 'Farmer' Gage, 'Hank' Kelly, and others who had been running engines before they came to the ED & BC. In those days most everybody got tagged with a nickname. Mine was 'Cy' because I had a habit of giving a big sigh as I sat down.
>
> Mark came to work on the road as a watchman in the spring of 1914. By the fall he was firing and he was running an engine in 1921. We never did hear what happened to the Swede.[13]

While Mark Barker, nicknamed "Cowboy," was a fireman for Engineer "Protestant Bill," Preston was fired for letting the water run low and burning the crown sheet of locomotive No. 1. He was eventually permitted to return to work on condition that there be no complaints about his standing on the seniority list.[14]

Locomotive No. 1
a wood burner converted to coal, 1912
Photo: Courtesy of Mrs. Ann Glaister

Shortly after the Barker brothers began their railway careers, the first steel was laid at the junction with the Grand Trunk Pacific at Edmonton. The *Edmonton Bulletin* of 6 July 1912 carried the headline: "First Rail Laid This Morning on Edmonton, Dunvegan and British Columbia Railway." The news story read: "The engineers are today putting in the stakes on the site of the roundhouse for the yards situated west of the Bronx in this City. The terminal of the line will also be constructed there."

At Dunvegan Yards there were a number of buildings in various stages of construction. Plans were on the table for a station, freight shed, engine and machine shops, stable, cookhouse, bunkhouse, blacksmith shop, and a large two-storey building to accommodate the office staff.[15] When the new office building was ready, the offices in the Alberta Block in downtown Edmonton

were vacated. To provide dining facilities for the staff a frame house, purchased on the right-of-way, was moved and placed near the station.[16]

By May 1912, work was progressing satisfactorily on the line. The D.F. McArthur Construction Company, owned by J.D.'s brother Duncan, had the contract for grading 125 miles of right-of-way from Dunvegan Yards to Mirror Landing, on the north bank of the Athabasca River.[17] Men, set up in gangs along the route, had cleared about 85 percent of the distance by the fall. Because of a strike on the Grand Trunk Pacific, McArthur was forced to send his own rolling stock east to get the steel.[18]

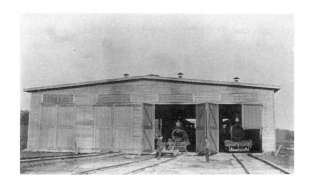

Engine house built at Dunvegan Yards in 1912.
Photo: Courtesy of Mrs. Ann Glaister

ED & BC office building, station, boarding house (partially showing), and Murray's Hotel at Dunvegan Yards in 1914.
Photo: Glenbow Archives, McDermid Collection, NC-6-842

The first major physical obstacle to be encountered was the Sturgeon River, 9.7 miles north of Dunvegan Yards. Work on a bridge to straddle the river, and on grading the right-of-way, was delayed by exceptionally heavy rains. Materials for the Mirror Landing portion of the railway were being shipped via the Canadian Northern Railway from Edmonton to Athabasca Landing, then by boat to Mirror Landing. Unusually low water in the Athabasca River slowed the movement of materials to their destination. Low wages caused a shortage of laborers.

Despite the problems, an article titled "To Complete 120 Miles of M'Arthur Line this Year," in the *Edmonton Bulletin* of 20 August 1912 reported, "Superintendent Galbraith stated yesterday that they would have no difficulty in getting track laid this season on all the grade that is constructed and the line will be laid as far as the Athabasca [River] this fall."

Hired by McArthur early in 1912, Alex Galbraith was a large heavy-set man, who had gained extensive experience as superintendent on the Great Northern Railway in

Spokane. [After the first 200 miles of the ED & BC were completed, Galbraith left McArthur's employment to undertake reconnaissance surveys for a proposed railway that was never built.[19]] Hearing that his old railway friend, Alex Galbraith, was involved in building a pioneer railway in Alberta, Jack Brown arrived in Edmonton in 1912 and lost no time in contacting him. Having received the promise of a locomotive engineer's job, Brown was soon involved in laying steel on the ED & BC.

Jack Brown, nicknamed "Chappie," had a wealth of experience behind him. He had started firing engines on the Great Northern out of Spokane in 1897 when gold was discovered in the Yukon. "Easy money" caught his imagination a year later and he joined the Klondike gold rush. After a couple of years without striking it rich, he returned to Spokane and railroading. His sense of adventure then lured him to Mexico where he worked as an engineer on the Mexican Central until the revolution in 1911 caused him to beat a hasty retreat back to Spokane.

In August 1912, the tall, bespectacled Brown was entrusted with the task of going to Winnipeg and bringing back engine No. 11, the first to run on the ED & BC's flimsy ribbons of steel.[20] A month later he made another trip to bring back engine No. 14. By October of that year he was at the throttle coaxing engines over the rough and newly laid railway. He held the distinction of being the first engineer on the railway's seniority list and the first to retire in 1938.

Locomotive No. 71, constructed
for the Lacombe and Northwestern
Railway, was decorated for Jack Brown's last trip.
Photo: Courtesy of E. Hagglund

To have 85 miles ready for track-laying before winter arrived, 530 men and 235 teams battled swarms of mosquitoes and blackflies as they worked on clearing and grading of the ED & BC.[21] Once the ground was frozen, laying of steel commenced in December 1912 with a heavy track-laying machine, called the Pioneer. Ungainly in appearance and resembling a guillotine, it was a marvel to watch how efficiently it operated. With it and 125 men working from Dunvegan Yards, 14 miles of track were laid by the end of the month; short of the stipulated 100 miles. Nevertheless, the public and the government seemed satisfied that a start had been made and McArthur was not held to the letter of his contract. By January 1913, the steel had reached Mile 26 [distance in railway parlance], seven miles beyond Morinville.[22]

To establish a townsite at Mile 52.5, the ED & BC purchased 80 acres of land from William Westgate and 60 adjoining acres of CPR land that had been squatted on by William Lockhart. Using the first four letters of each surname it was named "Westlock." The steel reached there in March 1913 and a station erected. It seemed that the entire population of the district was on the platform for the official opening in October. George MacKinlay, who had previously been station master and accountant with the Intercolonial Railway, was the first agent. While visiting Edmonton, the vibrant feeling and promise of opening up the West prevalent in the city at the time caught his imagination and he joined the ED & BC.

That same year, Valentine Whitman Rathbone Smith took over the reins as general manager and chief engineer on the departure of Thomas Turnbull.[23] Born in 1878 near Oshawa, Ontario, the civil engineer eventually moved south of the border. Shortly after his marriage to Reba Barrett, the daughter of a distinguished Virginia family, the Smiths came to western Canada.[24] He was engaged on building the Grand Trunk Pacific prior to joining the ED & BC[25] where his staff soon gave him the sobriquet of "Trombone Smith," or "T-bone Smith."[26]

W.R. Smith, General Manager ED & BC, CC, and A & GW railways, 1913-1920

During the winter of 1912-13, with 12 thousand tons of rails on order, contracts were let out for a total of 300 thousand railway ties and a camp was built for the tie cutters at Mile 101.1, which became known as Tieland. More than 100 teams were engaged hauling supplies over the right-of-way, and unloading them at caches reaching as far as Sawridge, on the east end of Lesser

Slave Lake.[27] [In 1922, after a shift in location, Sawridge was renamed Slave Lake].

As spring drew near, track-laying passed the present village of Dapp. A ballast pit was located east of Dapp, near the Pembina River, and a short spur was built into it. Glen Barker was fireman for engineer Mike Morgan on the track-layer at the time, and Jim Grover was the conductor. Barker remembered the ballast was a mixture of clay and sand with little gravel making it too soft for a proper roadbed. In this area of low lying land, engines resembled boats gliding over ocean waves as they travelled over miles of muskeg.

Barker recalled that on a cool spring day, without warning a locomotive publling a flat car arrived at the end of steel from Edmonton. In a shelter formed by ties sat J.D. McArthur with his back to the engine. Although he had a private car named "Alberta," he preferred this mode of travel over skeleton track. Without explanation McArthur ordered the ballasting to be halted and the workers to return to Dunvegan Yards by handcar over the rough, uneven, newly laid track.[28] Ballasting did not resume until the grade was extended and skeleton track laid to a

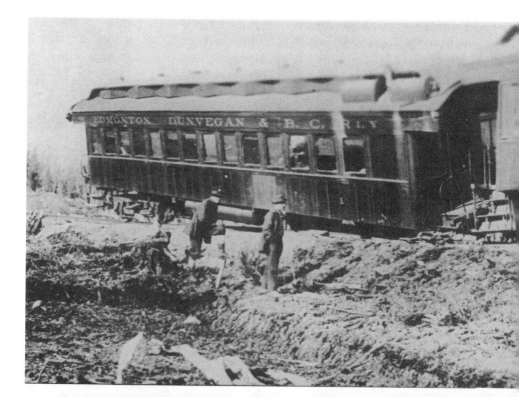

Derailment c. 1914.
Photo: Provincial Archives of Alberta A2232.

sand pit with better granular material at Kilsyth, some 21 miles beyond Dapp. Ballasting was completed from there back toward Dapp. Meanwhile work crews continued grading and ballasting towards the Athabasca River. When Chisholm Pit was reached at Mile 108.6, an excellent grade of ballasting gravel became available.

The settlement near the pit was named after Tom Chisholm, a moose of a man who stood six feet three inches and weighed 275 pounds. He was a contractor who provided many of the ties that built the ED & BC. Chisholm came west from Antigonish, Nova Scotia, with an expedition exploring western Canada. The Klondike Gold Rush enticed him to the Yukon where he was said to have owned the Aurora dance hall in Dawson City. He was a generous man who wore a watch chain made of gold nuggets and is reputed to have lost his fortune in Seattle.

"Each year some of his cronies from McLennan would take Tom Chisholm to Edmonton to meet with old friends from the North. Getting him into the confined space of a lower berth on the train needed the help of several men. This was accompanied by lusty comments from all involved. By the time Chisholm was in the berth and struggling to get out of his pants everybody in the sleeper was wide awake."[29] Often Eugene "Sandbar" McLaughlin, a conductor on the railway, was in the party. Chisholm's later days were lived out keeping house at McLennan for McLaughlin and Fireman Phillip "The Frog" Frigon. There many a railroader down on his luck found shelter.

By May 1913, large gangs of laborers were clearing the route, which skirted the south shore of Lesser Slave Lake. They were followed by men with teams of horses, wheelbarrows, scrapers, shovels and picks, building grade from the end of steel to Driftpile, Mile 204.5. Contracted out in stretches of approximately 100 feet, station work was heavy manual work, often taken on by several men together. The work had to be done by a certain time and how and when contractors did it was their affair. McArthur wanted to get the railway operational as far as the Athabasca River to eliminate the expense of shipping supplies over the Canadian Northern Railway to Athabasca Landing.[30] As soon as the ground was frozen in the fall, steel laying and ballasting began. In November 1913, the railway reached the south bank of the Athabasca.[31]

The small village of Mirror Landing, located at the mouth of the Lesser Slave River where it meets the Athabasca River, was briefly renamed Port Cornwall in December 1913 to honor J.K. Cornwall who owned the Northern Transportation Company.[32] It was a bustling, busy place during the steamboat season each year, but the coming of the railway taxed its resources to the limit. Soon its streets were livelier than they had ever been with rowdy railroaders. Many of them were "boomers," men who moved from one railway to another as they helped build railways across North America. With prosperity, Mirror Landing had to accept the seamier side of society. Gamblers, bootleggers and prostitutes did a flourishing business. When the railway building moved on they did too, but Mirror Landing was far too busy to realize that its decline and that of the steamboat era had begun.

Unscheduled train service between Dunvegan Yards and Smith began in January 1914, and construction rates were charged.[33] When the station was completed, the first agent appointed was a Mr. Hyslip.[34] He moved on with the steel shortly afterwards to Swan River [now Kinuso] and was replaced by McArthur's nephew Ewen Mac-

Back: *Allie D. and Ewen F. MacDonell (J.D.'s nephews).* Front: *Peter McArthur (J.D.'s cousin) and J.D. McArthur.* Photo: Courtesy of Agnes McArthur.

The railway company had surveyed a townsite on the south bank of the river opposite Mirror Landing and named the new community Smith, after Rathbone Smith. After a number of business places grew up near the railway station, the Post Office was moved to Smith, but Mirror Landing remained the name of the Post Office until 1957.

Donell, but he did not stay long either.[35] After filing on a homestead at Rio Grande near Beaverlodge in March 1915, he joined the 54th Highlanders and went overseas. On demobilization, he returned to Rio Grande where he and another of McArthur's nephews, Alex MacIntosh, opened the first store to serve the settlers attracted to the area now that a railway was being built.[36] –

As the railway pushed its way north, McArthur saw wealth in the timber lining its route and established the North West Lumber Company Limited. A sawmill, managed by Charles H. Blaikie,[37] was built at the east end of Dunvegan Yards in 1914. An office, stable, blacksmith shop, powerhouse and engine room were added later, and all were painted brick red to match the railway buildings. Across from the mill site, McArthur opened a boarding house to accommodate his workmen.

The tie between the logging-lumber operations and the railway was tight. McArthur acquired the rights to timber berths as early as 1912 and laid track into the areas to bring out the timber. Loads of logs piled high on flat cars arrived at the sawmill near Dunvegan Yards. From the saws and planers in this modern facility came the lumber used for railway buildings.

Neil Hyslop was a skinny, long-legged 14-year-old working as a delivery boy for Bingham & Beggs grocery store in Calder. He described the first time he made a trip to Dunvegan Yards to deliver lunch to Stationary Fireman Atkins: "I started out for the one and a half mile trip. . . . I was within the last half mile when I spotted the outline of the shop, standing alone in the middle of the prairie. To me it was a queer looking sight that bright moonlit night with the only sound the steam exhaust from a small air pump. The interior of the building was in semi-darkness with a few kerosene lamps burning."[38] Hyslop's curiosity was aroused as he wandered by examining various tools and gadgets. Like most youngsters, trains held a

Train of logs at North West Lumber Company's mill in 1914
Photo: Glenbow Archives, McDermid Collection, NC-6-1347a

fascination for him. To be a railroader became his ambition. In a few short years he was working in that very shop completing his apprenticeship in the trade of machinist.

The railway buildings did not stand alone for long. According to Hyslop, "A year or so later a small shack town grew up just north of the roundhouse. It was in the heavy bush with a winding road between the little houses. They looked rough on the outside, but inside they were comfortable and clean." These were the homes of railroaders built on a tract of land owned by the city of Edmonton and leased to a dairyman for pasture, who rented out plots of it to the squatters. McArthur built a number of houses for his employees on the east perimeter of the railway property along 135 Street, which became known as McArthur Row.

Locomotive No. 4 with Conductor David Tait and Engineer Charles Snyder
Photo: CP Rail Corporate Archives, 4994

3

Boom and Fall of Grouard

In December 1913, concrete piers were poured to support a 925 foot seven-span steel bridge across the Athabasca River at Smith. It would cost a quarter of a million dollars – an exorbitant amount in those days.[1] To enable construction trains to reach the other side, a temporary trestle bridge was laid on the solidly frozen river. The steel bridge was being built at Smith when William MacIntosh Donaldson, known to railroaders as "Moonshine" or "Mac," joined the ED & BC as locomotive engineer. His first assignment was operating a dinky locomotive to move materials and supplies across the temporary bridge to the crews on the other side. Following completion of the permanent bridge, Donaldson moved westward with construction to Sawridge.[2]

Like many others, Donaldson and his wife, Anna, lived in a tent. Although their home was humble, their warmth and hospitality were unsurpassed. Later, as residents of McLennan, they were well-known for their kindness to those less fortunate than themselves.

Soon clearing of the right-of-way had passed Sucker Creek at Mile 219.8. "As spring took the bite out of the air, the prevalent sounds were the ring of axes, the whine of crosscut saws, and the curses of men echoing across the bush."[3] The railway's progress was being closely watched by residents of Grouard, strategically located on the western extremity of Lesser Slave Lake.

The thriving community was mainly comprised of energetic young people with big dreams. Newspapers were bombarded with advertisements by unscrupulous promoters extolling the attractions of Grouard. Despite the fact that McArthur's ED & BC route map, dated 8 November 1911, showed the railway line running along the south shore of Lesser Slave Lake bypassing the town, Grouard believed differently. After all, it was the inland port into which the boats brought their passengers and freight. In wintertime, more than 250 teams of horses worked in and out of the town. Besides, every homesteader had to go to Grouard to file on a homestead because the Land Office was located there.

Newly laid track at Sawridge
Photo: Peace River Centennial Museum, 77.880.16

When the engineer in charge of the preliminary line of the ED & BC was questioned about the railway's route, the *Grouard News* of 4 January 1913 noted that Mr. Adamson "beat it at the first opportunity." He had good reason to be noncommittal. In February, Grouard residents discovered the ED & BC had filed plans with the Dominion government, projecting the line to be built 12 miles south of their town. Sensing the cold stealthy hand of death near, Grouard reacted angrily. The fight was on.

The battle raged back and forth between Grouard, Edmonton and Ottawa while the railway went doggedly ahead with its plans for clearing and grading on the route to the south. In an effort to calm the uproar, McArthur applied to the provincial government for a charter to build a branch line into the town,[4] but later reneged when the bonds could not be sold. While Grouard sat back to lick its wounds, its residents trickled out to settle in other towns. Meanwhile, the railway stole trade from the boats and the general depression of 1914 set in. By 1916, Grouard was but a shell of its former self. It awakened abruptly from its dreams to find that "progress had passed it by on two steel rails."[5]

PRINGLE & GUTHRIE,
BARRISTERS & SOLICITORS,
CITIZEN BUILDING,
OTTAWA, CANADA.

May 21, 1914.

re Edmonton, Dunvegan & British Columbia Railway

Sir,-

I beg to advise you that I am authorized by Mr. J. D. McArthur, the President of this Railway Company, to state that he will apply at the next Session of the Alberta Legislature for a Charter authorizing the construction of a line of railway from some point on the Edmonton, Dunvegan & British Columbia Railway to the Village of Grouard, and that upon the granting of such Charter the proposed Company will with reasonable despatch proceed with the construction of the said branch line.

I beg to remain

Yours respectfully,

Clive Pringle

The Honourable
The Minister of Railways,
Ottawa.

Letter re: Grouard's charter
Public Archives Canada, RG43,544,17277

Office Engineer, Ben Prest, who had emigrated from England in 1904, found the indecisiveness regarding Grouard disruptive and sighed with relief when the controversy was finally settled. The civil engineer, who had been with the ED & BC since 1912, was a stickler for detail both in his private life and in his work.[6] One of the more pleasant tasks assigned him was the naming of the new sidings and stations along the railway's route. He made some of the men on construction immortal by using their surnames. His own name went into the history books when his colleagues named a station Prestville.

Engineering department staff at Dunvegan Yards
Photo: Courtesy of Mrs. Ann Glaister

The spring rains of 1914 continued into June, slowing the grading on the low-lying land along Lesser Slave Lake. As the temporary bridge at Smith disintegrated into its swirling waters, the swollen Athabasca River threatened the partially built steel bridge.

Ferry service was the only substitute until the bridge was completed at the end of July 1914. Grading continued between Sawridge and the Smoky River. It was September before a track-layer arrived to replace the machine that had been sent to work on the Alberta and Great Waterways Railway.

An article in the *The Edmonton Bulletin* of 9 November 1914, titled "On the Northland, Limited," gave this account of the track-laying:

> The head of the steel is in the neighborhood of Driftpile River at Mile 206 . . . The [track-laying] gang consists of 150 men. First there is the big Pioneer track-layer right at the end of the steel followed by two cars of steel, eight cars of ties and two cars containing spikes and other material, with two engines – one in the centre and one in the rear. [The Pioneer generally operated with one engine.]
>
> On one side of the train is a carrier operated by steam from the Pioneer, along which run the ties, which are placed on the carrier by two men working on each tie car. As soon as each tie arrives at the front end of the Pioneer it is seized by a man known as a tie-layer, who throws it down on the grade, where it is placed in position by two men with long hooks [picaroons]. . . . While the Pioneer crawled slowly along and sometimes not stopping for half an hour at a time, the impression being given is that the busy men are all part of the big machine.
>
> Following the train there is a small army of spikers, who are never far behind, and at the rear there is another gang of men who straighten out the 'kinks' in the line.

J.D. McArthur's Pioneer track-laying machine laying steel
Photo: Provincial Archives of Alberta, A8271

William J. Pace, superintendent of construction, was known to McArthur because of his work with Mackenzie and Mann when he was employed by the Canadian Northern Railway [CNR].[7] Prior to joining the ED & BC, he had been superintendent of construction on the Edmonton, Yukon & Pacific Railway, when the CPR tried to prevent the installation of a switch connecting the Calgary & Edmonton and the EY & P Railways. His success in outwitting the CPR to get the job done is described by John Gilpin in *Edmonton – Gateway to the North*.[8] In 1906, Pace became Edmonton's Commissioner, Public Works, but his first love was the railway and in 1909 he returned to the CNR.[9] Needing his expertise, McArthur persuaded him to join his staff a few years later.

With the coming of the railway, a tent town with bootlegging establishments sprang up at High Prairie. Mixed trains on a nonscheduled basis were run in and out of the town and Mr. Napier, who had been with the construction department, was appointed the first station agent.[10] A wye was built to turn equipment and reverse the direction of trains.[11] The work train, with the Pioneer laying steel and Mike Morgan at the controls, returned there each night to coal the engine and fill the tender and wooden water car with water. Morgan's burly stature and bass voice, left no doubt as to the origin of his nickname "Big Mike." This robust character was one of a number of Americans who came to Canada during the railway building era.

One evening, Glen Barker, Morgan's fireman, was overseeing syphoning of water when Blackie Wagner, a well-known bootlegger, climbed up beside him on the engine. Generally, the good-looking, husky man was a congenial soul who was popular with the railway personnel, but there was a distinct note of anger in his voice as he told Barker, "I had a case of whiskey buried in the west end of that coal car and someone has stolen it." It was obvious from the tone of his voice that he suspected the train and engine crews were the culprits. Barker assured Wagner he knew nothing about his loot, but mentioned a car of coal had just been turned around on the wye. The bootlegger departed without a word to check the east end of the car and soon arrived back smiling to present Barker with a bottle of his brew.

EDMONTON, DUNVEGAN AND BRITISH COLUMBIA RAILWAY COMPANY

J. D. McARTHUR CO., LIMITED

(ALBERTA AND GREAT WATERWAYS RAILWAY CONTRACT)
(CENTRAL CANADA RAILWAY CONTRACT)

PRAIRIE DIVISION

TIME TABLE

TAKING EFFECT AT 24.01 O'CLOCK

SUNDAY, NOVEMBER 7TH, 1915

FOR THE INFORMATION AND GOVERNMENT OF EMPLOYEES ONLY.

GOVERNED BY MOUNTAIN STANDARD TIME.

THE SUPERIOR DIRECTION IS EAST OR SOUTH, AND EAST OR SOUTHBOUND TRAINS ARE SUPERIOR TO TRAINS OF THE SAME CLASS IN THE OPPOSITE (INFERIOR DIRECTION.)

The Company's Rules are printed separately in Book Form. Every Employee whose duties are connected with the movement of trains must have a copy of them and of the current Time Table accessible when on duty.

W. R. SMITH,
General Manager.

R. M. HALPENNY,
Superintendent.

Douglas Co., 31110. 500-2-11-15

Timetable No. 1

4

The Terminal that Should Not Be

While Grouard was on its death bed, the hamlet of McLennan was being born. At a distance of 130 miles from Smith, at Mile 262.2 on the shores of Round Lake, now known by the Indian name of Lake Kimiwan, the ED & BC bought land. A portion of it was earmarked as a townsite and in time this was subdivided into lots. The rest of the land was for the location of railway buildings and trackage. From there, the railway's main line would run west.

The new railway divisional point was named "McLennan," to honor Dr. John K. McLennan, whose titles included vice-president, secretary-treasurer and purchasing agent.[1] Dr. McLennan moved his family to Edmonton during his years with the northern railways. He was a deeply religious man,[2] well liked by the office staff and regarded as a gentleman. He was three years younger than J.D. McArthur and a first cousin of Mrs. McArthur. Besides being another Glengarry man, he was a close friend of the contractor and a member of the Board of the J.D. McArthur Company for 15 years.

When McArthur was building the Grand Trunk Pacific from Superior Junction to Winnipeg in 1907, he persuaded McLennan, who was then in medical practice around Paso Robles in California, to return to Canada and become business manager for the project. The doctor accepted the challenge.

Dr. McLennan was a tall, pompous-looking individual, who had the ability to handle large sums of money.[3] He had sound early training with smaller sums, when as the eldest child, he helped his mother raise his younger brother and sister after his father, a Presbyterian minister, was drowned "in attempting to cross a flooded river while ministering in his first parish."[4] Later, John McLennan moved to Winnipeg to study medicine at Manitoba Medical College, then moved to California after graduation. Upon his return to Canada, he remained associated with McArthur in railway construction for many years and stayed by his comrade's side through the difficult years until the railways in northern Alberta passed out of McArthur's hands. McLennan then returned to California with his family to resume his medical practise.

Before the railway's arrival, three stopping houses and some shacks were already on the shore of Round Lake, about a half mile west of the land designated for the McLennan townsite.[5] Soon there was an army of railway workers invading the little settlement. Close to the tracks, a jumble of shacks, tents, and poolrooms went up and the gamblers and their ilk moved in. Realizing customers were not going to trudge half a mile to reach them, often in mud, the stopping houses at Round Lake moved to the new townsite of McLennan where they bought lots for one thousand dollars each from the railway.

Early in January 1915, the steel reached McLennan. The first station was a boxcar, with an office in one end and living quarters in the other.[6] Later that year, a big two-storey structure was built. "As the carpenters put the finishing touches to the interior, the white spruce siding of the outside was coated with red paint and each gable had the name McLENNAN printed on it."[7]

The station building had a large waiting room, an office and freight shed. On the second floor were offices and bedrooms for the accommodation of passenger train crews laying over. Eleven coal-burning stoves heated the rambling building, necessitating the services of a full-time janitor.[8] Before the year was out, the station depot had a dining area with a lunch counter and eight tables. On the twice-a-week train days, because there were no dining facilities on the train, passengers who could afford this luxury jostled each other to reach the counter.

Station at McLennan
Photo: H.K. Williams

William Ellstock, who was installing channel blocks in switches along the line, arrived in McLennan shortly after the station was built in 1915. Expecting to take his lunch pail and go back to Edmonton on the next train, he was surprised when Superintendent Halpenny "stuck his head in the door of the waiting room and told [him] to take over the gang."[9]

Ellstock was working as section foreman when The Board of Railway Commissioners for Canada issued Order No. 23458 on 27 March 1915 authorizing the ED & BC "to open for the carriage of traffic its line of railway from Edmonton aforesaid to Mile 277 . . ."[10] The speed from Edmonton was restricted to a maximum of 20 mph. Beyond Wagner it was reduced further to 15 mph.

McLennan residents soon had a link to the world, with the erection of telegraph poles and stringing of wires as construction of the ED & BC progressed. By August 1915, 150 miles of flimsy telegraph line weaved through the countryside.[11] Its building was a feat in ingenuity and improvisation. The building crew consisted of a number of "boomers" whose work was seasonal. When the ground froze so did their jobs.

As the line progressed and the supply of standard poles decreased, trees were substituted. Holes were dug using a steel bar and long handled scoop and the poles erected with an insulator bracket already nailed to the top. Horses pulling a wagon carrying the coil of iron wire followed. A single strand of wire was thrown over the bracket to await the lineman's hand. He climbed the pole, tightened the wire and made the connection to the insulator, providing a link to the out-

Passenger train at Smith in 1915
Photo: Glenbow Archives, McDermid Collection, NC-6-1564

side world that was a lifeline for settlers and the men building the railway.

C.J. MacDonald was 34-years-old when he began working on the ED & BC's survey crew in 1913. He was soon familiar with every inch of the railway's route. A couple of years later, when he was offered a job as lineman in charge of the line between Smith and McLennan, he was certain he knew what to expect from the weather and the country. But there were always surprises and he soon discovered what a lad with a sling shot or .22 rifle could do to a glass insulator.

The ED & BC Railway's Prairie Division Time Table No. 1, took effect at 2401 on Sunday, 7 November 1915. A first class passenger train was scheduled to leave Edmonton at 1930 on Mondays and Thursdays, and arrive at McLennan at 0900 the following morning. Returning it was to leave McLennan at 1930 that same evening and arrive at Edmonton at 0900 on Wednesdays and Saturdays. Train movements were directed from the dispatching office at Dunvegan Yards under the guidance of Chief Train Dispatcher, Leonard Walton.[12]

During the early years, those trains seldom ran on time. Often they were late – sometimes a day or more late. Patrons, anticipating an immediate "class one" operation, were quick to criticize the poor performance and soon nicknamed the ED & BC the "Exceedingly Dangerous and Badly Constructed" or the "Easily Derailed and Badly Constructed" Railway. McArthur and Super-

intendent Robert Halpenny, who had come from the Grand Trunk Pacific, were not miracle workers; "Trackage was new; light weight, non-tieplated rail had been placed over a hastily built roadbed. Trains operated over miles of skeleton track where light ballast existed, it was far below standard, at times disappearing in areas of muskeg terrain. Washouts were frequent during spring and summer run-off."[13]

Although the ED & BC was not a class one railway in 1915, its senior conductor on the passenger train was nothing short of first class. The immaculately groomed, Kenny McLennan was born in Cobalt, Manitoba. Following similar employment with the CPR in Vancouver, he had hired on with the ED & BC.[14] McArthur must have been impressed with his abilities, because he was appointed superintendent for a short time. But McLennan preferred to remain in the running trades. The dignified, white haired man, tolerated no nonsense from the train crew and objected to any form of intoxication.[15] Myrtle Crowell recalled, "Everyone walked chalk when he was around."[16]

McLennan's son, Alan, also joined the railway, but when he was working as a brakeman on the wayfreight train, switching cars at Westlock, he was caught between the couplers and crushed to death. Upon his return on the passenger train, his heartbroken father picked up his son's body to transport it to Edmonton.

A railway circular, dated 15 November

1915, to all enginemen informed them "Effective this date, engineers and firemen will be paid on a mileage basis as follows: Passenger, thru freight, wayfreight – engineers: $4.20; firemen: $2.60. Switching and work train service – engineers: 42 cents per hour; firemen: 26 cents per hour." A "Schedule for Enginemen,"covering the rules governing their employment, was drawn up the following June. It provided for increases in pay rates. Wayfreight [local freight] engineers were the highest paid at $5.20 per 100 miles. Terminal detention pay was based on 12.5 miles per hour.[17]

Conductor Kenny McLennan, Fireman Bill Christian and Engineer Percy Brame, stand by locomotive No. 14, decorated for a special occasion
Photo: Courtesy of Bill Christian Jr.

In July 1916, the Radial Park Lodge No. 847 of the Brotherhood of Locomotive Firemen and Enginemen was formed. Among those who worked diligently on the first working agreement on the railway property

was James Gordon Fleming. A native of Hull, Quebec, he had come west to the ED & BC in 1913. Fleming had an Irish temper to match his red hair, which earned him the nickname "Pinky." Clarence Comrie recalls getting the fiery engineman's dander up when he suggested Fleming make changes to the way he was operating a locomotive. The railway veteran told him, "I am too old a turkey to be listening to any chicken."

A number of the train crews were housed at McLennan. The choice of this divisional point was made with the belief that Round Lake would provide a plentiful supply of water. The railway had the water analyzed before the final decision was made on the site for the terminal. The report received was that the water was potable and excellent for steam boilers and therein lay a tale.

Hughie Hunter was a staunch Liberal who had made his way to northern Alberta from Belfast in 1898 and settled for a time at Grouard.[18] Hunter remembered being asked by railway officials in the preconstruction days to obtain a water sample from Round Lake.[19] He was about to board the steamboat at Grouard, after riding over a rough trail, when he discovered the water container empty. Faced with a long, tiresome journey back to Round Lake, and having an abundance of water right where he was, the man made a quick decision. He filled the receptacle from the waters of Lesser Slave Lake.[20] The analysis, which recorded the water as excellent for drinking and use in locomotive boilers, was correct.

Charter Radial Lodge No. 847
Courtesy of M. MacFarlane

After the terminal was established, it was realized that something was seriously wrong. The water could not be used in locomotive boilers even when heavily treated with chemical compounds. This resulted in water being hauled in tank cars, by train, for locomotives and public consumption for many years. Notwithstanding this serious drawback, McLennan was to become the railway's second most important divisional point. The town relied on the railway's stationary fireman to blow the whistle to arouse its populace from slumber each morning. The railway payroll sustained the community whereas others relied on agriculture.

Many of the new community's residents were seasoned railroaders, but there also were those just learning railroading skills. With so many single men around, the restaurant in the Giroux Hotel did a flourishing business. Operating it were Trainman Don Praught and his wife, Maude. Shortly afterwards, Praught lost a leg in a train accident at Wembley when he fell during switching operations.[21] Later, the Praughts operated their own restaurant on main street.[22]

*Engineer Gordon Fleming and
Fireman Sam Jones in 1920s.*
Photo: Courtesy of D. Baker

On the peripheral edges of the railway community were people like Peggy Kyne. Before the arrival of the ED & BC, she cooked for teamsters and travellers at Leon Giroux's stopping house at Round Lake. She moved when Giroux, who became very influential in McLennan's early business development, purchased two lots in the new townsite. When the Praughts left McLennan, Kyne saw an opportunity in the little restaurant, where railroaders were the backbone of her clientele. On the door she had a poster that read: "EAT HERE IF IT KILLS YOU. I NEED THE MONEY!"[23]

When the last customer was gone and she had some quiet moments, Kyne would sit down in the eating area with "its half-dozen, redchecker clothed tables and write verse about the men who came in to eat."[24] The following piece of unpolished verse tells much about some of the characters who helped to build McLennan and the railway.

THE LUCKY SEVEN

Way back in the year nineteen-thirteen
  when the Peace River country was new,
And the old Dunvegan railroad
  was slowly crowding through;
Seven husky boomers
  signed on as engineers,
And they've stuck it out through thick
and thin, for 21 long years.

They came here from all over,
  Just why they do not know,
Hank Kelly from north of Lac La Biche
  Jack Brown from Mexico,
Jinks Frizzell looks Irish,
  blue eyes and curly hair,
When he's not running engines
  he's a pilot of the air,
But he says it's not exciting and
  claims his biggest thrill,
Was when the old bear stole the bacon
from his tent on Smoky Hill.

There's Percy Brame – the envy
  of the boys along the route
For he's always clean and shining
  coming in or going out,
But he says – there's nothing to it,
  it's all because he knows,
How to put oil on his engine,
  instead of on his clothes.

Hank Pentzer is one of the boys
  who claims he's working hard,
But his fireman just sniffs and says,
  "Huh, yeah! in his backyard,
For when he's on the engine
  if the trip be short or far,
He just waves at all the natives
  and leans on the Johnson bar."

Carl Gage, another one, declares
  railroading has lost its charm,
And he's going to leave it flat some day
  and move out on his farm,
But the boys all say when his train
  pulls out, and he stays on the homestead
They will order up the roses
  for they will know that he is dead.

But for a really clever fellow
  Mike Morgan is at the head,
Though he's had a score of sweethearts
  he still remains unwed.
He says railroading taught him
  from first to very last,
When a fellow starts in running,
  it pays to do it fast.

And though they are just as different,

as seven men can be,
They have worked together all these
  years, in perfect harmony.
And we know that when the time shall
  come, that they have finished here,
And started on that last great run
  they'll make it in the clear.

Mrs. Peggy Kyne,
McLennan, 1934.

It was said that Kyne had cooked in the gold camps of Nevada, Colorado and the Yukon. Occasionally, her patrons saw her dance around her restaurant with a tumbler full of water perched upon her head without spilling a drop.[25] In spite of being a plump little woman, she was as light as a feather on her feet as she twirled across the floor, and some claimed that she had been one of Tom Chisholm's dance hall girls in Dawson City during the gold rush days.

Ernest Rietze, a German immigrant, opened McLennan's first Post Office in 1915. When the Rietzes arrived at Round Lake the previous year mail was carried by a man on foot or on horseback from Grouard. Rietze built a log rooming house with a restaurant there but, like Leon Giroux, he moved when he realized his location was too far from the railway station. He built a new hotel of lumber in McLennan, across the street from the Giroux Hotel with space for the Post Office, but it burned down in 1917. When the Post Office reopened, it was in the Giroux establishment.[26]

The Rietzes' daughter, Beatrice, who was 14 when they came to Round Lake, became one of the early teachers in McLennan. Handsome young Claus "Dutch" Turninga caught her eye when he came to the village in 1919 to work on the railway. They had both left McLennan, Turninga quitting the railway, when they met again in Calgary. Against the wishes of Mrs. Rietze, the young couple eloped to Vancouver where they married. They had two children by the time they decided to return to McLennan, where all was forgiven, and Turninga rejoined the railway and eventually became a conductor.

Another well-known character in McLennan was Louis Benoit, who hailed from Quebec. He was a resident of Grouard in 1912 and when the railway bypassed the town, he moved to McLennan where he opened a poolroom and barbershop. It is rumored that he also did a good trade as a bootlegger. "Benoit was a gregarious soul who dearly loved a joke. He was an excellent actor and would disguise himself and sally out to play pranks. One time he appeared on main street as a crippled beggar passing through town. Nobody recognized him. He successfully touched a number of the railroaders for contributions. Then he rounded them up, took off his disguise"[27] and bought them beer with the donations at Giroux's Hotel. With so many railroaders around it was inevitable that Benoit's daughter, Annette, would marry one. She worked with her father in his barbershop until her marriage to Joe Breault, who was station agent at Donnelly for 21 years.[28]

Louis Benoit made life in the pioneer community more bearable by every week or so stacking the pooltables at one side, sprinkling shavings from wax candles on the floor to make it slippery, and turning his establishment into a dance hall. The children, wrapped in overcoats, often slept on the pool tables while their parents kicked up their heels.

What is a dance without music? Operator A.L. "Pot" Potentier, an Englishman in spite of his surname, was a piano thumper who often came to the rescue. His repertoire consisted of hymns. Undaunted, he would jazz them up and the lively crowd would twirl to "When he cometh, when he cometh to make up his jewels" as it was pounded out on the piano with "a lot more verve than the hymn ever got in church."[29]

Meanwhile, a number of men who would spend the rest of their lives working for the railway were putting down roots in McLennan. Among them was Fred Crowell who had joined the railway at Dunvegan Yards as a steam fitter in the roundhouse. By May 1916, he was working as a fireman and in time he became expert as a locomotive engineer. Myrtle Crowell recalled one of her early trips to McLennan, when she was pregnant with her first child. She asked Bert Carrick, the agent at Dunvegan Yards, for a pass. When she picked it up, she blushed. Carrick had written on it "Mrs. Fred Crowell and family."[30]

Crowell was a slim, sinewy man whose infectious grin hinted that he found the world a huge joke and was continually laughing at it. He loved to tease and play tricks on people. His bachelor days earned him the title of "Count." "The Count," said Mrs. Crowell, "never had any clothes. I used to think it strange that he had a different overcoat on every time he came to visit me. There was a character in the comics that was called Count Fewclothes ... Fred's pals, from whom he borrowed clothes, named him 'Count Fewclothes'."[31] The character in the funnies was short-lived, but the first part of the name stayed with Fred Crowell. Mrs. Crowell was McLennan's only "countess."

Another lady who came to McLennan as a bride and is still living there some 70 years later is Margaret Jones. On Thanksgiving Day in October 1918, she married a tall, handsome brakeman, Percy Jones. The young couple took the train to McLennan and stayed at the hotel while their home was being built. They were still there when Armistice was signed on 11 November 1918. Margaret Jones recalls that a special train was sent to Peace River and "returned well supplied with liquid refreshments for the dance that was held that night in Louis Benoit's poolhall."[32]

Born on a farm in Uxbridge, Ontario, Percy Jones had little interest in railroading until he visited a sister married to a CPR trainman at Moose Jaw, Saskatchewan. He was soon aboard a caboose working for that railway, but some years later developed an interest in neuropathy and left to attend Davis College of Neuropathy in Los Angeles. After graduation in March 1912, he returned to Moose Jaw and set up a practise, but the outbreak of World War I changed the economic picture. He went west to Prince Rupert, then backtracked to Edmonton, where he signed on with the ED & BC.[33] Throughout his life, Jones was meticulous about his appearance and careful about his

weight, and when an accident befell a railway comrade he always knew what poultice to use or what medicine to administer.

As railroaders settled in McLennan they played significant roles in the community and civic affairs of the town. In 1918, locomotive foreman Fred Bellis was a member of the first school board. At various times, Agent Harry Swift, Engineer Ed Faust, Conductor Percy Jones, Dispatchers George Thompson, Ernie Bromley, and Pat Brown served on the school board. When the hamlet was incor-

At McLennan, "Count" Crowell, on the occasion of his last trip. L to R: *Fireman Jack Griffith, CNR Engineer B.B. Shaw, Engineer George Malloy, Machinist Jimmy Hagan, Engineer Fred Crowell, Conductor Claus Turninga, Conductor Jack Carley, Engineer Wm. Donaldson, Conductor Jens Hansen, Brakeman Bill Wintermute, Conductor Harry Chausse, Brakeman George Hughes.*
Photo: Courtesy of R.D.C. Comrie

porated as a village on 1 February 1944, Station Agent Harry Swift was elected mayor. Master Mechanic Archie Wotherspoon was a councillor and Express Messenger Leon R. Kvittem secretary treasurer.

When the village was incorporated as a town four years later, Locomotive Foreman William Kirkland was elected Mayor. He served in this capacity for 20 years.[34] Seeing the need for progress, Bill Van Buskirk bought a small diesel electric plant in the 1930s to supply the town with electric light and power. He had been a lineman prior to transferring to train service and his training came in useful in the new enterprise. Later, Conductor Tom Bradner[35] became his partner until the business was sold to Henri Charbonneau, who also had worked on the building of the railway. Throughout the years, railroaders continued to be in the forefront of everything that happened in McLennan.

Bridge and Building Foreman Jack Rouse on bridge building at
Mile 345, Smoky subdivision, c. 1916.
Photo: Courtesy of J.G. Rouse

5

End of Steel

With lightening speed, construction towns sprung up along the railway route to accommodate the army of men engaged on railway construction. As the line crept forward, new locations became end of steel. Many of the construction towns disappeared overnight as the workers and "boomers" moved on, leaving the debris of construction camps and abandoned shacks in their wake. Labor problems, combined with financial difficulties and the engineers' indecision about the best route into Peace River Crossing, must have made it a turbulent period for McArthur. For a time he concentrated on pushing the main line of the ED & BC west from McLennan.

Quigley and McPherson won the contract to build all the bridges for J.D. McArthur. Locomotive Engineer Cy Barker remembered them as a Mutt and Jeff team of bachelors; one was tall and lanky and the other short and stocky. It was no small feat for them to keep their men working ahead of the steel laying gang. In addition to wooden trestle bridges, Quigley and McPherson built the concrete piers for the Smith and Peace River steel bridges. Piles for bridges were driven by horse power. A man by the name of Sanky was their key horseman. While the piles were being driven, workers often stopped working to watch in awe as he controlled the horses by voice command.

As grading continued, caches were established along the right-of-way by Allie MacDonell, a nephew of J.D. McArthur.[1] The last one was near the present site of Culp, named after an ED & BC conductor Joe Culp. Syd Thompson, whose integrity was respected by the settlers, was in charge.[2] He later became "postmaster at Watino and people in the district with problems came to him for advice."[3] He was an outdoorsman who loved the Smoky Valley through which the railway was pushing forward.

The end of steel was in the vicinity of Culp early in June 1915. Ahead, the steep hills of the Smoky Valley necessitated a 10 mile descent to the valley, crossing the river, then a similar ascent the other side to cover a distance of 3.5 miles as the crow flies. This territory was similar to that found in mountainous areas. A steam shovel, six graders, scrapers, and manned wheelbarrows were used as a wave of straining, sweating men toiled to build the grade.[4]

George Robinson had come north on the railway's construction with C.S. Wilson Construction of Edmonton. He wrote, "Our contract was across the Smoky and a couple of miles up the hill from where the bridge was to be built."[5] Farther on, other contractors were building other sections of the grade toward Spirit River. Robinson was a timekeeper, a position that carried a good deal of responsibility. It was imperative that the timekeeper be honest and reliable. If the man hired for this position was unknown to the company, enquiries were made into his background.

In the summer of 1915, the notorious "Baldy Red" came on the scene. Not many knew him by his real name, George Yeoman, but his name became linked with bootlegging. Although he was not the only bootlegger by any means, he became one of the best known in northern communities.[6] Yeoman, whose nickname is said to be derived from the ring of reddish hair surrounding his bald crown, had moved west with railway construction.[7] Few could tell a story like Baldy Red and this sometimes was useful in his frequent brushes with the law.

When Baldy arrived at the Smoky River, Contractor Charlie Wilson, who had known him on the Grand Trunk Pacific Railway, warned Timekeeper Robinson to keep an eye on him. Robinson recalls, "Baldy hauled a load of sacked oats from the supply depot at Cache 19 and, of course, I checked them when he delivered them at our camp. Two bags were missing! Baldy drove horses! And he also tried to charge freight on the two bags he pinched."[8]

The locations of the first settlements along the east banks of the Smoky River have long since disappeared. At Pruden's Crossing a small cable ferry crossed the river. Beaver Landing was located a short distance downstream from Pruden's Crossing.[9] Many of the high-rollers who had descended on Mirror Landing and High Prairie moved to where the action was just beginning. Buildings were in various stages of erection to cater to a predominantly youthful, boisterous clientele.[10] George Robinson describes Pruden's Crossing as "quite a place in 1915, some 25 to 30 buildings and all logs. One street ran parallel with the river with buildings on both sides, there were a few stores . . . and many other log shanties occupied by ladies who carried on business which was not advertised in the papers."[11] There was also an abundance of those we would now call 'hustlers,' card sharpers and gamblers.

Although liquor was banned north of the 55th parallel, it seemed to be in plentiful supply from bootleggers and those who manufactured moonshine. Whiskey could be bought at 50 cents a shot. The Royal North West Mounted Police had a post in the vicinity and at intervals they staged raids of the bootlegging establishments and brothels. If the ladies received advance warning, they escaped to a hideaway in the hills, leaving a telltale trail of silk fragments torn from their dresses.

Construction town on east side of Smoky River, looking toward river, 1915
Photo: Glenbow Archives, McDermid Collection, NC6-1568

Later that summer, Quigley and McPherson began building the bridge over the Smoky River two miles upstream from Pruden's Crossing. Close by, a settlement with similar activities sprang up. With virtually no recreational facilities for a population largely made up of young, virile, single males, the brothels and poolrooms offered the only social activities for most of them and

brawls and fist fights often erupted. It was impossible for the few members of the Royal North West Mounted Police, scattered across the country, to keep control. As construction moved on, realizing the era of railway building was coming to an end, many of the professional gamblers sought other ways to earn a living. A number of them even became railroaders. Many of the old "rails" who remained in northern Alberta were top-notch poker players.

During the summer of 1915, another hamlet sprang up on the west side of the Smoky River. Most of the business places of Pruden's Crossing moved to the new village of Smoky, which at that time consisted mainly of tarpaper shacks and tents, but this was a more respectable community.[12]

New Smoky, later named Watino, on the west side of the Smoky River
Photo: Glenbow Archives, McDermid Collection, NC6-1563

In later years, Agent Operator A.P. "Bert" Bott was involved in changing the town's name to Watino. He had spent his boyhood in England, his army service in France and time as a prisoner-of-war in Germany before emigrating to Canada and joining the ED & BC. He had married a girl from Donnelly and they made their first home in Smoky. A number of towns had Smoky in their name and Bott decided to end the confusion this caused. Frank Eagan, then agent at Enilda, suggested a number of Indian names. They were all much too long, so the two men shortened one of the names to the more manageable Watino. The Post Office liked it and so did the railway. Watino appeared on timetables from then on.

To cross the Smoky River more easily while building the permanent bridge, Quigley and McPherson used the same tactics they had used at Smith. A temporary trestle bridge was built on the ice and by the end of 1915 the steel crossed the Smoky River on it. As the track-layer edged toward Spirit River, two shifts of men were used to keep the work on schedule. In April 1916, when the ice went out and most of the temporary bridge with it, the new bridge was still under construction. The first train crossed the completed bridge in May 1916, ringing the death knell for settlements on the east side of the Smoky.

Meanwhile, 600 men and 60 teams worked on the grade from the top of the west Smoky Hill to Spirit River, and on a branch

Station at Smoky, 1925. L to R: Engineers Henry "Hank" Pentzer and "Protestant" Bill Preston, Conductor Jack Carley, Agent "Bert" Bott and Ralph Fullerton, agent at Clairmont.
Photo: Holden Swift

line from Rycroft, 5.3 miles east of Spirit River, south to Grande Prairie.[13] Grading was completed to Spirit River Station in May 1914.[14] By the end of January 1916, the steel had been laid to there, bypassing the original settlement at Spirit River and Dunvegan to its north.

already aware of the real estate speculation there, his land scouts should have apprised him of the situation. Macintyre eloquently described the area in his diary of 1912: "What do you know about Dunvegan? Great Scot! Half a dozen buildings mostly in connection with the Hudson's Bay Store and that's all –

Remains of trestle bridge after the Smoky River flooded in spring, 1916.
Photo: Provincial Archives of Alberta, Acc. 76.283

It is doubtful whether or not McArthur ever intended building through Dunvegan. A route map filed in November 1911 showed the line running south of the settlement. "Dunvegan" was already in the railway's name when he took over control of the ED & BC. Before the railway became a reality, land values escalated and if McArthur was not

but oh the hills and ravines – sheer drop of 700 feet. . . . Such an utterly impossible place for a townsite."[15]

The railway brought a dismal end to Dunvegan which had made history as a fur trading post, fort and Protestant mission. When building began on the ED & BC, real estate speculators in Edmonton used the

"Dunvegan" in the railway's name to their advantage. They advertised the settlement as the Eldorado of the North. A modern city, with paved streets, avenues of prosperous homes, bridges, and bustling hotels, was described to sell lots.[16] Lots that did not exist and some on steep hillsides were bought and sold to unsuspecting buyers, many of whom lost their savings in the venture.[17]

There is a story told of one investor who travelled to Dunvegan to look over his purchase. On his return a friend accosted him in Edmonton and said, "I thought you went to live on your land at Dunvegan." "I can't say as how I actually lived on it," was the curt reply. "I only leaned up against it." Now the railway had bypassed it, the closure of the Hudson's Bay Post in May 1918 was the second severe blow.[18] All Dunvegan had left was its ghosts, a ferry and some empty buildings. By 1922, Dunvegan had returned to its original state.[19]

Grande Prairie might have suffered the same fate as Dunvegan had its settlers not relentlessly pressured the federal and provincial governments for years to authorize financing for a railway.[20] In July 1911, Grande Prairie City had risen in importance when the Dominion government moved its land office from Grouard. Now its inhabitants wanted a railway and they did not care who built it. After repeated requests by the minister of Railway and Canals at Ottawa, McArthur agreed to build a branch line to Grande Prairie City.[21] To ensure that this branch reached its destination, the provincial government guaranteed the bonds to the extent of $20 thousand per mile; but had to dispose of the securities at a very low price.

The ED & BC had preliminary survey parties in the Grande Prairie area by June 1915 under the direction of locating engineer G. Murray.[22] George H. Webster was awarded the grading contract from Rycroft. Webster, at Mile 27.2, was named after the contractor, who later became a Member of the Legislative Assembly. After blasting through the Saddle Mountains, grading moved faster and was completed by 1 November.

The shrill whistle of the track-layer train was music to the settlers' ears as rails neared Grande Prairie early in 1916. In March, the steel reached the hamlet with Dymetro "Mike" Obniawka in charge of the steel gang.[23] Obniawka, Austrian by birth, was orphaned at an early age and emigrated to Canada in 1910. The strapping young man was soon working for the Grand Trunk Pacific, but the railway building in the Peace River country, where land was available, attracted him. He joined the steel gang at Smoky. Although he filed on a homestead two miles west of Sexsmith, he continued to work for the railway until 1929.

A temporary station was erected at Grande Prairie in April 1916.[24] B.F. Hall arrived from Spirit River in the fall of 1917 to build the new station one block east of the first structure. He stayed on until May 1918 to assist the new station agent, Ben Harmer. But the genial and accommodating Harmer was not a telegrapher, and when this skill became a requirement for the agent at Grande Prairie, he transferred to the CPR.

On 22 March 1916, Obniawka watched the throngs of eager faces lining the right-of-way in Grande Prairie as the track-layer completed its task ahead of schedule to the sound of a brass band.[25] The last mile of track was being laid when a special passenger train moved slowly along the skeleton track carrying railway officials and dignitaries for the special celebrations. Margaret Benson, one of the first white women to live in the area, drove the symbolic golden spike held by a railway employee. For years, Arsen Student liked to exhibit a mark on his hand caused when Mrs. Benson missed the spike on the first try.[26]

Mrs. Margaret Benson driving the last spike on the ED & BC at Grande Prairie on 22 March 1916
Photo: Courtesy of Pioneer Museum
Society of Grande Prairie

In his speech, General Manager Rathbone Smith told travellers what they could expect when they travelled the newly laid track: "We wish to call your attention to the fact that we are now operating on over 100 miles of skeleton track. There will be delays and our trains will have to run slowly, but we will do our best and we hope you will not be too hasty with your criticism."[27] The inhabitants of Grande Prairie City did not care. They had the railway for which they had fought so hard. But the general manager's warnings came true all too soon.

To celebrate the railway's arrival, Grande Prairie hosted a Frontier Exhibition and Agricultural Fair from 1 to 5 July 1916. A special train decorated with union jack flags, red ensigns and banners took dignitaries to the event. Doctor McLennan and Rathbone Smith travelled in the private car "Lac La Biche."[28] Everything was arranged, but no one could plan the weather. Some revellers were stranded for nearly a week when torrential rains washed out track on the Grande Prairie line.[29] Clay and dirt had been used as ballast due to the long haul and difficulty of transporting gravel from the Smoky pit with its steep grades. As the rains subsided crews worked frantically to rebuild small bridges and restore the damaged roadbed.

Trains were operating again when the Willis family arrived from Exeter, Ontario with household possessions, purebred heifers, chickens and ducks. On their way north, one of the ducks escaped from the car. Although the train was travelling at normal speed, Mr. Willis hopped off, captured the bird and managed to catch up to the train.[30] The Willis family detrained at Sexsmith, where another son, Orville, made his appearance into the world on 28 August 1916. He must have liked the rock and roll of the train because he became a railway conductor in later years.

Roadmaster Charlie Johnson and Conductor John Carley at Watino Pit.
Photo: Courtesy of R.D.C. Comrie

6

Clouds on the Horizon

Construction of the branch from Rycroft to Grande Prairie halted temporarily the construction of the main line of the ED & BC westward, and Spirit River became an end of steel town. Grain for shipment by train was hauled to the bustling community from as far west as the Pouce Coupe area.[1] In mid-June 1916, McArthur announced that Quigley and McPherson had been awarded a contract for construction of the main line from Spirit River Station to the British Columbia border.[2] Grading was done on 80 percent of the distance and bridges built over several creeks.[3] Due to the war effort, steel was a scarce commodity, and by the time it became available, McArthur was fighting to save his railways. Consequently, this extension was abandoned.

On the land not taken up by the Spirit River townsite, McArthur set up a "model" farm in an attempt to show incoming settlers what could be done by raising high quality livestock.[4] The farm, located at the top of the hill south of the railway station, was operated by his cousin, J. Arthur McArthur until it passed from J.D.'s hands.[5]

Spirit River townsite with McArthur farm and home in foreground, 22 August 1917
Photo: J. Martinos, courtesy of Don Moore

By the spring of 1916, passenger trains were doing a brisk business. The railway operated its own sleeping cars on the twice weekly trains and seldom was a berth empty. On 9 June 1916, the *Edmonton Bulletin* carried a story about the new cafe service managed by Sam Freeman. "Not only is the service good," said the newspaper, "but the dining car is so well arranged that it is a pleasure to eat in it. Fine napery and beautiful flowers show the excellent taste of the caterer and the reasonable prices make the service a decided convenience to the trip to the northland." The railway had leased the cafe car privileges to Freeman for $800 per year.

Although apparently prosperous, the railways were struggling financially. McArthur had managed to build railways despite a depression and a war that was making increasing demands on Canada's money, manpower and supplies. The effects of these demands were beginning to show in late 1916, but the public was not yet aware of the difficulties they were causing the contractor.[6]

In April 1916 the government of Canada voted for the subsidy promised for the Grande Prairie branch.[7] By June 1917 McArthur had received only 78.08 percent of the $160 352 subsidy.[8] This resulted from the report of the inspecting engineer from the Department of Railway and Canals in Ottawa whose inspection of the construction revealed serious deviations from the agreed specifications.[9] The engineer estimated the cost per mile at $11 726.93, far below the $27 780.52 per mile claimed to be the average cost by the railway.

Gradually, the cool breezes of criticism began to blow.[10] There was censure by the opposition in the Alberta Legislature of the government's financial backing of the contractor. There were complaints about the railway's quality of service, its cost and its elastic schedule. The war had effectively curtailed immigration and the number of settlers travelling north. Track maintenance forces fought a losing battle with ballast and new rails in short supply. Passengers' help was often enlisted to get the equipment back on track when an accident occurred.

In the summer of 1917, A.G. Sutherland joined the railway as general superintendent, but the condition of the railway track was already in a sorry state. In desperation, Roadmaster Jim Mulcahy devised a method of replacing damaged rails. On 6 September 1917, he wrote from Spirit River to Frank Donis, extra gang foreman,

> I have made requisitions for rails to Mr. Sutherland and he claims that he cannot give me any rails between McLennan and Grande Prairie, so when you find a very bad one go to the nearest siding, take out

rails from side track and put in main line and put your bad rails in side track that you take from main line. Leave a man to protect the track until you return with bent rail to replace good rail taken out.[11]

Later that month, Donis was operating a track motor when it jumped the track about a mile from Spirit River. The impact caused a wood and iron seat back to spring forward and strike Roadmaster Mulcahy in the back. He felt the injuries were severe enough to sue the railway. The dreadful condition of the roadbed was described in the court room: "The track east of Spirit River was in bad condition, being a skeleton track, in many places sunken in mud, the rails surface-bent and kinked, or perhaps I might make the condition clearer by saying the rails were bent both vertically and horizontally."[12]

During 1918, as the cash flow shortage became more acute, the contractor tried to effect economies. Because of the railways' dependency on borrowed capital and the scarcity of money, bond receipts fell far below face value and interest rates rose.[13] Interest payments alone were crippling. There was a slowing of construction work and a curtailment of the amount of money spent on maintenance work on roadbeds already built. This was to prove costly in the future.

With the optimism of a true pioneer and entrepreneur McArthur made numerous trips to Ottawa. He still felt the colonization grants that would solve his money problems would be forthcoming. William Burns and Thomas Turnbull travelled into the Peace River country to inspect line conditions. It must have been with some sadness that Turnbull reported the deterioration of the railway which he had nurtured in infancy. In the report to the government of Canada, it was estimated that it would cost approximately $425 thousand to bring the properties up to proper operating standards.[14]

In March 1919, to get cash to keep the railways operating, McArthur was forced to issue, against his $3.5 million equity, $2.4 million in debenture stock to the Union Bank of Canada.[15] This brought the bank into the railway picture along with the provincial government. That spring the government of Canada granted an additional subsidy of $258 797.16 to be used on reconditioning the line.[16] It was stipulated that the improvements would be inspected and approved by an engineer appointed by the Board of Railway Commissioners.

In July 1919, when the inspection was made, McArthur accompanied the engineer. The subsequent report said the road was still in bad shape and many places on the line had rotted ties and lacked ballast. Also noted was the deplorable condition of the track west of Smoky [Watino] and the branch from Rycroft to Grande Prairie. Spring rains had softened the soil. Rails were sinking in the clay roadbed, which the passage of trains churned into mud.[17] The engineer estimated that $950 thousand was needed to recondition the road. He also noted the scarcity of rolling stock and subsequent loss of business due to overcrowding on trains. The war was over and people were on the move.

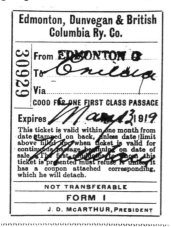

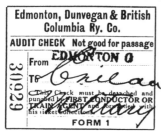

First Class ticket to Enilda

Richard Hazlewood's arrival from Winnipeg early in May, to look over the McArthur lines, indicates the builder was trying to obtain the best possible advice about the roadbeds on his lines.[18] Hazlewood was one of the best known railway engineers in Canada. He was the son of an engineer who had been allied with Sir Sanford Fleming during the construction of the Intercolonial Railway. The younger Hazlewood had been associated with the CPR, and since 1904, had worked for J.D. McArthur on a number of his construction projects.[19]

During this time, there had been growing unrest in the ranks of western labor. Wages and collective bargaining rights were key issues.[20] In mid-May 1919, a general strike had broken out crippling Winnipeg within a couple of days. Railway shopmen were among those who responded to the strike call. At this time, McArthur was in Ottawa trying to reach an agreement with the government. In comparison with this new development, McArthur's problems were minuscule and he returned to Winnipeg. In a letter to his general manager dated 31 May 1919 McArthur said: "I hope the strike will be settled by the time you receive this letter. Things are cleaning up nicely in Winnipeg. I think by the beginning of the week the strike will be a thing of the past." McArthur was overly optimistic. It was 26 June before there was a back to work movement after Premier Norris of Manitoba had agreed to appoint a Royal Commission. After a protracted and bitter struggle, the Trades and Labor Council called off the strike which had lasted six weeks.[21]

The work stoppage appears to have had little effect on McArthur's rail lines, although the agreement signed by the shopmen the previous year was due to expire at the end of June.[22] The centre of this unrest remained in Winnipeg, but there were sympathetic work stoppages in other cities such as Edmonton and Calgary, and by members of other railway unions.

Locomotive No. 5 siphoning water
Photo: Courtesy of Public Archives of Canada,
Department of Interior Collection, PA 40685

A casualty of the sympathetic strike was Albert Whiteman.[23] He had arrived in Edmonton in 1909 to start a job with the Grand Trunk Pacific in Calder. His expertise was airbrakes, and he was soon local chairman of the carmen's organization.[24] The GTP gave Whiteman and some others their walking papers when the dust had settled from the strike. Whiteman set up a wood and coal hauling business; however, some years later when he was told of a vacancy for a carman on the ED & BC he grabbed the opportunity to return to his trade.[25]

In the summer of 1919, bumper crops were reported in the Peace River country.[26] The roadbeds deteriorated further due to inadequate maintenance. In September, train service on the Grande Prairie branch was suspended entirely and a track motor had to be used to transport what was said to be a "hunting" party of CPR operating officers from Rycroft to Grande Prairie. It seems it was actually an inspection trip and the report that followed blasted the railway builder.

> The difficulties of the system are due to the fact that it was evidently built by the contractor with a view to selling it at once to the Grand Trunk Pacific, or some other system, and the construction was of the cheapest possible type. When the builder found himself saddled with the responsibility of operation, it was then impossible to do the necessary financing to enable him to put the property in condition for handling traffic. He had no proper organization for operating a railway and it is not unfair to say that the road has been managed in a scandalously inefficient way.[27]

The CPR report was harsh in its criticism of McArthur, and one wonders if it was completely fair. There is evidence that he had dreams for the country that went beyond lining his own pockets. Had the war not intervened, the result might have been the opposite. "It cannot be overlooked that McArthur put rail lines into the north country while others talked about it, but never acted," and opened up a vast, rich economic territory.[28] As a railway contractor, McArthur expected to make a profit from construction of the lines; but, must have known that he could not operate them without obtaining a government subsidy.

However, on 5 October, Alberta's premier was in Ottawa accompanied by provincial treasurer, Hon. C.R. Mitchell. Reports persisted that they were there to obtain assistance for McArthur's rail lines.[29] In fact, McArthur was also there pleading for financial relief. He appears to have been confident that Ottawa would provide the money needed to rescue his railway, or arrange for a takeover by the national railways. If those options failed he hoped that the CPR would buy his lines. After the Ottawa trip, the Alberta premier said the province would pay the interest due on the railway's bonds out of the general revenue if no takeover of the lines was imminent.

As the ground froze and the roadbed firmed in the fall of 1919, the Board of Railway Commissioners instructed other railways to rent sufficient equipment to the ED & BC to ensure that the crop was moved out of the Peace country.[30] The passing of the Cow Bill Act by the government of Alberta and the drought in southern Alberta prompted a sharp increase in the number of cattle shipped north. Returning on 12 November from a trip to Spirit River, McArthur told the press that the amount of business in the north now "amply justified the optimism of 1913." He mentioned that there were exceptional difficulties facing the railways but that all the traffic would be handled.

That McArthur was anxious to improve efficiency of operations was evident in a letter to his general manager dated 25 November 1919: "Your letter of the 19th re: appointment Judge as Assistant Superintendent. . . . What I want is that every trip will show results." Jack Judge's experience made him well qualified for the position of assistant superintendent. He had moved up through the ranks from rodman, instrumentman, transit man, resident and maintenance engineer, to roadmaster. Experience gained on the Northern Ontario Railway and CPR had been useful when he joined the ED & BC in 1912.[31] His article, "Early Railroading in Northern Alberta," gave an interesting account of the early years of the ED & BC.[32] When he left the railway in 1922, it was to take a position with the government of Alberta where he was eventually appointed Deputy Minister of Municipal Affairs.

The completed Heart River Bridge
Photo: McDermid Studios, Edmonton

Packard is transported on a J.D. McArthur Co. Ltd. flat car.
Photo: Courtesy of R.D.C. Comrie

Part Two

The Central Canada Railway and
Alberta & Great Waterways Railway: 1905-1919

Train No. 6 on Peace River Bridge on route to McLennan.
Photo: Courtesy of Peace River Centennial Museum

7

The Railway Reaches the Mighty Peace

According to a Beaver Indian legend, those who drink from the clear waters of the Mighty Peace River are destined to return.[1] The Athabasca River bridge at Smith was still being built when McArthur was making plans for reaching districts in the Peace River country where vast agricultural lands were being developed. Settlers had been trickling into this area from 1905, and with the promise of a railway the trickle became a steady stream.

In 1913, the ambitious railway builder became president of yet another company. The Central Canada Railway was incorporated to construct a branch from the ED & BC main line north to Peace River Crossing, then west toward the settlement of Waterhole, on the steep banks of the Peace River, about 13 miles north and east of Dunvegan, and a branch line north into the Battle River area, but the latter was never built.[2] That fall, 100 miles of railway from McLennan to Waterhole were guaranteed at $20 thousand per mile.[3] Work on the Central Canada Rail-

way grade began at Winagami Junction on the ED & BC, 1.3 miles west of McLennan during the winter of 1913. The right-of-way was staked and cleared for a distance of 30 miles under the direction of G. Murray, the locating engineer. Townsite land at Peace River Crossing was purchased in the name of the ED & BC Railway.[4] Caches were set up and stocked with supplies in readiness for grading.[5]

With the arrival of spring, grading commenced. Tie contractors unable to meet their commitments, impeded track-laying on the ED & BC early in 1915, releasing the Pioneer for work on the Central Canada Railway. By April, 21 miles of steel were laid,[6] reaching Reno, where a station agent was located to handle the business. That fall the first carload of wheat was shipped south. It had been brought to the rail head by sleigh from the Vanrena district, beyond Waterhole.[7]

John Timothy had the grading contract from Reno to Peace River Crossing, and

Quigley and McPherson took the contract for the laying of steel and bridge building. The first 30 miles were fairly straight forward, but the next 16 required negotiation of a 2.6 percent grade down to Peace River Crossing. Its setting – in a deep valley at the confluence of the Heart, Smoky and Peace rivers surrounded by majestic hills – was a nightmare for civil engineers. Surveys gave a choice between two routes. Disagreement over the route down the hills, and financial problems, brought a halt to construction work on the branch. In a telegram dated 8 March 1915, Rathbone Smith assured the residents that no change affecting the Crossing was contemplated.[8]

By 1915, McArthur admitted he was unable to sell the railway bonds and attributed his failure to the closure of the London money market in England and the depression that followed the outbreak of hostilities in Europe. By raising interest rates from 4.5 to 5 percent in April 1915, the provincial government was able to peddle bonds that enabled it to provide the J.D. McArthur Company with a loan of $2 million for building of the branch from Winagami to Peace River Crossing.[9]

Once the problems of financing and route had been resolved, work began again with the objective of reaching Peace River Crossing by November 1915. Contractors, Timothy and Riley, attempted to meet the schedule. Henry Dimsdale had taken over as locating engineer. By mid-October 1915, residents of the Peace River Valley welcomed the sight of the smoke curling skywards from the stacks of steam locomotives on Judah Hill.

Judah was named after the railway's auditor, who spent his days juggling railway finances. Noel Fulton Judah, who preferred to be called Tom, had been coaxed west from Montreal that year by McArthur.[10] He had worked for other railways and his expertise in freight rates was second to none. When the office building at Dunvegan Yards burned down three years later, only the huge eight foot high cement safe and its contents remained intact. The staff promptly dubbed it "Judah's monument," and so it remained for almost 50 years.

The number of settlers increased as the steel inched closer to Peace River Crossing. They complained about the type of transportation and its cost from the city of Edmonton to Dunvegan Yards, a six mile distance. "The service provided by John McNeill's Twin City buses over a dirt road for 50 cents per person" was fairly comfortable in fine weather, but "after a heavy rain storm it was a jolting, uncertain trip" and it was even less pleasant during a winter snow storm.[11] This difficulty was resolved by arranging with the Grand Trunk Pacific to travel over their tracks to facilities at 107 Avenue and 121 Street.[12] A temporary shelter was erected and a block office built, as early as 1914 for the joint service of the railways concerned. Trains obtained clearances and all arrivals were registered there.[13] At that location, George Lomas was one of the earliest operators.[14]

*Surrounded by a slough, the station at 121 Street in
Edmonton was built on stilts.*
Photo: Glenbow Archives, NA-639-5

Twin City Transfer No. 3
Photo: Glenbow Archives, McDermid Collection, NC-6-1312

On train days, Agent Bill Adams or Assistant Agent Frank Poole from Dunvegan Yards arrived there an hour ahead of train time to sell passenger tickets.[15] Adams had no training as a telegraph operator, but in later years he succeeded in mastering the key. He spent five years at Dunvegan Yards before switching jobs with Bert Carrick at Peace River.

The increase in passenger business to the north prompted the purchase of sleeping cars. The services of Twin City Transfer were enlisted to operate the new sleeping cars and to handle the ticket business from their downtown offices. The transfer company also inaugurated a special stage service from the end of steel to Peace River Crossing, which changed its name to Peace River shortly afterwards.

As crews worked around the clock, kerosene lanterns twinkled like fireflies along the grade down the hill from the end of steel. The bouyant, expectant feeling in the town of Peace River, dissipated when freeze-up arrived with the steel still more than a mile from the station site. Because there was insufficient ballast on the track downhill from Judah, only work trains ventured the descent.[16] The 590 foot long and 140 foot high steel bridge over the North Heart was not finished when the *Peace River Record* reported on 10 December 1915, "Steel Completed to Heart River Bridge." Residents were disappointed to learn that service would remain at the top of the hill until completion of the Heart River Bridge.

Nevertheless, the steel was close enough for Premier Sifton to be a passenger on the first train that went that far when the ground was frozen early in December 1915.[17] Some freight was also handled to the Heart River rail head. Until trains could run into Peace River, the nearest water supply for locomotives was at Tank near Nampa, Mile 30.[18] Consequently, to obtain railway service patrons travelled up the steep hill from Peace River to Judah. The spring of 1916 brought more settlers on the lurching, swaying, rattling trains as they negotiated the unsettled, poorly ballasted roadbed to the end of steel. They detrained in a small clearing in the bush at a temporary platform. By May 1916, the last bent was placed in the Heart River bridge and it was opened for traffic.

Track tipped by a slide on the East Peace River Hill in 1916
Photo: Glenbow Archives, NA-1830-6

About this time, McArthur was organizing the Central Canada Express Company, with himself as president.[19] The closed corporation handled express over the McArthur railways. The new company's General Superintendent Chris Dowling and Assistant Superintendent C. Hope had offices in Edmonton's Quebec Bank Building where a ticket office was also opened. Toward the end of May 1916, Charles Cockroft arrived in Peace River to arrange for the opening of a branch office. On 26 May 1916, an article titled "Central Canada Express Company" in the *Peace River Record* announced: "The office of the company at Peace River will be at the Central Canada depot, where all the parcels will be delivered, and the delivery from the depot will be handled by the Palace Livery barn as agents for the company."

Small, youthful looking Albert Craig Carrick was the agent in charge of the Peace River depot. He had begun railroading at 14 years of age in a small station outside London, England. When the experienced ticket agent was sleeping off the effects of a "night on the town," Carrick would handle ticket sales. Market days were the busiest and to have sufficient height at the ticket wicket he stood on a wooden crate.[20]

Bert Carrick was a survivor of the devastating Regina cyclone on Dominion Day 1912, which destroyed the CPR roundhouse and station where he was working.[21] Later, a conflict with Carrick's superiors culminated in his transfer to Edmonton, where he heard about the railway being pushed north by J.D. McArthur. He applied for an agent's position at a starting salary of $52 per month for ten

Peace River station was built in 1916. Temporary station is at the left.
Photo: Glenbow Archives, NA-2812-18

hours a day, six days a week. A few years later, he was joined in the Peace River station by Assistant Agent, Bill Moore. It was a job he expected to last a few months but Moore, who had an artificial leg, remained there for 44 years.[22]

Carrick also had a wooden leg. Nevertheless, he was quick of glance and movement. He also possessed a prodigious memory. Recognizing his abilities the railway transferred him from Peace River to Dunvegan Yards in 1921, where he remained until retirement: "He could recall dates and numbers of rail cars that had come into the yards, been sent out, returned and transferred to other roads. If something happened to a car while on the railway, or if it had a particular load, he could recall the details after a year or more had elapsed."[23] A train moving out of the Dunvegan Yards terminal at a much slower pace than usual would try Carrick's patience. Watching it from the side window he would hop up and down on his good leg muttering his closest approach to profanity, "The sons of butches, the sons of butches! What in hell are they doing now?"[24]

For Bert Carrick and the other residents of The Crossing, it must have been a treat to watch the laying of steel in July 1916 on the last stretch of grade between the Heart River Bridge and the depot site. A modern railway station, with a basement, was built that year at a cost of $4 500. Two years later, stockyards also graced the station grounds to handle the livestock which, along with grain and lumber, comprised the bulk of outgoing traffic.

Carload shipments to and from the north were hand led at the Grand Trunk Pacific freight sheds on Namayo Avenue, 97th Street, in Edmonton. The cost of the long haul to Dunvegan Yards for less-than-carload shipments caused complaints. McArthur arranged for the National Paving Company of Winnipeg, a company in which he was a major stockholder, to pave the St. Albert Road, but still the charges continued.[25] From 19 September 1916, all freight shipments were handled at the GTP.[26] An agreement was signed between the railways the following year and remained in effect until 1920.[27]

Ever the entrepreneur, McArthur had begun another fledgling business venture. He was drilling for oil at Tar Island, north of Peace River. On 31 July 1916, the *Edmonton Bulletin*, in a story titled, "Oil Strike At M'Arthur Well," reported: "Oil in considerable quantity was struck at the J.D. McArthur well, 14 miles north of this place on the Peace River on Friday, the 27th., at the depth of 886 feet. The oil is heavy and is pronounced by oil men to be of good quality." The Peace River Oil Company was financed by a group of businessmen, headed by McArthur, and drilled four wells between 1916 and 1923.[28] McArthur had the means to get the valuable commodity to market. All that was necessary was well ballasted railway track. Gravel trains were rushed to the area. A year later, surveys were undertaken to locate a line from Peace River to the oil well.[29] Unfortunately, salt water and an uncontrolled flow of gas dashed McArthur's hopes for a producing oil well.

The first special train arrived in Peace River on 11 August 1916. Aboard was the first cabinet member to visit the Peace River country, Hon. Dr. Roche, minister of the Interior. He was accompanied by Dr. McLennan, and other railway officials. This was only one of a number of special trains into Peace River before the year was out.

Early in September, McArthur accompanied a group of Union Bank of Canada officials from Winnipeg. As the railways' bankers, these gentlemen had a particular interest in the progress being made by McArthur's railways and oil wells. Less than a week later, another special train, consisting of three coaches and a diner, carried 47 Edmonton Board of Trade members to Peace River. Dr. McLennan showed them the town and one of the McArthur oil wells, before taking them by motor car across country to Spirit River Station [changed to Spirit River in 1920]. There they were met by the same train and travelled on to Grande Prairie.

J.D. McArthur's dependence on his friendship with Premier Arthur Sifton and the financial support of his Liberal government is indicated by a report in the Peace River newspaper in June 1917, which states that he spent several days campaigning on behalf of the local Liberal candidate. This personal approach to the farmers left with them "the inference that should they not do his bidding at the polls it is all off with their chances for a railway past the Peace River."[30] Although out of character for McArthur, this seems to have been something he was willing to do in an effort to save his railways.

McArthur did not stop pressuring the federal government for a colonization railway subsidy. Undoubtedly, having its own difficulties obtaining sufficient money to support the war effort, Ottawa refused. But a $175 thousand subsidy was voted toward the building of a bridge to span Peace River.[31] This was McArthur's last major construction project. Contracts for its construction were let out in December 1916. The substructure of the bridge was designed by the railway's assistant chief engineer, William Jackson, and preparatory work began in January 1917. The following year, a veteran western bridge builder from Winnipeg, S.C. Hill, arrived to replace the superintendent of construction.[32] The contract for the superstructure was let to the Canadian Bridge Company. Construction began in the latter part of May 1918, under the direction of L.E. Mahon, who had superintended the erection of several large bridges.

Crews worked in shifts on the bridge. An electric light plant supplied current for powerful arc lamps used for night operations. The construction noises became the backdrop against which residents lived. Townspeople had the opportunity to earn some extra money as laborers, while others used their teams of horses to haul gravel to make cement for the bridge piers.[33] The crane swung the last girder into place in mid-October. Dr. McLennan made his final inspection of the completed bridge on 8 November 1918. It had cost about $900 thousand.[34]

It was a proud day for Joe Hawkins when he drove the first work train over the newly built Peace River bridge.[35] Hawkins had arrived in McLennan a few months earlier, with his wife and children, and was hired by the railway as a locomotive engineer using as reference experience gained at the throttle of CPR locomotives. He eventually worked in the McLennan shops as night locomotive foreman, where his calm temperament kept tempers under control.[36] In time he tried homesteading, but returned to the railway during the manpower shortage of the war years.

When completed, the Peace River Bridge was 1 736 feet long with 11 steel spans set on concrete piers and abutments. The structure had no guard rails or decking to enable horse teams and vehicles to cross safely. A sign warned those who used the bridge that they did so at their own risk. Vigorous lobbying by the local board of trade for its planking was eventually successful. In April 1918, an appropriation for $175 thousand was approved by the Alberta government for the project.[37] Shortly afterwards, vehicular traffic moved back and forth across the structure. River boats plied the river during the months of open water and larger vessels, such as the "D.A. Thomas," had hinged smoke stacks to enable it to pass beneath the bridge.[38]

While the bridge was being built, railway construction continued westward toward Waterhole under the direction of Contractor, W.T. Craig. Floyd Kresge, who had worked on the Peace River bridge, built one mile of this grade in 1917 and did some more work in 1918 on the 10 miles that were graded. Peter McArthur, a nephew of J.D. McArthur and a director of the Central Canada Railway, had purchased 140 acres of farm land in the Vanrena area for townsite purposes.[39] Because rails were not available, nothing further was done on this portion of the line until later years.

Passenger service was not immediately established to Peace River Crossing. Travellers detraining from ED & BC passenger trains were transferred at McLennan to a locomotive and caboose for the trip. The caboose was equipped with seats along the sides of the back section and a rack above held belongings.[40] McArthur used his Packard car instead of the train to make an inspection trip of his northern lines in July 1919.[41]

8

The Railway Scandal that Toppled a Government

The Alberta and Great Waterways Railway was the most controversial of the lines built by J.D. McArthur. Its construction caused dissension that led to the resignation of Premier Rutherford and several cabinet ministers, a rift in the Liberal party in Alberta, and a disillusioned public. Its history dates back to 1905, the year Alberta became a province, some years before McArthur appeared on the scene.

The A & GW began as another of James Kennedy Cornwall's schemes to develop the north country. Along with several others, Cornwall obtained a Dominion government charter to build a railway. The Athabasca Railway Company was to run from Edmonton to near Fort McMurray.[1] Cornwall was the only incorporator with any substantial interest in the railway which he planned to link up with a new steamboat transportation enterprise he was embarking on.[2] A railway was needed to circumvent the Grand Rapids between Athabasca Landing and Fort McMurray.

Cornwall was in his mid-thirties when the railway charter was acquired. He had been a sailor, mail carrier, trapper, fur trader, riverman and businessman. Known as "Peace River Jim," few white men knew the north like he did. In spite of attempting to interest everyone from newspaper publishers to politicians, he was unsuccessful in obtaining financial support for the railway.[3]

In an attempt to salvage the charter, Cornwall gave an option for $2 500 to Faulkner & Emerson of Winnipeg.[4] It was taken up by the formation of The Athabasca Syndicate. Toward the end of 1906, the syndicate commenced negotiations with the government of Alberta and on 18 October 1907 announced financing could be arranged if the government would guarantee the bonds for $13 thousand per mile. William H. Cushing, minister of Public Works, said the government was not interested.

On 5 June 1908, William R. and Bertrand R. Clarke, bankers from Kansas City, Missouri, obtained an option from syndicate members to purchase all rights under the Athabasca Railway Company charter.[5] Soon afterwards, William Clarke entered into negotiations with the government of Alberta and made a separate arrangement with Cornwall. If the railway enterprise succeeded, he would pay $25 thousand for a controlling share in Cornwall's new steamship enterprise. In return, Cornwall would release his interest in the railway. [He received only $14 500.]

As a precaution, the government investigated the financial stability of the Clarke brothers. Since they were both vice-presidents of The United States Trust Co., their credentials seemed irreproachable.[6] The trust company had been established in 1888 by their father William Bingham Clarke, a Kansas City financier with an excellent reputation. Besides, William was a graduate of Yale University and Bertrand a graduate of Williams College.

Once negotiations with the Alberta government appeared to be progressing satisfactorily, William Clarke looked for a chief engineer for the railway. Dr. John A.L. Waddell, a consulting engineer from Kansas City with impeccable credentials, accepted Clarke's offer and assured him the railway could be built for $17 thousand per mile.[7] His services did not come at bargain prices. The first year he operated on a per diem fee of $50 and expenses. From 1 October 1909, his salary was $25 thousand a year, plus a bonus of $75 thousand for advisory services, an exorbitant amount for those times.

John Waddell was no stranger to Canada. He was Canadian by birth and one of three brothers who were civil engineers.[8] An innovative engineer and prolific writer of articles and books, he relished being in the limelight.[9] He was a widely acclaimed expert on bridge structures.[10] A good deal of his work had been done on railway bridges, and he had been chief engineer on several railway projects.[11] His overseas work occasionally brought him decorations and medals, which he liked to wear when posing for formal photographs. But he left the A & GW with a blot on an otherwise distinguished career.

William Clarke entrusted the Athabasca Syndicate's engineer, J. Woodman, with making arrangements for a survey of the proposed route. Woodman hired Cecil Goddard as assistant chief engineer. He was aware of Goddard's integrity and his experience with railway surveys. Goddard received instructions from Dr. Waddell to keep a low profile, particularly with regard to the press. The railway's lawyer, George Minty had further instructions from Clarke for Goddard, ". . . impress upon him the necessity of securing for us an absolutely conservative report. We want to know from the beginning because it will be suicidal if we deceive ourselves, and I do not want any suggestions he may receive later to change this order, or to betray him into giving us too rosy a story. We want plain, hard, unbiased facts."[12]

By August 1908, the thrill of discovery buoyed Goddard's spirits as the survey crew proceeded toward the Hudson's Bay post at the southeast end of Lac La Biche, then continued on through rough terrain toward Fort McMurray. Meanwhile, Waddell had hired J.M. Phillips, whom he had known in Kansas, to do an independent reconnaissance survey.[13] Clarke's instructions were that it was to be a first class railway – one that would bear up under the strictest criticism and investigation. After his return from the survey, Goddard concluded that Dr. Waddell was willing to settle for an inferior railway. At that time, Waddell drafted a report on the information given to him by Goddard using his own figures in certain places. Goddard refused to sign it until Waddell had made several alterations and assured him the report would not commit him. To Goddard's surprise it later appeared on government files.[14]

By February 1909, William Clarke had abandoned the Dominion charter in favor of one granted by the province and changed the name of the railway to the Alberta and Great Waterways Railway.[15] The principals were the Clarke brothers and William Bain. Bain, a Winnipeg accountant and brother-in-law of Minty, was a director in name only. At the same time, the government of Alberta guaranteed the railway's bonds to the amount of $20 thousand per mile for an estimated distance of 350 miles, plus $400 thousand for establishment of a terminal at Edmonton, retaining an option to purchase at any time.[16] The railway legislation was pushed through on the last day of the session, along with an amendment to the Railway Act transferring the control of railways to the premier from the minister of Public Works.

Clarke, a complete stranger and an American, must have been a promotor with excellent powers of persuasion to succeed where Cornwall and the Athabasca Syndicate, with its large complement of Canadians, had failed. He also obtained concessions vastly in excess of what had been asked for by the Syndicate. Now Clarke set about selling the railway bonds and forming a construction company.

E.A. James, General Manager, Alberta & Great Waterways Railway, 1909-1910
Photo: International Press, courtesy of City of Edmonton Archives

Meanwhile, A & GW offices were established at 21 Jasper Avenue West. Edwin Alfred James was persuaded to take the position of general manager in April 1909, at a salary of $12 thousand a year.[17] James knew something about railroading all right. He had moved up through the ranks and served in official capacities with the Grand Trunk Pacific and the Canadian Northern, taking early retirement in 1907 from the position of general superintendent. The post with the A & GW was a challenge he could not resist tackling. In later years, this period in his life was one James preferred to forget.[18]

In July 1909, James introduced J.D. McArthur to William Clarke, who attempted to persuade him to put up $1 million of his own money to start a construction company. In October 1909, McArthur told Clarke, "No deal." McArthur was candid about his reasons: "He [Clarke] was not a railway builder and I did not want to be connected with him and him have any say in something he didn't know anything about."[19] The rejection did not prevent Clarke from borrowing $5 thousand from McArthur. When he repaid the loan he included an extra $500 for expenses, but McArthur returned the money explaining, "I feel that it is my business to stand my own expenses when looking into a proposition."[20]

On 7 October 1909, the agreement between the province and the A & GW railway was signed. A month later the railway company was organized. The $50 thousand of paid up capital stock was subscribed for by an unusual method. It was arranged by an overdraft, by which Clarke drew the cheque for that amount and deposited it to the credit of the company. No money was actually paid out of the bank.[21]

At the same time, the Canada West Construction Company, formed under a Dominion of Canada charter, was organized to build the railway.[22] Its first incorporators were George Minty, Charles S. Tupper and H.W. Hollis, all from the same law office. Their nominal interests were subsequently transferred to Bertrand Clarke. Although Clarke was the president of the construction company, his brother, William, firmly held the reins of control. Both the railway and the construction company were run as one, using the same staff. James A. McKinnon was hired as right-of-way agent on 1 November 1909. His previous employment with the Liberal Club in Edmonton and then as election agent in the north, had given him no experience in the purchase of land, but had provided excellent contacts.

The railways' entire issue of bonds was sold to J.S. Morgan and Co. of New York and then resold on the London stock exchange for $7.4 million on 1 November 1909, allegedly at par.[23] Shortly afterwards, it was learned that the bonds had been sold at 110 percent instead of at par.[24] The $740 thousand difference was never satisfactorily explained.

About this time the Hudson's Bay Company, realizing their land grants would be worthless if the railway by-passed them at Lac La Biche, approached the promoter with a proposal. The HBC would give the railway the necessary land for their right-of-way and yards, and five lake front lots. In return, the A & GW would build a hotel worth $50 thousand and both companies would share equally in the profits from the sale of town-site lots. It was settled. The railway would change its route.

On 15 November 1909, the first sod was turned on the A & GW 16 miles north of Edmonton.[25] Contractor E. Manders had 40 men with 35 teams brushing and clearing the right-of-way. By mid-December grading was completed on a portion of the first seven miles and about two-thirds of the route from Edmonton to Fort McMurray had been cleared, although the route had not yet been approved by the government.

During the winter, discord in the Liberal ranks increased. There was criticism of the railway contract and the methods used to arrive at it.[26] When the legislature met in February 1910, Cushing resigned as minister of Public Works and J.R. Boyle, member for Sturgeon, gave notice of a resolution to expropriate the A & GW and set the wheels in motion for an examination of the government's actions in this regard.

On 25 February, the debate began. Cushing firmly maintained that the guarantee of the railway bonds had been made without his consent, which was disputed by the other ministers, who had attended the Cabinet meeting.[27] What followed was the most sensational week-long legislature debate in the province's history. The opposition, led by the Hon. R.B. Bennett, hinted the missing money was in Clarke's pocket. There were even

E. Manders and his crew breaking ground for A & GW
Photo: Provincial Archives of Alberta, Ref. 69.128/5b

whisperings that some of it had made its way into those of Cabinet ministers. There was also the unsettling puzzle of the small number of documents found on government files regarding negotiations for such a major undertaking. Some claimed documents had been disposed of quietly when the first rumblings of discontent arose.

On the afternoon of March 9, Attorney General Cross and his deputy, Sydney Woods resigned. The following morning, W.A. Buchannan, minister without portfolio, withdrew.[28] Cross claimed his own resignation was because Cushing had been invited to reenter the Cabinet.[29] Cushing did not return and three days later Cross was back in his seat. A vote of confidence, which passed by 20 votes to 17, revealed a split in the Liberal ranks.[30]

On 14 March, hoping to clear himself and his government, Dr. Rutherford appointed a royal commission to investigate the A & GW transactions.[31] Its members were Hon. D.L. Scott, Hon. H. Harvey and Hon. N.D. Beck, justices of the Alberta Supreme Court. The hearing commenced on 29 March 1910. William Clarke failed to appear, reasoning that the controversy did not concern him directly, but was initiated by enemies of the present government. Dr. Waddell was questioned closely about a discrepancy in estimated costs on file at the A & GW offices and those supplied to the government. He insisted the changes were made as a result of his best judgment and not to cheat the government. The route map submitted to the

Manders' construction camp
Photo: Provincial Archives of Alberta,11252, Ref. 69.128/4b

government and tabled in the legislature during the famous debate could not be located.

When the House sat on 26 May 1910, the Lieutenant-Governor announced the resignation of Premier Rutherford.[32] It was a lethal political blow to a man who was widely respected for his honesty and integrity. He was succeeded as premier by the Hon. Arthur Lewis Sifton, formerly chief justice of Alberta. The commission hearings concluded on 7 July 1910 and produced 3 225 pages of convoluted evidence and 255 exhibits. In November, a majority report signed by Harvey and Scott was presented along with Beck's minority report.[33] Although the commission exonerated the government ministers of any personal implication, the reports were inconclusive and the evidence did little to allay the public's suspicions of wrongdoing.

During this time, the A & GW office staff dwindled as it became obvious that the project was at a standstill. Smaller quarters were rented in the Alberta Block and Allan R. Buddo, Dr. Waddell's stenographer, remained on as the company's representative in Edmonton.[34] In July 1910, the A & GW failed to pay the first instalment of interest on its bonds and the province was obliged to do so. In November, Clarke resurfaced in Winnipeg to condemn the commission and Sifton's railway policy. The government of Alberta, he said, declined to accept the company's offer of 1.5 percent which, with the bank's interest, would have met the 5 percent obligation.

In an odd quirk of fate, the missing route plan of the A & GW was discovered stashed away on top of the Speaker's cupboard the following month. It bore no signature of approval by Dr. Rutherford, indicating that the former government had not officially endorsed the railway's plans.[35]

As the rift in the Liberal party narrowed, a new difficulty arose. Hoping to end the controversy, Sifton's government decided to cancel the contract with the railway company and introduce an act by which the proceeds from the sale of the bonds would become part of the provincial revenues. The result was costly lawsuits. Early in January 1912, lawyers for the bondholders, the Royal Bank, the railway, Clarke and the Province of Alberta attended hearings. Lower courts held government appropriation valid.[36] Clarke took the case to England. In January 1913, the Privy Council of England declared the act ultra vires. The funds could be used only for railway construction and Premier Sifton was obligated to repeal the Act.

The $7.4 million for railway construction must have appealed to a number of railway builders. In the fall of 1913, J.D. McArthur publicly laid his cards on the table when he wrote his friend Premier Sifton, "On behalf of myself and associates, I propose to take over the Alberta & Great Waterways Railway on terms satisfactory to representatives of the bondholders, and the Bank. . . . The Government will, of course, waive any default of the

Railway Company to date. . . ."[37] Premier Sifton presented McArthur's proposed plan to the Legislature. After debate, it was given approval. It provided for work to commence on or before 31 December 1913 and to be completed within two years of that date. Dunvegan Yards would be used as the terminal for both lines. A settlement must have been made with the Clarkes. They dropped out of the picture.

9

Lac La Biche Welcomes Rails

At the end of December 1913, the "turning of the sod" on the A & GW got off to a rocky start. The special train carrying a number of visitors was delayed awaiting the general manager, whose car had sustained a collapsed wheel en route to the railway station. Eventually, Rathbone Smith arrived and the train was on its way to Carbondale on the ED & BC, which became the junction with the A & GW.[1]

The guest list included J.L. Cote, MPP for Grouard; A.C. Galbraith and W.J. Pace, superintendents of construction; R.H. Douglas, provincial railway engineer; N.L. Harvey, secretary to the provincial department of railway and telephones; and D.A. Pennicuick, accountant for the McArthur railways.[2] Although there was no formal ceremony, Mr. Cote climbed a mound of earth and marked the occasion with a few words. In what seemed to be a rerun of events in November 1909, a gang of 30 men set to work with picks and shovels, but cold

weather soon put a stop to further progress until the spring.

McArthur may have considered what the building of the A & GW would mean to the settlers en route, but he had more pressing problems. Access had to be gained to the vast sand deposits north of Bon Accord. A good supply of ballast was essential to the building of his railways. As a lumberman, McArthur was also keenly aware of the value of the timber reserves waiting to be tapped south of Lac La Biche.

During the pitiless low temperatures of the winter months of 1913-1914, McArthur's survey teams retraced the steps of their predecessors of 1908 and 1909 along an overgrown route and staked alternate lines. Early in 1914, the contract for 150 miles of the A & GW was let to the D.F. McArthur Co. of Winnipeg, which was owned by McArthur's brother Duncan, who was the main subcontractor.[3]

Civil Engineer Philip L. Debney
Photo: Courtesy of Mrs. Ann Glaister

Philip Debney arrived from the ED & BC as resident engineer located at Bon Accord. Standing six feet three inches tall, the Englishman had immigrated in 1912 and after a short time with the Canadian Northern, joined the McArthur railways. The ED & BC had honored him by naming a station "Debney" [later renamed Pibroch].[4] He left to serve overseas in the First World War, and upon discharge in 1919 joined the staff of the Lacombe and Northwestern Railway [L & NW], then owned by the Government of Alberta.

From Carbondale, the land was fairly well populated for some 10 miles, and settlers were thankful for the jobs the railway offered; $1.25 a day was like gold dust.[5] Oth-

ers profited from sales of farm produce, moonshine and feed for the teams of horses. As on the ED & BC, the A & GW grade was built manually by large gangs of workmen. Among them were cousins, Andrew Hoglund, Rudolf Lindstrom and Anton Gustafson. [6] They bought their supplies from the railway and when the contract was completed and they had paid their bills, to their dismay they found they had made no profit.

The first townsite to be surveyed was 8.4 miles beyond Carbondale in the vicinity of Bon Accord. Residents of the original settlement purchased lots and moved their homes there when the station was erected about 1914.[7] The quarter section chosen for the townsite was purchased from James Mulcahy, who became the local section foreman and caretaker of the train station and was later promoted to roadmaster.[8]

Rails followed closely behind as the grade was built. Sidings and townsites were spaced from seven to eight miles apart. Until the track-layer arrived from the ED & BC, steel was laid by hand. At Mile 14 lay the immense sand deposits that the railway was anxious to exploit. Several service tracks were laid to accommodate the steam shovel and ballast loading. That summer Glen Barker was fireman for Locomotive Engineer Jack Brown on a work train at the pit.

Throughout the summer, ballast trains operated around the clock. Once the pit had been reached, progress on the A & GW slowed. By February 1915, there were only 24 miles of the track ballasted north of Carbondale. Most of the ballast was taken for use on the ED & BC. Construction supplies were shipped via the Canadian Northern Railway to Colinton, near Athabasca.[9] For 35 cents a hundred weight, homesteaders were contracted to tote supplies, using team and sleigh, overland to Cache 3 at Alpen Siding.

The settlement at siding 10 was named after the Hon. Justice J.R. Boyle, who had been involved in the controversy regarding the construction of the A & GW back in 1910. Boyle grew to be one of the larger centres on the line. A railway station was built to serve the district in 1915.[10]

The Boyle area was where the Lindstrom family settled on their arrival from Sweden. Tony Lindstrom, Rudolf's brother, preferred the steady wage earned as a sectionman to that of homesteading. Later, he was promoted to section foreman at Boyle and Ellscott, and two of his sons, Ernest and Lawrence, also joined the railway. The Lindstroms watched with interest the building of the grade past their settlement.

By the end of 1914, the grade was completed to Mile 93.3,[11] where the siding was named Bondiss. Beyond this siding, a large gravel deposit became a valuable source of ballast. The approach of the railway attracted

Steam shovel loads up car No. 547 marked J.D. McArthur Co., Ltd.
Photo: Courtesy of Miss Mary Watson

homesteaders to the arable land between Hylo and Venice. The settlement that developed was a predominantly Italian community.

Otto Michetti recalls arriving at Hylo in April 1917. The train trip from Edmonton took 12 hours. Michetti came from Italy with his mother and brother, to join his father, who was homesteading in the area.[12] Joseph Michetti brought his city born family to his log house with its sod roof, and while his young children initially suffered from some culture shock, it was a malady from which they soon recovered. Otto Michetti saw something of railroading at an early age. His father and uncle took out tie contracts and Otto and his brother helped with the work. This was good training in the value of hard work and for Otto it was a stepping stone to a career in the railway industry.

In the vicinity of Hylo, McArthur's North West Lumber Company had about 200 men at work cutting logs for the sawmill in Edmonton. Henry Thompson worked as a bushman and logger before hiring on the A & GW as a sectionman. He learned to hack ties for which he received 15 cents each. With hard work he could earn four and a half dollars a day. McArthur built spur lines off the main line to reach logging limits. These never appeared on any maps as branch lines and their construction was paid for by the North West Lumber Company.[13] One was an eight mile stretch built southwest from Hylo at Mile 100, to reach timber berths leased by McArthur.[14]

There were also large stands of mature, spruce trees in the St. Lina region. In 1915 surveys were undertaken in this area. By September that year, McArthur was building a branch line easterly from near Dewar at Mile 101, toward St. Lina.[15] It was constructed under the charter of the Central Canada Railway.[16] Although never officially named, the branch became known as McArthur's Railway, the St. Lina Line and the Egg Lake Branch.

A reconnaissance survey was conducted by G. Murray for approximately 200 miles to a point in the vicinity of Prince Albert, Saskatchewan. The contract for construction of the St. Lina branch was let to the D.F. McArthur Company. On 17 May 1917, the *Edmonton Bulletin* reported on its progress: "The grading outfit of Felix Negro [sic], with about 25 teams, is expected to join the outfit working. Messrs. Foley Brothers are subcontracting for 10 miles of construction and Mr. W. Grant 7 miles. Mr. P.A. James is the walking boss, looking after the McArthur interests in general on this construction."[17] From Mile 8, a six mile spur line was built in a northerly direction to tap another timber limit.

Although 41 miles of the St. Lina branch were graded, only 11 miles of steel were laid.[18] Felix Nigro and his brother-in-law, James Anselmo, were partners in the grading contract. Nigro's knowledge of reading and writing was limited but his integrity gained him the respect of his employees. He became a successful contractor and went on to handle larger contracts. He enjoyed the challenge of helping to open up the country to homesteaders.

By this time, the railway grade on the main line of the A & GW had reached one of Alberta's oldest settlements, located on the southeast shore of the sparkling lake of the same name.[19] The history of Lac La Biche as a trading post dates back to 1798.[20] A Hudson's Bay trading post was still in operation when the railway tracks reached Lac La Biche in 1915. A Roman Catholic mission was established there in 1853, where many of the local children were educated.[21] The decline of Lac La Biche began with the emergence of the steamboat era. Freight bypassed the settlement and overland trails fell into disuse.[22] With the advent of the railway, a new townsite developed seven miles from the mission site and Lac La Biche began a rapid regrowth.

On 6 February 1915, the *Edmonton Bulletin* acknowledged the arrival of rails at Lac La Biche with its headline "Lac La Biche Turns Out to Welcome Steel." Almost the entire population of the area witnessed the Pioneer track-layer edge toward the new townsite with Jinkle Frizzell at the controls, and the last rail laid in place. But it was not until 14 July 1916 that the A. & GW became operational as far as Lac La Biche and 10 miles beyond.

As the railway approached Lac La Biche, McArthur made plans to build a resort hotel. An agreement along the same terms negotiated with the original charter members in 1909 was signed by McArthur and the Hudson's Bay Company. It seemed an idyllic location with the lake's clear blue waters lapping at white sandy beaches and providing excellent fishing. A resort hotel could only be reached by rail since roads and automobile traffic were still in the future. Roland E. Lines, a well-known Edmonton architect who later lost his life in World War I, was hired to design the hotel.[23] Workmanship was of the highest calibre. It cost $53 thousand to build and $13 thousand to furnish and equip, a cost that today astounds, since everything from linens to furnishing was of the finest quality.[24]

Lac La Biche Inn facing on to the lake

Built facing the picturesque lake, the inn was of frame and fieldstone construction, completely modern for the times with a lookout tower, dining room, bathrooms, 22 bedrooms and its own electric generating plant. It was managed by Harry Cole, who had been McArthur's valet on his private car.[25] With its manicured lawns and tennis courts giving a good first impression, the Lac La Biche Inn was ready for guests in late June 1916.[26]

the McKeen Company where some modifications were made prior to delivery to the A & GW.[29] The front of the cars resembled the bow of a submarine, and the attractive interior had round windows, resembling portholes. Excellent craftsmanship was evident in the inlaid panelling and woodwork.

Conductor Fred Martin worked on the cars for many years and was proud to answer the questions of those curious about the cars or the countryside. Martin was a robust,

Entrance of Lac La Biche Inn. Front: *cook and helper, unidentified man, Manager Harry Cole and son Percy.* Back: *Mrs. H. Cole and chambermaids, c. 1916.*
Photo: Glenbow Archives, NA-4049-4

To provide transportation from Edmonton, two self-propelled coaches, powered by gasoline motors were purchased in 1914.[27] Built by the McKeen Car Company, Omaha, Nebraska, in 1910, they were numbered 709 and 711.[28] They had been used for less than four years by The Woodstock and Sycamore Traction Company before being sold back to

barrel-chested bachelor in his forties, who liked to chew tobacco. Agents sometimes complained that his paperwork arrived splattered with tobacco juice. Passengers missed his familiar face when he died suddenly of heart failure in later years.

In preparation for the opening season, advertisements extolling the vacation facilities at the Lac La Biche Inn ran in the Edmonton papers in June and July 1916. Weekend excursion fares of $3.45 return were offered. The inn was in full operation in time to cater to the 1 July 1916 Dominion Day picnic of the employees of the *Edmonton Bulletin*. The story in the newspaper the following Monday commented that the gasoline cars were "comfortable and speedy." Nevertheless, locals nicknamed them the "skunk" cars because the fumes from the residue of poorly refined gasoline issued from the often leaking exhaust systems.

The McKeen cars were ahead of their time, but their one glaring weakness was the transmission. Manually actuated, they were a constant source of trouble. To compound the mechanical failures, parts were very difficult to obtain following the bankruptcy of the McKeen Car Company. Eventually, to keep one running, parts were taken from the other. In 1917, Henry "Hank" Kelly was the engineer operating one of the McKeen cars when a sleeve of his overalls became tangled in a gear. His arm was badly torn and he sustained injuries to his chest. Fortunately, the

McKeen No. 711 with Engineer Hank Kelly and Conductor Frank Waite, c. 1916
Photo: Courtesy of M. Maccagno

railway doctor was among the passengers.[30]

Kelly alternated between several occupations in Wyoming until the sobering thought of marriage to his childhood sweetheart settled his mind on railroading. In 1912, he became involved in union organization, which caused friction with his superintendent, and eventually headed north to Canada.[31] When he got a job with the ED & BC the following year he sent for his wife and two sons. His son, Glenn, became interested in railroading when he travelled with his Dad in the McKeen cars. He later became an agent and dispatcher.

While building of the Lac La Biche Inn was in progress, workmen were erecting a station, a two stall round house and other railway buildings. The station was of the larger, terminal type of building, painted boxcar red, similar to those at Smith and McLennan on the ED & BC. Set on a surface foundation of spongy ground, it eventually started to lean toward the track, a condition that was costly to straighten.[32] There is some disagreement as to who was the first station agent. *Lac La Biche, Oasis of the North*, compiled for Canada's Centennial year, mentioned, "Mr. Piteblado was the first station agent appointed in 1915." Railway records indicate that John Watson was the first agent. Possibly Mr. Piteblado was the station caretaker and not a qualified agent.

John Watson worked for the railway from 15 June 1915 as a timekeeper and in other capacities, before becoming the permanent station agent at Lac La Biche. His wife was a niece of Mrs. J.D. McArthur and a cousin of Dr. J. McLennan.[33] Watson was a dedicated, hard working Scot, who had been a master weaver before coming to Canada. Involving himself in community activities, he served as justice of the peace and police magistrate for Lac La Biche for a number of years and was chairman of the board of trade, secretary-treasurer and mayor of the town.

Two stall engine house at Lac La Biche.
Section foreman's home to the right.
Photo: Courtesy of M. Maccagno

Once, after he became justice of the peace, a man came into the station and bought a ticket. John Watson gave him change for five dollars. The man protested, "But I gave you a ten dollar bill." Watson checked the till. There were no tens in it. Glaring at the man from under bushy brows he roared: "Do you want to go to gaol, laddie? Because if you do, I'm the man who can put you there!"[34]

In the summer of 1916, the Lac La Biche Inn's opening weeks were successful. At the height of the tourist season, tragedy struck. In the second week of August 1916 a number of prominent Edmontonians were vacationing at the Inn. On 9 August, Harry Flowers, manager of the Sommerville Hardware Company, took his wife and two other ladies out on the lake in one of the hotel's wide beamed row boats. A sudden storm blew up capsizing the Flowers' boat. The upturned boat was found rolling from side to side a few yards off the shore.[35] When McArthur heard the tragic news he arranged for a special train from Edmonton to Lac La Biche to accommodate relatives and friends of those drowned.

This tragedy in the Inn's first season, along with the scarcity of money because of the war, and the fact that Edmonton was still small made the operation of the Inn less successful than had been hoped. McArthur decided not to reopen it in 1918. When the Cole family departed for Edmonton, the station agent's family undertook its care. In winter, the few rooms the Watsons occupied on the ground floor formed an island of warmth, and in the summer, they enjoyed the spaciousness of the large structure, particularly their daughter Mary, who played in the rooms. For her stewardship, Mrs. Christina Watson received $50 per month in the early days. In March 1933, as the Depression deepened, this was reduced to $10 per month. From the fall of 1918 the Inn stayed idle, except for the occasional non-paying guest, until it was sold along with its contents. The sale was completed on 4 October 1937 for $8 thousand to Les Filles de Jesus,[36] a Roman Catholic order of nuns, who began renovations to convert it into St. Catherine's Hospital.

On 19 May 1919, a forest fire levelled McArthur's logging operation near Hylo. Camp Four was completely destroyed, along with 14 cars of green logs.[37] Many of the ties on the Egg Lake branch were burned out from under the rails. The steel was later used in the extension to Fort McMurray.[38] The fire was a disastrous blow to McArthur's plans.[39]

The flames that left McArthur's camp in ashes continued to destroy 42 ballast cars. At Lac La Biche, the fire devastated the village. Businesses, homes and belongings were all destroyed. The flames provided the only light in the mid-afternoon. Among the buildings left standing were the railway depot and the Lac La Biche Inn. It was a terrifying experience for all involved. While no casualties occurred, a number of people survived only by wading into the lake and with wet blankets escaped death by suffocation, or from the heat.

Christina Watson is remembered as being at the forefront in the rescue operations as the flames died down. She threw open the doors of the inn to accommodate the homeless and helped to organize food and clothing. With telephone and telegraph lines destroyed, the community was completely isolated from the outside world. Word of the disaster reached Edmonton the next day when a delegation of four arrived seeking aid for Lac La Biche. A train was on its way to the town when the fire broke out. It ran into heavy forest fires 40 miles south of the town. The intense heat burned the paint off the coaches and the train had to stop at intervals to remove debris deposited by the winds fanning the flames. The passengers were terrified but arrived safely to see the desolation of Lac La Biche. The return train was packed with homeless escaping the devastation.

The railway rushed a special train with Red Cross and Army supplies to the site. Most of the stricken people had only the clothes on their backs. Many homes were destroyed; and residents were grateful for the army tents provided. The railway's doctor W.O. Farquharson was accompanied by Doctor McLennan and they offered medical services to the injured. The *Edmonton Bulletin* of 15 July 1919 reported: "Lac La Biche Rapidly Rising from the Ashes," and beneath the headline stated: "while a great deal of suffering was caused in connection with the recent disastrous fire at Lac La Biche the conflagration is having the effect of creating a new town far away ahead in its number of modern buildings that existed before."

Undated A & GW cheque for $1 402 088.11 signed by J.K. McLennan
Photo: Courtesy of K. McLennan

10

Arriving – God Willing

Dog team was the mode of transportation most commonly used by those who lived north of Lac La Biche. The thought of a railway displacing them was an exciting one. With a better means of transportation linked to the northern waterways, supplies could reach the Arctic faster and with regularity. A railway to take furs and fish south to market could open up a whole new world of possibilities.

By March 1915, track had been laid to Mile 135.3 north of Lac La Biche. As rails were spiked, the A & GW entered a world of sand hills, muskeg, and small trees. The stretches of muskeg became longer, deeper and softer, and it was obvious there was little to produce revenue except trapping, fishing and a few small lumber mills. All weather roads were nonexistent. Fort McMurray was a fur trading and transportation centre for provisioning the far north and the Arctic. McArthur wanted his railway to be the gateway to the water transportation systems connecting these areas. [The mineral wealth of the tar sands had not yet been tapped.]

Construction work on the railway leading north was hard and frustrating. Engines and equipment were frequently derailed. By March 1916, the railway had arrived at the Christina River, Mile 199. W.F. Stevenson had been locating engineer between Carbondale and Lac La Biche and again took over from Mile 199 to Mile 272, 18 miles from Fort McMurray. William Christian, whose interest in weightlifting earned him the nickname "Dumbbell," was then locomotive watchman. He recalled the train seemed to be off the track more than on it.

I was called about 16K [1600 hours] on April 10 1916 to go watching on the 10 spot [engine number 10]. Destination was the end of steel on the A & GW. Lon Weaver, nicknamed "Daddy," was the engineer and Mark ["Cowboy"] Barker the fireman. The trip from when we left Dunvegan Yards until we got back . . . consumed a total time of three weeks.[1]

As the grade was built, both men and beasts were beset by hordes of vigorous mosquitoes, black flies and "bulldog" flies. In May 1916, the blood thirsty insects tormented the men working north from Mile 202, the end of steel, on the last 92 miles. Most of the men were eastern Europeans and spoke little English. Wages were 15 cents an hour for a 10 hour day. Bed and board cost $1 per day, which they also paid on Sundays and on days when it was too wet to work. In addition, there was a doctor's fee of $1 per month.

Dr. W.O. Farquharson was head of the railway's medical service. The monthly fee paid by workers went directly to the doctor, who contracted to supply all medicines and drugs. Hnat Barabash was among those paying the fee who claimed they never saw the recipient. In his memoirs, Dr. Morrish says a hospital, consisting of a large tent, was erected that spring near the Christina River.[2] Dr. Morrish was then a medical student and went further north to provide medical services to the men.

When steel became scarce, the men were put to building grade with wheelbarrows. Living conditions were cramped in the old converted boxcars used as bunk cars. The bunks were built in tiers on both sides, leaving a narrow aisle in the centre. Mattresses were made by topping straw with a bedroll, and fatigue made it feel fairly comfortable. Each car housed 16 men in an area of 334 square feet.[3] There were no sanitary facilities other than two pailfuls of water and two washbasins in each car. In spring, there was mud everywhere and it was carried into the bunkhouse on the soles of boots and on overalls. Wet clothing was hung about the stove to dry.

Anna Barabash recalls her husband describing the terrible working conditions endured by the men. Dissatisfied with their wages, the men demanded a five cent per hour increase to 20 cents.[4] It was refused and the men went on strike. They were fired. The timekeeper did not have enough cash on hand to pay them and they had to find their own way back to Edmonton, if they intended to collect their pay at the Dunvegan Yards office.

Barabash's son, William, remembers his father and the other men were stranded in the bush. With nothing but their bedrolls, they started walking along the tracks. A train passed them, heading north to pick up those still in camp. On the return trip the men tried to climb on to a flat car, but RCMP officers brutally kicked them off. Some fell by the wayside and died from exhaustion and hunger. The others continued to walk until they reached Lac La Biche and food. From there those who could afford it caught the train to Edmonton. "The thing I find hard to accept is how individuals are treated today and the kind of treatment our pioneers received."[5] Hnat Barabash and Ed Dembrawski were among the men to survive the ordeal.[6]

This strike effectively stopped work on

the railway until late 1916. In early 1917 steel again became available and several carloads were sent to Lac La Biche. Travellers bound for the far north also arrived. Getting to Fort McMurray was an ordeal. North of Lac La Biche the railway was under construction and during the summer, travel was restricted to hopping work trains and speeders to reach the end of steel. After freeze-up in the fall, trains carried freight and passengers that far. Mickey and Pat Ryan, who freighted from the end of steel to Fort McMurray, had ideas for a solution to the problem.

Speeder operated by "Gasoline Gus" for Mickey Ryan.
Photo: Provincial Archives of Alberta, A3890

The Ryan brothers are probably best known for the 16 mile portage they built between Fort Smith and Fort Fitzgerald on the Slave River. Mickey Ryan got the government contract for hauling mail from Athabasca to Fort McMurray. Soon after the steel reached Lac La Biche, the mail arrived via the A & GW. Mickey made arrangements with McArthur to carry the mail and small perishable freight by speeder north from Lac La Biche.[7] This often included the occasional passenger or two. To allow him access to one of its speeders, the railway gave him the designation of lineman.[8]

There is no record of whether or not Mickey Ryan ever did any line work, but C. Lynn and his outfit did. The telephone construction crew battled mud and muskeg to string telephone wires. In places, the muskeg was so deep that the poles sunk to their crossarms. Where the muskeg was too soft to support telephone poles, a log about 25 feet long was attached five feet from the bottom of the pole. This was braced with a piece of wood at each side, which provided a tripod means of support.[9] By the spring of 1917, the communications system was in operation as far as Mile 229 and Quigley and McPherson had completed building all the bridges and culverts to within four miles of Fort McMurray.

Track-laying was not moving as quickly and a series of accidents plagued the railway when the ground began to thaw. Work ground to a halt for a time in April 1917 when a landslide occurred about eight miles from Fort McMurray. A lidgerwood was rushed forward to clear the line. That summer a locomotive overturned at Mile 257. Conductor Peterson was reported hurt. Superintendent J.D. Murray immediately proceeded north on a speeder with Doctor Farquharson. En route, he had a head-on collision with another speeder manned by Section Foreman Chorney. Both Murray and Chorney were hurt and were taken to hospital. By then the steel was 18 miles from Fort McMurray.

on the work extra and recalls willing hands built a raft from logs to ferry supplies across to the stranded crews and extra gang. The telephone line that straddled the river, was

Locomotive No. 6 on its side on A & GW, north of Lac La Biche.
Photo: Courtesy of Miss Mary Watson

Rails were no closer to Fort McMurray by the spring of 1918 when massive ice jams occurred simultaneously on the Christina and Athabasca rivers. On the Christina River, water and ice swept toward the Clearwater River taking out the bridge, north of Conklin.[10] A Métis man seeing it being washed away, had the presence of mind to flag down the train with a lighted candle.[11] A mixed train, a freight train and a work train were stranded north of the river. Glen Barker was

used as an anchor to keep the raft from disappearing downstream. Rebuilding began almost immediately on the bridge.

McArthur and Rathbone Smith made a inspection trip in the Packard car at the end of May 1918 to see the difficulties encountered with the grade on the Clearwater Hill. There was still no scheduled train service into Fort McMurray. Smith endeavored to explain why to William Pearce, from the CPR's Statistical Branch: "It is impossible for us to arrange any regular schedule north of Lac La Biche, as this part of the line is still in the hands of the contractors and the track is not in shape that any regular schedule could be maintained."[12] Nine years earlier, after a tour of the north, Pearce had told a CPR official, "The Great Waterways Railway, I do not think in the next 20 years, will get freight enough to pay for the axle grease used on it."[13] At the time of Pearce's trip, the train only stayed at the end of steel for a sufficient time to do necessary work. The end of the First World War came too late to make any change in the railway's operations. In fact, construction work was moving at a snail's pace. By the end of 1918, the steel was near Cache 23 at Lynton.[14]

McArthur's enthusiasm must have been subdued as one year ran into the next. Freight for the north had been piling up in Edmonton and at Lac La Biche for months, but by the end of March 1919, it was on its way north. The steel had finally reached old Cache 24 near Sappre siding, Mile 283.[15] The article in the *Edmonton Bulletin* of April 2, "A & GW Steel is Advanced to Cache 24," reported that, "Owing to heavy grade and the new track, it is not feasible to bring down more than a few cars at a time . . ." From the foot of the hill, it was loaded on boats or freighted into Fort McMurray.

On 5 April 1919, the 10 Spot was returning south to the material yard near Mile 272 when suddenly the rails were swept from the grade. The locomotive and a flat car went hurtling down the embankment at Mile 276.

The caboose turned completely over.[16] Engineer James Donley, and Construction Foreman, Grant Thorburn were crushed to death beneath the wreckage. Brakeman, R.E. Hartman and four others were injured. The *Edmonton Bulletin* of 8 April says the others were "three foreigners, whose names could not be obtained."

Locomotive No. 10 on its side after accident in which Donley and Thorburn died. Railroaders erected a monument using the side of cab support.

Donley had begun his career with the Sante Fe Railway and had come north from the U.S. with Bert Hornbeck and J.L. Nichols about 1916. His widow sued the railway for $20 thousand, claiming negligence on the part of the company and was awarded $11 500 in damages by the Supreme Court of Alberta.[17]

Because of soft track, a three week embargo was placed against freight and passenger service on the A & GW. In April, I.A. Larmer wired the general manager to say both crews of engine 10 and dinky 100 were continuously working at the wreck: "They have engine 10 nearly in position to pull up and expect to have her on main line tomorrow noon."

Because people living north of Fort McMurray had no boat transportation in the winter, most travelling was done during the summer months. Getting passengers from Lac La Biche to Fort McMurray by train in the spring and summer remained a problem and Mickey Ryan solved it by making a proposal the railway liked.[18] In the railway shops at Dunvegan Yards, a Packard automobile was fitted with new flange wheels. It had a seating capacity of seven and pulled a trailer for baggage and express. After the ground was frozen trains could take the freight to the end of steel, now eight miles from Fort McMurray. When they could not, Ryan could.

Mickey Ryan met the train from Edmonton at Lac La Biche once a week and drove passengers to Mile 274, the end of solid grade. From there they travelled over the next three miles of unreliable track by speeder. Horse teams then carried passengers downhill to the boat landing, where they were met by a gas boat for the 16 mile run down the Clearwater to Fort McMurray. The cost of the total trip was $18.[19]

It was a wet summer in 1919. Rail freight was getting no further than Mile 274 where it was stockpiled. Getting it that far was an accomplishment because of muskeg between Mile 264 and 274. Where there was no foundation for ballast, corduroy and brush were sometimes used to keep the track from sinking from sight.[20] With this type of track who could resist spreading the rumor that the initials A & GW stood for "Arriving – God Willing." Years later, when Otto Michetti was

Packard car, operated by Ryan, preparing for departure from the Lac La Biche station.
Photo: University of Alberta Archives, John A. Allan Collection, Acc. No. 79-23-2990

roadmaster, 35 feet pilings were driven and track trestled just above muskeg level for about one eighth of a mile.[21]

Provincial engineers Harry Warner and Bill Jackson inspect track.
Photo: Provincial Archives of Alberta, A4000

Old-timers like Jack Brown were accomplished at guiding their black steeds over the rough track. One day when heading north, gale force winds buffeted the engine as though it was a toy. When a tree, ripped out by its roots, crashed across the track in front of the engine Brown was forced to a stop. He and Fireman Phillip "Frog" Frigon decided the safest place was under the tender. As they waited out the storm, Brown, who was a devout Catholic, began saying the Rosary. Frigon, not so staunchly Catholic, concluded that it could not hurt to have a word with the Lord on his own behalf. So, as Brown finished each Hail Mary, "Frog" would say, "And the same over here, Father." The prayers must have reached their destination – the pair lived to tell the tale.

Storms were not the only problems that summer. As August neared and the end of navigation to far northern points was in sight, Premier Stewart sent Harry Warner, an engineer with the provincial department of railways, and a party of men to get the stockpiled freight to the river for loading on the boats and barges.[22] Some work had to be done to improve the track, particularly on the hill down. The supplies were needed in the north, without them it would be a long hard winter.

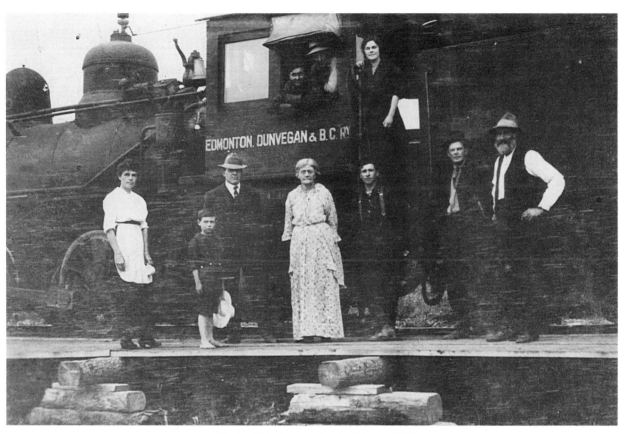

Photo: CP Corporate Archives, 4998

Part Three

The Lean Years-1920-1929

The snow plough, equipped with flanger blades, throwing snow off track was a common sight in winter after a heavy snowfall.
Photo: Courtesy of S. Deakin

11
Shattered Dreams

Winter set in early in 1919. Toward the end of September there was snow which stayed. It was one of the most severe winters on record. In northern Alberta there was more livestock than usual due to the number of cattle shipped north from the drought stricken areas of the province. In addition, the Alberta government's Cow Bill had resulted in settlers owning larger herds. Feed was soon depleted and animals perished in the deep snowdrifts from cold, exhaustion and starvation. It was always the government cows that died.

This was the type of winter J.D. McArthur and his struggling rail lines could have done without. A subsidy payment of $78 851.37 received from the Government of Canada in August 1919 had done little to ease the financial morass into which McArthur was sinking.[1] January 1920 was bitterly cold. It was also the month when Fireman Lee "Cutie" Walton, Len Walton's son, received his nickname.

Headlines in the *Grande Prairie Herald* of 20 January read: "HYTHE MURDER CASE HELD AT GRANDE PRAIRIE" and the subheading below said: "Henrietta Dougherty Confesses to Having Shot her Husband John Dougherty in Self-Defense – Jury brings in Verdict of Manslaughter – His Lordship Judge Stuart gives Sentence of Twenty Years Imprisonment."[2] John Doherty, had disappeared at the end of May 1919. His wife's inconsistent explanations of his absence came to the attention of the Alberta Provincial Police. Constable Sullivan, posing as a cattle buyer, gained Mrs. Doherty's confidence and she finally told him that Jack was dead and buried in the cellar. The body, buried under a pile of rutabagas, was found in a remarkable state of preservation. After the trial, the prisoner delivered a few choice words as she passed Constable Sullivan, "As for you, you son-of-a-bitch, when I get out I'll be looking for you."

While the court was in session, outside a

blinding snowstorm was raging. Snow was still falling as Locomotive Engineer Hank Kelly and Walton prepared to leave Grande Prairie on 20 January. As she passed the locomotive to entrain, Mrs. Doherty noticed the young, handsome fireman's curiosity as he watched her through the open cab window. "Hi, Cutie," she called. The story spread quickly and Walton was known by the nickname for as long as he worked on the railway.[3]

When train No. 2 finally left Grande Prairie, temperatures ranged between minus 50 and minus 60 degrees fahrenheit, playing havoc with steam power and rolling stock. Among the passengers were Judge A. Stuart, Crown Prosecutor E.B. Cogswell, Mrs. Doherty and the police escort taking her to Fort Saskatchewan prison. The passengers had a long, delay-plagued journey ahead. They did not know it then, but it would be Sunday, 25 January before they reached Edmonton.[4]

Progress was slow in places where several feet of snow covered the rails. Conductor Jack Carley was relieved to reach McLennan, but more delays were in store. Train No. 6 from Peace River, with which it connected, had not yet arrived. The shops, in the charge of Locomotive Foreman Fred Bellis, were a beehive of activity. The small staff had difficulty keeping the motive power in running condition and Bellis had every available man on duty.

Fred Bellis was a Welshman who had

honed his hunting skills in the surrounding bush. His daughter, Lillian Donlevy, remembers the bear cub he once brought home as a pet from one of his hunting forays.[5] Although the Bellis home was close to the shops, there was no time for a full night's sleep during that winter of 1920. While Bellis worked to keep equipment operational, Chief Dispatcher Reginald Lee, known as "R.L.," worried about keeping it rolling. The inclement weather prevented adherence to the timetable. Nothing was moving as it should on the railway. Lee had replaced Len Walton the previous October and now he wished he was any place but McLennan. He had learned telegraphy in Ontario and came west with the Grand Trunk Pacific.[6] He was well liked, respected and sometimes feared by the railway men. The men knew that no matter how he denounced them when something went wrong, he remained fiercely loyal, defending them against management when necessary.

Lee's zealous political activities placed him in an untenable position with management.[7] Dismissal followed an unfortunate incident at Peace River in 1929, but he was later reinstated with full seniority.[8] Although he finished his career as second trick dispatcher, the fire in his soul that made him stand out as a leader had been doused.

In the terrible winter of 1920, keeping trains on schedule was impossible for Reg Lee and his dispatching staff, and train No. 6 was no exception. Deep snowdrifts and leaky stay bolts on a locomotive were the cause of the Peace River passenger train's delay. Boilermaker Richard Rathbone, who had been working on locomotives all day, was dispatched to solve the problem. By the time Rathbone arrived back at McLennan on the Peace River train he was exhausted, but there was no time to rest. Within five minutes of the fire being put out, he had thrown his frozen overalls and sweater into the hot firebox of another locomotive, then climbed in to caulk its leaking flues. To add to the delay, switching took longer than usual because of the cold weather which made it difficult to see hand signals through the steam. Meanwhile, the boilermaker was having his second meal in 72 hours.[9] He had no sooner finished eating than he had to set to work caulking a locomotive on the passenger train. When it was finally ready to depart, every available engine was used to get the train on its way to Edmonton, preceded by a locomotive and snow plow. The company loyalty of railroaders like Rathbone was remarkable. Like many a boomer, the Welsh immigrant was good at his job. In Canada he had moved around from one railway to another before joining the ED & BC but the confirmed bachelor did not stay long. He finished out his days with the CNR.

The *Peace River Record* of 20 February 1920 ran the headline, "Railroad Crew goes Joy Riding with Locomotive." It was not just the train crew, it was nearly every adult in McLennan.[10] On 16 February, the predominantly French-Canadian settlement of Donnelly was holding a Valentine's Day dance in

Henry Christoffel shimming track near Hondo.
Photo: Courtesy of Mrs. Elsie Christoffel

the hotel owned by the Gravel family.[11] Their neighbors from McLennan, eight miles away, were invited. Not everyone in McLennan went to that dance, but those who could go, did. Because he was "on call," Myrtle Crowell and the Count stayed home. In the wee hours of the morning the Count was called to take his first trip as a locomotive engineer. After climbing into his work clothes, he called out, "Open the door, Woman, and let the ENGINEER out," then went rushing past her.[12] At the station he discovered an accident was the reason he was called and that he was to take the injured to Peace River.

As the tired revellers high-tailed it back to McLennan the locomotive jumped the less than perfect track. Locomotive Foreman Bill "Sledge Hammer" Henderson and Fireman

Sam Jones were scalded. Both men recovered, but Jones bore the marks on his face throughout his life. Henderson and the railway parted company a few years afterwards, but Jones worked on and was promoted to locomotive engineer 20 years later. He was dubbed with the nickname "Streamline," because when he was running a locomotive he would hunch over with his hand high on the throttle as though he was riding a race horse.

Snow dwarfs track motor.
Photo: C.A. Carlson

The harsh January of 1920 had been preceded by a year in which the financial muskeg around J.D. McArthur had become more uncertain. If he had any hopes of selling his railway to the CPR they were soon dashed. CPR President Beatty claimed excessive interest charges and depreciation were prohibitive. Besides, the route was too circuitous and the equity of $3.5 million, which McArthur wanted, was too high. With the CPR out of the picture, McArthur still clung to the hope that the Dominion govern-

ment would provide the much needed subsidies for his railways or nationalize them. On 24 February, Ed Rankin wrote from McArthur's Winnipeg office to Rathbone Smith that J.D. was still in Ottawa and "we do not expect him back for a week or ten days."

When McArthur contacted his general manager the following month, it was apparent that he planned to continue operation and construction on the railways. His letter of 23 March reads,

> Go ahead with erection of bridges west of Spirit River. . . . My idea is for you to try and rent 25 or 30 flat cars from the GTP, use them for a few days distributing ties. . . . What are the chances of rounding the hart cars up and putting them in service from Smokey West with gravel? I do not suppose there will be very many repairs necessary on the steam shovel. Just keep your eyes on that shovel as we may run it out about the 10th or 12th of April to the Smokey and finish the track from there to Spirit River and nine or ten miles in on the Grande Prairie Branch. . . . Glad to hear that you are still getting the freight in. I am having my own troubles with the Railway Commission on holding them off the job.[13]

Tired of waiting for the federal government to make a decision, the government of Alberta passed an Act enabling it to borrow one million dollars to reservice the line under government management in the event negotiations between McArthur and Ottawa failed.[14] A letter, written by McArthur to

Rathbone Smith on 10 April, hints at how acute the shortage of money had become, "Re: the tools for the sectionmen. I suppose that you will have to get some. As you say men cannot work without tools."

In April 1920, watchman Edward "Doo-dad" Hewitt relieved the fireman between Rycroft and Grande Prairie. While standing on the coal tender of an engine, as it pulled out of Clairmont, Hewitt was hit by a sand-pipe and fell between the tender and the baggage car.[15] A wheel of the baggage car passed over his arm. Fortunately, the engineer witnessed the accident and stopped the train. From Clairmont an engine and caboose were used to take the injured man to Grande Prairie. At the hospital staff refused admittance, claiming there was no room. Hewitt was taken to the Grande Prairie Hotel. In one of the rooms Glen Barker held the man's mangled arm while Dr. O'Brien amputated it. Eventually a hook was fitted to Hewitt's arm, and he became adept at its use.[16]

During the month following Hewitt's accident, McArthur was once again in Ottawa seeking authority from the Board of Railway Commissioners for a 50 percent increase in freight rates and one cent per mile extra in passenger fares.[17] He argued that revenues from existing rate levels were insufficient to properly maintain the operation. Increases would be used on maintenance, fixed charges and reasonable operating expenses. The increases were vehemently opposed. Lawyers Frank Ford, K.C., and A.F. Ewing represented the boards of trade for Grande Prairie and Peace River respectively at the hearing held in Edmonton in June 1920. They argued, "The ED & BC should not be shown any more consideration than any other railway system or corporation and that the application should not be considered except as part of a general increase of freight and passenger tariffs throughout the country."[18]

F.H. Phippen, K.C., of Winnipeg, represented the railway. Rathbone Smith, Tom Judah, and James McVicar, chief clerk in the traffic department, appeared as witnesses. [Traffic Manager C. Dowling had resigned the previous year and Rathbone Smith had shouldered the additional responsibilities.][19] Both Phippen and Smith claimed that McArthur had invested his entire fortune in the ventures, "to provide and maintain a railway service into the great and fertile northland in which he has unlimited confidence as to the future."[20] McArthur's application was refused on the premise that increases would be a hardship on the people of northern Alberta, even though the Board was on the verge of generally raising freight and passenger rates.[21]

Although late, the spring of 1920 brought with it torrential rains which created havoc on the Peace River and Smoky hills. A portion of the steep Judah Hill became a sliding mass of jelly as earth slides occurred one after another halting traffic at Judah for ten days.[22] A massive slide occurred on the Smoky Hill. Starting above the right-of-way it carried one mile of track and piling down into the valley, effectively closed the line to Grande Prairie until the fall.[23]

While this was happening, the need for transportation into the Peace River country was becoming more acute. By June, the railway's equipment was inadequate to cope with the volume of traffic and settlers. To compound matters, that month the federal government refused to take McArthur's railways into the Canadian National Railways system.[24] The ball was back in the provincial government's court. The government of Alberta was prepared for the eventuality of self-management of the lines using the advance of one million dollars voted for this purpose back in April.[25]

Settlers unload at temporary terminus at Judah siding on Central Canada Ry. during the summer of 1920.
Photo: Public Archives of Canada, PA 18371

12

CPR – The Savior

In July 1920, an agreement was reached between the government of Alberta and the Canadian Pacific Railway for the management of the Edmonton, Dunvegan and British Columbia, and the Central Canada railways.[1] The CPR held an option on the common stock of the companies at the end of the five year term.[2] Although the province of Alberta was the outright owner, McArthur retained a seven-year option to regain possession of both railways.[3] To upgrade them "to a reasonable standard of operating efficiency," the government of Alberta lent the CPR $2.5 million.[4] The bargain did not include the Alberta and Great Waterways Railway, which the Department of Railway and Telephones decided to operate.

Negotiations had been going on for some weeks with full expectancy of the settlement reached. The CPR had work equipment waiting at its Strathcona yards ready to be sent out and large quantities of ties stockpiled. James Alexander Macgregor, CPR super-intendent at Edmonton, replaced Rathbone Smith as general manager. Macgregor lost no time in naming the new officials. Among them were Colonel J. Garnet Reid, chief engineer and superintendent; N.F. Judah, auditor; Stanley Lamb, resident engineer; Archie Beaton, bridge and building master; and roadmasters, E. "Teddy" Edmundson, J.C. McLean, Jimmy Bain and Fred Kinnert.[5] W.H. Wortman was named master mechanic shortly afterwards.

J.A. Macgregor, General Manager, ED & BC and Central Canada railways, 1920-1926.
Photo: Courtesy of Mrs. Helen Hill

Judah was the only official who had been with the McArthur railways, but his pleasure at being part of the new management team was short lived. Stenographer Nellie Wright, who later married office engineer Ben Prest, was in the office the day the announcement appeared in the newspaper. Judah was happily accepting congratulations on his good fortune when a letter was delivered telling him his services were no longer required. Mrs. Prest recalls, "He lost out in a most undignified way." Shortly afterwards, E.J. Bulgin presented himself as the new auditor.[6]

Chief Clerk George Latter felt good about the fact that he received no letter of dismissal, instead he got a promotion. The Montreal native started "earning his place at the table" at an early age. In 1904 he joined the Algoma Central & Hudson's Bay Railway and two years later, he moved west to the Grand Trunk Pacific. By 1910, he was in Edmonton, dabbling in real estate, but the war ended the boom and he joined the ED & BC. With this background, few eyebrows were raised when he was promoted to right-of-way, townsite and claims agent. Margaret Nix describes her father as "a 'bulldog' Englishman [with] very firm ideas about how things should be done. . . . I think that in the office he was probably seen as being a hard taskmaster. He expected people to do their jobs and he expected the same of us, his children."[7]

Other changes followed. By 26 July 1920, it was revealed that D'Alton C. Coleman,

George Latter, Right of Way, Townsite and Claims Agent.
Photo: Courtesy of Miss Gwen Vigus

vice-president of the CPR, was replacing McArthur as president of the two railways and Charles Murphy of Winnipeg was the new vice-president, taking over from Doctor McLennan. Directors included the Hon. Charles Stewart, Alberta's minister of Railways, W.M. Kirkpatrick of Winnipeg and George A. Walker of Calgary, both from the CPR.

In a speech given in Edmonton a few days later, Coleman expressed regret that McArthur's plans did not materialize. He went on to say, "He made a game and gallant fight against odds which were too heavy for him, and when he did realize that he had to relinquish control, for a time at least, he did it with the good grace and in the fine spirit which we would expect from a citizen, who throughout his life has been decent and honorable and who is, in all respects, a lovable character."[8] Coleman also stated that the railways were in a "deplorable condition" and the CPR had a "gigantic" amount of work ahead of it, "but nevertheless the impossible will be attempted – and, who knows – perhaps will be accomplished."[9]

The reins of management were firmly in the capable hands of a Scotsman, and the CPR tuscan red soon became a familiar sight. Almost immediately, Macgregor went on an inspection trip to become acquainted with his new staff. Accompanying him was Colonel Reid, who had a great deal of experience, much of it gained in construction work on the CPR. Reid had broadened his expertise when he succeeded Colonel Ramsay in the command of the Canadian Railway Construction Corps during World War I. As they travelled, he and Macgregor plotted strategies for the efficient operation of the railways.

Known as "Wee Macgregor" or "Mac" to his close friends and J.A.M. to his employees, Macgregor was an able railroader, well skilled in handling people.[10] Macgregor was in his late teens when he came to Montreal where he joined the CPR as a clerk. After gaining experience in several positions, he moved west in 1914 as superintendent at Edmonton, Alberta.[11] In July 1920, he found himself with his greatest challenge when appointed general manager of the ED & BC and Central Canada railways.

Macgregor was also a musician, and there are tales about him by playing the piano as fellow executives clustered around

him, glasses in hand and voices lifted in song, after a long day at the conference table.[12] He frequently adjudicated at music festivals in Alberta, and daughter, Helen, was often the accompanist for participants and travelled with her father. Along with Macgregor, Charles E. Cox, then Edmonton's city clerk, was involved in organizing the first music festivals held in the Peace River country.[13]

G.W.E. "Billy" Smith, then storeman at McLennan, recalled a trip Helen Macgregor made as accompanist, along with Welsh singer and violinist Vaughan Williams, who was adjudicator at the music festivals that year. Hugh Humphries, a Welsh machinist at McLennan, was on the platform as the train from Peace River pulled in. Humphries introduced himself, then invited Williams and Miss Macgregor to his shack while they waited for the connecting train from Grande Prairie. In the shack they drank tea and sang songs. Later, Miss Macgregor wrote a letter thanking Humphries for the pleasant hours spent at his home. Smith said bachelor Humphries seemed to have romantic notions about her from then on. If he did they came to naught.[14]

Those who worked for Macgregor remember him as a very understanding human being, but one who could be strict. A few years later Holden "Harry" Swift was sent to Smith to relieve the night operator. He arrived to find the man had held the job until the previous evening when the way freight pulled in with Coleman and Macgre-

Left to Right: *Machinist Hughie Humphries,*
Boilermaker "Smoky" Edgett, Boilermaker
Helper Roy Gall, Car Foreman Bill Dickson and
Carman Andy "Hotbox" Hancharyk at McLennan
Photo: Courtesy of G.W.E. Smith

gor in the business car. It was a bitterly cold, windy evening, and the night operator was fond of a drop of warming, spirits. On this particular evening he imbibed more "warmth" than was good for him. He also copied some messages for the men in the business car and went to deliver them. Noticing the two railway officials talking in the lounge, without pausing to knock, he burst in exclaiming: "Why, D.C. you old so-and-so, the last time I saw you, you was checking cars in Fernie yard." Coleman turned to Macgregor and enquired coldly, "Who is this man?" Macgregor replied, "Up to one minute ago he was night operator at Smith."[15]

In the tradition of CPR executives, Macgregor was intensely loyal to the company he served and his company was eager to demonstrate its worth by upgrading the pioneer lines. Macgregor's efforts were greatly appreciated by northern residents. Some years later, after the CPR lease on the two railways had expired, Macgregor was asked to take over the management of the Pacific Great Eastern Railway, the forerunner of the British Columbia Railway. He refused, saying, "I've had one white elephant, that's enough for a lifetime."[16] His response indicates those years must have been difficult ones.

There were not many idle moments for the general manager as the CPR began rebuilding the McArthur lines. On 17 August 1920, in the wake of a storm, high waters submerged the low-lying meadow lands around the shores of Lesser Slave Lake. The railway tracks were washed out in several places between Wagner and Widewater. Sectionmen working in shifts had the tracks repaired and service restored by 22 August.

However, railways keep operating despite the wiles of Mother Nature. Upgrading of the Peace River railways continued, and gradually began to show results. On 15 September 1920, the first train since 8 June pulled into Grande Prairie. Service over the whole line was improving and three new stations were opened.[17] One of them was at Jarvie. The station agent in charge was William J. Reid, a telegrapher who had pounded brass on many railways in the U.S. and

North of Sexsmith poles are used as ties to repair track ahead of train pulled by Locomotive No. 23.
Photo: Public Archives of Canada, *PA 18215*

Canada. Unconfirmed stories said that the stoutish, red-faced man had been one of the early organizers for the Order of Railroad Telegraphers [ORT] in the U.S. In those days many union organizers on the railways south of the Canadian border were blackballed. This is said to have brought Bill Reid to Canada.[18]

Reid's organizational abilities were soon evident in the Jarvie community. He used his Liberal political connections in Edmonton to aid the district. Roy Newnham, one of the Jarvie district pioneers says, "W.J. Reid had as much to do with bringing education to the young people at Jarvie as anyone. . . . As well,

he got the town site surveyed and became the only local magistrate in Jarvie's history."[19] With his experience and background, Reid was a natural choice as local chairman of the ED & BC telegraphers union, following Bert French. In 1920, the two Peace River railways came under the Order of Railroad Telegraphers and followed the CPR Division No. 7 agreement, which Reid considered cumbersome. When he believed it was necessary, he bent the rules. Reid continued to battle for his union members until his untimely death in November 1928.

Even with CPR at the helm, the lines continued to operate at a loss in 1920, but the

CPR management was bringing some efficiency into the service. By December, train speeds were increased and the running time for passenger trains from Edmonton to Grande Prairie reduced from 39.5 hours to 27 hours.[20] In spite of the improved service, the opposition continued to find fault with the government's railway policy. The federal government had taken over the guarantees on the Canadian Northern and the Grand Trunk railways, reducing the provincial government guarantees to $17 million of which $11.4 million was for reconditioning of the ED & BC and Central Canada railways.

To take care of expenditures for interest and railway maintenance on the railways it operated, the Department of Railways and Telephones requested $4.75 million from the government of Alberta when the total budget for the province in 1921 was less than $13 million.[21] In spite of Premier Stewart's alarm at the expenditures required to assist the northern railways, the Legislature approved the budget. It was unthinkable that the railways should be shut down.

Auditor Bulgin was juggling the finances of the ED & BC and Central Canada railways. He had the unenviable task of bringing order to the accounting system. The Board of Railroad Commissioners was endeavoring to implement accounting procedures on Canadian railways patterned after those followed by U.S. lines. Needing assistance, Bulgin sent a note to a young travelling auditor of timekeepers on the CPR, Frederick J. Kavanagh: "The next time you are in Edmon-

ton, drop in and see me." When Fred Kavanagh walked into his office in December 1920 Bulgin offered him a job saying, "I will teach you all I know about railway accounting."[22] Kavanagh accepted the offer.

Kavanagh was the son of a CPR locomotive foreman at the shops in Farnham, Quebec. In November 1898, he was placed on permanent staff as a call boy. Eventually, he became a timekeeper and later travelling auditor. To the Peace River railways, Bulgin and Kavanagh brought different kinds of accounting expertise. Bulgin was a master of revenue accounting while Kavanagh's experience was in disbursement accounting. "For the railway, it was a fortuitous blending of skills."[23] Under Bulgin's tutelage, Kavanagh mastered revenue accounting procedures. A few years later, upon Bulgin's appointment to auditor of passenger revenues for the CPR in Montreal, Kavanagh filled the vacancy as auditor of the ED & BC and Central Canada railways.[24]

Fred Kavanagh was in his 101st year when he passed away in 1985. Time had not dimmed his perception of an auditor's duty and responsibility: "During his working years he was scrupulous in all his accounting practises. He was also adamant that the auditor did not work under the jurisdiction of the general manager, but reported directly to the Board of Directors, and was on occasion the watchdog over management practises. This viewpoint was not always popular with management but it worked to the overall benefit of the railway."[25]

The opposition continued to berate the government of Alberta for its operating agreement with the CPR in spite of Premier Stewart's assurances that the province was protected and that the CPR would absorb all costs in connection with the Peace River railways.[26] The decision to charge mountain, instead of prairie rate tariffs on the ED & BC came under scrutiny in the legislature early in April 1921. The outcome was that mountain rates were a federal matter and that they would prevail for a time. Northbound merchandise was generally assessed at mountain rates and it was a fact that costs involved in handling traffic on the Peace River and Smoky hills were similar to those incurred in mountainous areas.[27]

By this time, the ED & BC had extended sleeping car services to Grande Prairie. The *Edmonton Bulletin* reported that the new service "is very much appreciated by the travelling public. Train service is slow, but trains arrive and depart on time, and freight service is prompt and satisfactory."[28] Gerald Carveth was an express messenger on the twice weekly run between Grande Prairie and McLennan. There was usually such a big cargo of shipments that he seldom had time for his scheduled rest at McLennan.[29] In 1922 the Dominion Express Company took over the operations of the Central Canada Express Company. Since the company handled the express business of the CPR, it seemed a logical progression.

The Liberal government, which had been in power since Alberta became a province in September 1905, gave the impression of confidence and complacency. They handled the Conservative opposition seemingly oblivious to the threat posed by the United Farmers of Alberta. When Premier Stewart called an election for June 1921, the UFA had a candidate running in almost every riding. The electorate voted for a change in government and Herbert Greenfield, a farmer from the Westlock district, became premier.

Premier Greenfield named the Honorable Vernor W. Smith, a farmer from the Camrose district, minister of Railways and Telephones. Smith had some railway expertise having at one time worked for the railway construction firm of Stewart and Welch,[30] and been a partner in the Smith and Sheady Construction Company.[31] Shortly after his appointment, Smith persuaded his friend John Callaghan to come to Edmonton as his deputy minister and as general manager of the government railways. He had a long, distinguished career in railway construction behind him.[32] Born in Iowa, he began his career as a construction engineer in 1889 in the U.S. and Canada. Prior to his government appointment, he was superintendent for Stewart and Welch, railway contractors located in Calgary.

The UFA government was committed to a railway policy similar to that of the Liberal party and it pledged support for extensions. The Legislature had in 1921 voted $600 thousand for extension of the Central Canada Railway from Peace River to Berwyn, a distance of 21.7 miles to be built by the CPR. After relocating a portion of the right-of-way, this extension was officially opened for traffic on 4 February 1922.[33]

Ira Card was the first station agent at the new end of steel town. As a 16-year-old he had been introduced to station work on the Canadian Northern Railway. In September 1919, after two years with the Great Northwest Telegraph Company in their Calgary commercial telegraph office, he came to the ED & BC; "He was of chunky build, with stubby-fingered hands that had great dexterity."[34] He was a very organized man who tried to teach his assistants his system, but he did not succeed in making them all orderly people. They tried to imitate his telegrapher's freehand style where the wrist never touches the paper, and the pencil is grasped halfway along its length, but were not always successful.[35]

When the Cards went to Berwyn they were temporarily housed in cold, draughty converted boxcars. Their baby daughter succumbed to pneumonia. The morning after the funeral, the general manager arrived on the passenger train. After eating lunch with the Card family Macgregor said, "Ira, as soon as train No. 6 leaves this afternoon, and you have sent the OS,[36] I want you to put up a notice stating the station is closed for the balance of the day, on my instructions. Then lock the doors and take your family away from here for a few hours."[37] Macgregor's kindness was always remembered by the Card family.

Agent Ira Card with Assistant Agents Ed Bailey and Jack Swift at Grande Prairie in 1928.

In addition to caring for the personal welfare of his workers, Macgregor also confronted problems with the provincial government. The deputy minister of the Department of Railways began what amounted to a crusade against the CPR management of the Peace River railways. The seat of his office chair was barely warm when Callaghan attacked the CPR verbally. In a 16 page letter to his minister dated 14 November 1921, he wrote: "In applying the CPR system to a line like the ED & BC or the A & GW it is like using a six horse team to do the work of a two horse team." The $2.5 million advance from the government of Alberta was exhausted by the end of 1922 and there was still much to be done.[38] The CPR needed more funding to continue the upgrading program. New extensions on both the ED & BC and the Central Canada Railway were under construction and financed by the provincial government. In the annual report of the railways branch for 1922, Callaghan made allegations of CPR mismanagement of the $2.5 million, that caused a ruckus in the Legislature. President D.C. Coleman angrily refuted Callaghan's accusations.[39]

In July 1923, at Callaghan's insistence, the government hired two civil engineers from Vancouver to conduct an inspection of the two railways managed by the CPR. The report submitted by James H. Kennedy and C.E. Cartwright was not complimentary. In November, government members went north to see the progress for themselves. The annual report of the provincial department of railways for the year 1923 was labelled "Tame and Innocuous" by the *Edmonton Journal*. No mention was made of the investigation into the CPR management of the northern railways.

Toward the end of September, an accident near Northwest Lumber's pond at Dunvegan Yards cost Conductor William Kirkland his life.[40] While a log train was switching, he rode the footboard of the engine. A log caught Kirkland's leg as he passed, toppling him beneath the train. The 40-year-old man, who had been with the railway for eight years, left a wife and five children.[41]

Meanwhile, a 13 mile extension from Berwyn to Whitelaw on the Central Canada Railway was under construction.[42] The Alberta Government had secured the services of Cecil Crysdale as locating engineer. Henry Dimsdale, from the Department of Railways, was the engineer in charge of construction and it was ready for operation in December 1924. The agent who opened the station doors at Whitelaw was Phillip Filion, whose easily aroused temper became legendary. In fact, it was to be the death of him when he experienced a heart attack in the midst of an argument with crew members on a train at Rycroft.

Clarke "Knothole" McCombs, Conductor Ross McCombs' son, became Filion's assistant at Whitelaw. Filion had a way with words. Once, he riled McCombs so much that before he realized what he had done, McComb's fist had made contact with Filion's face. The eye had blackened by the time McCombs was removed from the station and sent to McLennan.

Station at Whitelaw
Photo: Courtesy of M. Mahood

At McLennan, M. Wilson Boucher was assistant superintendent for the duration of the CPR's lease. The big framed man was a strict disciplinarian. Wishing to introduce economies, he substituted newspaper torn into squares and hung by a string for toilet tissue in the outhouse. Incensed at the increase in the length of time his men spent in the facility and the discussions that followed on news gleaned from there, Chargehand Duncan MacDonald confronted Boucher saying, "It is no longer a toilet we have, but a flipping library."[43] The newspapers were replaced shortly afterwards with regular tissue.

In the meantime, the 15 mile extension from Grande Prairie west toward Lake Saskatoon on the ED & BC was under construction. Although approved in 1922,[44] construction was delayed until difficulties regarding permission from McArthur and the Union Bank were resolved. When grading commenced in September 1923, Henry Dimsdale was the division engineer in charge.[45] The railway was built south of Saskatoon Mountain, bypassing the thriving settlement of Lake Saskatoon and bringing about its decline. The area had gained some notoriety because of Hermann Trelle who owned a farm in the vicinity. His wheat and oats won World Wheat Championships and numerous awards.[46] The ED & BC benefitted from the unsolicited publicity as the movement of settlers into the area more than doubled.

Lake Saskatoon picked itself up and moved to the railway townsite of Wembley. The extension was officially opened for traffic on 9 December 1924, and Vince Talbot was the first agent. As an end of steel station, Wembley was a busy terminal. It had insufficient space, equipment and was understaffed. Talbot was a first class telegrapher, but the bookkeeping became a nightmare. Agent Berube arrived to take over the station with Assistant Agent Maurice Mahood.

Not too enthralled about sitting on apple boxes to work, because the chairs were broken, the men decided to repair them. Carpentry was one of Berube's talents. Mahood waded into the pile. He writes, "One yank and the greatest army of mice I ever laid eyes upon were running all over the freight shed. Berube had both pant legs hitched up over his knees and was yelling at the top of his voice, 'Maurice, Maurice, kill them, kill them.' I stood laughing, and then caught the note of panic. The man was really afraid of them. I grabbed an old broom, opened the back door of the shed, and as I smacked ineffectively at them the mice scooted for the great outdoors. . . . "[47] Harry Swift arrived about three weeks later to take over management of the agency.

At Wembley, Swift taught Mahood agency work. Mahood remembered him saying, "Now listen carefully, kid, I'll show you thoroughly, but I expect to show you only once. After that you're on your own."[48] A man who worked in spurts, Swift could do the equivalent of an hour and a half's work in

45 minutes, then he liked to stop and relax for 10 minutes.

In addition to the station, a water tank and a two stall engine shop were erected at Wembley. Locomotive Foreman 'Sledge Hammer' Bill Henderson, who had been scalded in the accident after the Donnelly dance in 1920, and Locomotive Watchman Francis Schenk were transferred from Grande Prairie to work in the new facilities. It was here that Henderson lost part of his leg. After he had left the railway, he was riding a locomotive down to the water tank, when he slipped off and a wheel crushed his leg.

A & GW bridge collapsing at Mile 275.
Photo: University of Alberta Archives, John Allen Collection,
Acc. No. 79-23-3001

13

Alberta Manages the A & GW

Because it did not appear to have revenue producing prospects, the CPR was not interested in managing the Alberta and Great Waterways Railway. With no other bidders on the horizon, the government of Alberta decided to manage the railway along with the Lacombe and Northwestern Railway [L & NW], which it had assumed responsibility for in 1918.[1] An agreement signed on 23 July 1920, provided for the absolute release and discharge of the A & GW's liabilities to the J.D. McArthur Company Ltd. and the Union Bank of Canada. As with the ED & BC, McArthur retained the option to regain control exercisable at any time prior to the first day of July 1927. The 500 par value shares were transferred to the government of Alberta.

Premier Charles Stewart became the railway's president. Norman L. Harvey, deputy minister of Railways and Telephones, was named general manager of the A & GW and L & NW railways.[2] Henry A.O.

Warner, an engineer with the Department of Railways, became superintendent and chief engineer. Louis Scott, another engineer in the department, was appointed secretary of the government board of management and purchasing agent. Section Foreman Walter Bryant was promoted to Roadmaster.

Norman Harvey had spent seven years with the Canadian Northern Railway in the accounting and executive departments prior to joining the government of Alberta in 1912.[3] As secretary to Premier Sifton, and then to the Department of Railways and Telephones, he had been involved with the Peace River railways since their inception and this continued after his promotion to deputy minister in 1918. Although Harvey was general manager, the actual management of the A & GW and L & NW was for the most part in the hands of Harry Warner.

The new management team set out to improve the roadbed and service on the A & GW. The track north of Lac La Biche was

N.L. Harvey, Deputy Minister of Railways and Telephones and General Manager, A & GW and L & NW Rys., July 1920-March 1921.
Photo: Courtesy of Alberta
Government Telephones

little more than skeletal. The portion down the Clearwater Hill was still not operational as a result of slides. It was decided to abandon the line beyond Mile 272 and to relocate by way of Deep Creek.[4] This did not deter Premier Stewart from optimistically declaring in early September 1920, "Trains will be running directly into Fort McMurray within a year."[5]

To get the track north of Lac La Biche into shape, an agreement was reached with the Northern Construction Company,[6] which held contracts for some large drainage projects in the province. The firm also operated the train service over that portion of the road, under the direction of government officials, during the period of the construction work.

Train crews were on loan from the ED & BC and A & GW. The staff of Northern Construction and their families swelled the population of Lac La Biche. The company was formed in Winnipeg in 1904 by the renowned railway builders Andrew Robert Mann, brother of Sir Donald Mann, and Archibald Cameron MacKenzie who was related to Sir William Mackenzie.[7]

Locomotive No. 30 syphoning water from Horse Creek between Waterways and Lynton, c. 1920.
Photo: Courtesy of R.D.C. Comrie

Lineman Hugh J. "Slim" Bowman lived at Lac La Biche. He enjoyed squiring the new school teachers when he was in town, but his job kept the tall, popular bachelor out on the line a good deal. The battle to keep old decaying poles upright between Carbondale and Lac La Biche was never ending. While A. Lambert and his men built the telephone line between Mile 272 and Fort McMurray, it was Bowman's responsibility to make it work. He had difficulty getting satisfactory service between Edmonton and Waterways.

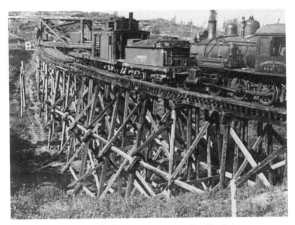

This self-propelled, steam powered pile driver was designed by J.E. Deakin and operated by Jack Hudson.
Photo: Courtesy of Bill Christian Jr.

Service was good from Lac La Biche in either direction, but not all the way through.

To assist the construction work in progress the A & GW purchased a 12 passenger, 30 foot launch called "Moberly." The $4 thousand boat was used on exploratory work between the end of steel and Fort McMurray. Jack McClung, a student at the University of Alberta and son of the famous Nellie McClung, was the skipper.[8] He joined the attorney general's department in 1927 and later was appointed King's Counsel. The "Moberly" did not fare so well. Used only for one summer, once the railway reached its destination, there was no further use for the boat. During the following years all offers to purchase the launch were declined. By 1937, it was obvious its glory days were over as its hulk lay rotting on the banks of the Clearwa-

ter River.

Because of his considerable experience, Harry Warner understood the problems faced by Northern Construction. He had been on the original survey of the route. Warner and Louis Scott had worked together in the ED & BC drafting office as early as 1914. The English-born Scott enlisted in the Princess Patricia Canadian Light Infantry in 1915 and was commissioned overseas.[9] Later, he was seconded to the Royal Air Force and returned to Edmonton in 1919 to find his friend Warner had joined the Department of Railways in the interim.[10] Warner became acting general manager upon the resignation of Norman Harvey on 29 March 1921.[11] At a meeting of the railway's Board of Directors, held on 4 August 1921, he was appointed general manager and chief engineer, "retroactive to 30 March 1921."

Walter Hill was a friend of Scott and Warners' and served with Scott overseas in World War I. He was a druggist in the Griffin drug store which was owned by Harry Warner.[12] He sometimes accompanied Warner and Scott on trips over the railway. Consequently, he was happy to oblige when Harry Warner stopped by the drug store one day in 1920 and invited him to help name some of the sidings.[13] Walter said, "We spread a map out on the table. There were four of us; Harry Warner, Louis Scott, Sammy Brand and myself... .[Brand was auditor of traffic accounting.] Newbrook we called after an old Englishman who homesteaded there ... Venice we thought looked like Venice because the whole darned place was under water."[14] Several other sidings were also named at this gathering.

At that time, Hill had no idea that two years later he would move to Fort McMurray to work in Sutherland Drugs and spend the rest of his life there. His plans were to head south to California. Until his death in 1986, Walter Hill continued to be active in running Hill's Drugs and telling yarns.

John Callaghan, who replaced Warner, was a heavy-set, barrel-chested man, about five feet ten inches tall, who liked to sign his correspondence Jno. Callaghan. He was the last of a breed of railway managers from a generation where the boss was BOSS. The bachelor had few close friends.[15] He was not much concerned about what the public thought of his actions, nor those who worked for him.[16] Callaghan treated the office staff with little respect and most feared his moods. Diminutive Stan Morgan was his secretary for a number of years and recalls being summoned to the general manager's office to pick up the signed payroll sheets. He picked them up, but from the floor. As soon as Morgan appeared in the doorway Callaghan started pitching.[17]

An incident occurred one morning that caused much merriment among staff members when Callaghan was out of earshot. Hearing some rattling outside, Stan Kenworthy, a new time keeper, yanked the entrance door open. He discovered a key

from a key chain in the lock but to his dismay the other end was still attached to Callaghan's trousers. The strain had been too much for the buttons, and as the general manager struggled to hold the front of his pants together, his roars of anger drowned out the young man's apologies. To his surprise Kenworthy still had a job the following day.[18]

Jno. Callaghan, Deputy Minister of Railways and Telephones and General Manager, A & GW and L & NW Rys., 1921-1926, ED & BC, CC, A & GW and L & NW Rys., 1926-1928, ED & BC, CC, A & GW and PV Rys., 1928-1929. NAR's General Manager, 1929-1937. Photo: International Press

In spite of his caustic nature, Callaghan was fond of children. When Agent Alvin "Kelly" Olstad was a boy he bagged several mallards while hunting one day near his home at New Norway, Alberta. As he trudged homeward, he met Callaghan, who had also been hunting but with less success. The hunters chatted. Then Callaghan bought Kelly's ducks. Before they parted, he told the lad if he wanted a job when he grew up, he should write to him personally. Kelly tried banking, then "I wrote to Mr. Callaghan and almost immediately had a letter telling me to report to Chief Clerk, M.E. Collins. I got a job as an assistant agent."[19]

Callaghan was not an easy man to work with. Nevertheless, Bill Reid, local chairman of the Order of Railway Telegraphers, managed to hammer out an agreement with him that was the envy of other railways. It was said that during Callaghan's tenure he had more labor disputes before the Board of Arbitration than either the CPR or CNR railways.[20] This may have been the result of changing attitudes in the relationship between employers and labor. With economic recovery after World War I the growing strength of the bargaining power of unions and their acceptance as a legitimate part of society was increasingly evident.[21] Adjusting to this different management approach must have been difficult for men accustomed, as Callaghan was, to holding almost autocratic power.

Soon after taking over the A & GW reins, Callaghan affected economies, starting with a reduction in staff. He dismissed the entire engineering staff involved with maintenance work between Mile 0 and 272. A large number of section foremen were replaced and salaries for operating personnel were reduced.[22] A number of the replacements were people who previously had worked for Callaghan. Northern Construction was taken off the job of reconditioning the A & GW at the end of October 1921.[23] The contract had cost the government $3 million in total.[24] Stationmen employed by the company were allowed to complete the ditching work in progress. Running crews for the construction company had the opportunity to transfer to the railway. Among them was J.R. "Jack" Smith. He hailed from Nova Scotia, and had railway experience dating from 1909, first with the Grand Trunk Pacific and later the Pacific Great Eastern Railway's construction department in British Columbia. In 1922, the A & GW welcomed him into the engine service ranks, and eventually promoted him to locomotive engineer.

Henry G. Dimsdale replaced S.E. Reaugh as resident engineer on the extension to the town being located at the junction of Deep Creek and the Clearwater River. In October 1921, the government announced that Waterways would be the name of the new railway terminus, some six miles from Fort McMurray. The choice was dictated by the fact it owned 840 acres there and very little land beyond that point.[25]

The outraged residents of Fort McMurray sent a delegation with a petition to the provincial government deploring that, "The railway company, the creature of the government, should end its line six miles short of

Fort McMurray and should promote and encourage the development of a new townsite there in apparent competition with the old establishment of McMurray; and that too, on a location which offers no peculiar advantages for a townsite, steamboat landing or railway terminus, and can only be hewn from the dense bush at a considerable expenditure of time and money."[26]

Turning coaches on wye at the end of steel, Waterways
Photo: Courtesy of R.D.C. Comrie

The anger of Fort McMurray's citizens was justified. Only one month before, Premier Greenfield had made an inspection trip over the line in "Rosemere," the ED & BC general manager's business car. In his entourage were Vernor Smith, John Callaghan and J.M. Mercer, general superintendent of Northern Construction Co. When interviewed, the premier was enthusiastic about the prospects of an extension to the town, "Steel will be laid to Hangingstone

Creek, about four miles from McMurray, this fall."[27] He expressed a desire to have all track work and ballasting completed by fall. A month later the government announced that the steel would end at Deep Creek and not continue to Fort McMurray. Shortly afterwards a tie contractor lost his stockpile of several thousand ties in a bush fire that happened to sweep through the storage area. That the ties were insured came as no surprise.[28] Warnings from Fort McMurray that the junction of the Clearwater River and Deep Creek was not practical because uncertain water conditions hampered navigation proved to be correct.

Karl "Charlie" Eymundson, who owned a small store in Waterways, built and operated a telephone line between Waterways and Fort McMurray. The station and a log hotel in Fort McMurray owned by Angus Sutherland, the druggist, were connected to it. The telephone was later moved to Sutherland's drug store, which later became Hill's Drugs, where telegrams phoned from the station were accepted and delivered on a commission basis.[29]

There was much socializing on trains going north to Waterways. Everyone knew everyone. Rule G, prohibiting the use of alcoholic beverages among staff, was sometimes bent. Once, a passenger overcome by the refreshments, retired early to her lower berth. She awoke to find herself surrounded by empty bottles. Eyeing them with a jaundiced eye she proclaimed loud and clear that she "knew damned well she had not consumed that much."[30] By then bootlegging was a profitable business in Aberta, even though Prohibition was still in effect.[31] The A & GW fell under suspicion when a whiskey still was discovered in the section house at Thorhild. The section foreman claimed his wife was responsible. The roadmaster did not dismiss the section foreman, but when Callaghan heard about it both men had to hit the road.

It was in the summer of 1923 that 14-year-old Otto Michetti got a job as an extra gang laborer. It was 60 hours a week of back-breaking work under the supervision of Foreman Frank Dunnigan. Dunnigan was a stern Irishman who seldom smiled. If he did, his enormous blonde handle-bar moustache hid it. One day, while the men each trimmed four ties, Dunnigan called Michetti. The frightened boy wondered how he had

Locomotive No. 28, Conductor Fred Martin and Engineer Charles Snyder
at Waterways(later Draper) c. 1925
Photo: Provincial Archives of Alberta, A3936

sinned. His fear turned to inspiration when Dunnigan said, "Otto, from where I stand, I can see each of the four ties trimmed by you around this curve. Keep this up and you will surely become a roadmaster some day."[32] The prophesy came true some years later.

After struggling for a few years with the vagaries of the Clearwater River, in 1925 the railway did move 3.7 miles down the hill.[33] Cecil Crysdale was the locating engineer and R.M. "Bob" Martin was the resident engineer. H.K. "Pat" Williams, who was only 17, was a member of the crew surveying the wye at the end of steel. Lack of space necessitated a 24 degree curve – a 12 degree curve was considered sharp. Mannix and Walgren were the contractors.

The survey crew had Saturday afternoon off, but there was little to do on a summer's day in Waterways where the main street was just a trail peppered with tree stumps. For the young men the best entertainment was at the boat dock where they might see the Northland Echo or the shipyards where independent fur traders were building barges to take goods down north to trade with the Indians. Pat Williams and Jim Thom were not adverse to earning an easy $10 when asked to guide a barge down the Clearwater to the Snye, adjacent to Fort McMurray.

The hamlet of Waterways was moved to where the Hangingstone Creek flows into the Clearwater River. Its previous location was renamed Draper after Thomas Draper. He

erected an experimental plant alongside the railway at Deep Creek for oil extraction from tar sands in the vicinity. The railway still did not cross the Hangingstone into Fort McMurray. The combined station and warehouse at the old terminus was partially dismantled. A portion was moved to the new site and the remainder was converted into a temporary station building.[34] The name Waterways stayed with it.

Agent Herbert Victory Viney arrived at Waterways in 1925 as George Palmer's bridge and building gang put the finishing touches to the two storey station building.[35] Viney had no idea then that he would spend 20 years in charge of what was the railway's

Dr. Karl A. Clark, Research Council of Alberta, established this experimental pilot plant at Dunvegan Yards for the extraction of oil from tar sands. Dismantled in 1930 it was re-erected at Waterways.
Photo: Provincial Archives of Alberta, A11227

busiest station in the summer season of navigation. Carloads of freight and express for the Arctic went by rail to Waterways. From there, they continued their journey down north by barge.

Until completed, a slow order of four miles per hour was placed on the extension between Draper and Waterways. Charlie Snyder eased his locomotive slowly over the uneven track. Both Snyder and his fireman, Bill Lindgren, had been with the railway since 1916. That did not impress an irate reporter from eastern Canada, nor did the slow speed. The crowd on the platform listened as he roared, "This would never do in the East." Agent Viney, who was watching the performance, saw the stranger check his watch, then peer through the office window. The station clock was in Edmonton for repairs. The reporter demanded, "Where's your clock?" The audience exploded in laughter as Viney replied, "We don't use one here, sir. We just use a calendar."[36]

There was no mistaking Viney's nationality. His accent could not be disguised. The fragile looking frame of the tall,

Bridge and Building crew at Waterways. Left to right:
Lorin "Andy" Carnochan, Albert Robinson, Frank Loewen
Bill White, Kunte Knutson and Jim Currie.
Photo: Courtesy of Lorin Carnochan

A shaved head helped Agent Bert Viney
keep his cool in the summer heat.
Photo: Courtesy of Wm. J. Donlevy.

Waterways. In his leisure hours Viney liked reading and gardening, but spare time became scarce at Waterways as the way-freight business increased. Because of his obliging ways and his ready ear, he was well liked by the northerners.

Another accommodating employee was young Express Messenger Harry McAfee.[37] Like those who would follow in his footsteps, he knew everyone along the route north of Lac La Biche. Besides sectionmen and pump-men, there were trappers and the local population of the scattered settlements. They always needed something – shells for a gun, a part for a camera, money orders or a pay cheque cashed. McAfee never let them down and they came to depend on him.

Viney and McAfee listened to many a gripe before the citizens of Fort McMurray reluctantly accepted the new location of the railhead. It was, after all, only about three miles from the settlement and the railway used that to advantage. On the premise that it was still being built, construction rates were charged on freight for many years.

Between 1925 and 1928 the A & GW carried an unusual cargo - buffalo. Stock cars loaded with the shaggy coated animals from Wainwright Buffalo Park were shipped to Waterways. Occasionally, it took close to eight hours to empty the cars of the stubborn creatures. Then they were held in specially constructed corrals until loaded in scows for the river trip to Wood Buffalo National Park.[38] From Waterways, J.K. Cornwall had the contract for transporting the animals to their final destination.

A stubbornness similar to that of the buffalo surfaced in the turbulent relationship between the general managers of the A & GW and the ED & BC. A major bone of contention was the terminal facilities at Dunvegan Yards where the two railways shared the same terminal and both operated over the ED & BC tracks north to Carbondale.[39] To be successful, the terminal agreement required a harmonious relationship and both men had very different interpretations. Callaghan wanted to manage all the railways himself. It was his recommendation that the ED & BC and Central Canada Railways be taken over by the government at the expiration of the operating contract. In 1926 the government finally agreed.

Buffalo in corrals at Waterways prior to shipment by scow to Wood Buffalo Park.
Photo: Courtesy of R.D.C. Comrie.

In 1928 spring floods washed the track up against the unloading chute for buffalo.
Photo: Courtesy of R.D.C. Comrie

Mixed train descending hill between Lynton and Waterways.
Photo: Courtesy of R.D.C. Comrie

6V

14

The Alberta Railways

On 30 July 1926, the *Edmonton Bulletin* carried the headline "Notice is Given CPR." This announcement ended months of speculation about the management of the Edmonton, Dunvegan and British Columbia and Central Canada railways. The CPR was given three months notice of termination of the operating lease agreement of 1920. The government had secured ownership rights of the northern roads with the payment of $1 275 000 to the Royal Bank. By settlement, the province of Alberta obtained a transfer of debentures issued by the ED & BC Railway to J.D. McArthur. The trust deed mortgage securing these debentures was also transferred to the province, along with the capital stock issued by the railways.

To avoid media pressure, General Manager Macgregor immediately left on vacation. When he returned to Edmonton, the press hounded him for a statement. He declined to comment except to deny reports that the ED & BC was allowed to deteriorate under CPR management. He claimed, "The ED & BC is being maintained to the highest standard of branch line maintenance in this or any other country."[1]

A trip to Winnipeg by Premier Brownlee and Hon. Vernor Smith in November 1926 finalized the transfer of the railways. All qualifying shares in the ED & BC held in trust by the CPR were transferred to the Province of Alberta and the resignations of the CPR directors were accepted. The premier's optimistic comment was "Officials of the Railway Department are confident of their ability to operate the road and see a substantial operating profit."[2] John Callaghan had got what he had been angling for and he was now firmly in the saddle as general manager of the ED & BC, the CC, the A & GW, and the L & NW railways.

News of the settlement was met with sighs of relief by most employees. They were weary of rumors surfacing every few months regarding the railway situation. Nevertheless, they wondered how it would affect their careers. Harry Frechette was then a young man, operating a crane at Dunvegan Yards. He had a family to support and what became of the A & GW was of great concern to him. Frechette had left CPR's Transcona shops in Winnipeg and come west after a recruitment blitz by J.D. McArthur. His son, Joe Frechette recalled his mother came west in the spring of the following year. They lived in Rossdale Flats in Edmonton until the 1915 "flood put their house awash so they moved out to Dunvegan Yards."[3] There they built a small lean-to shack, which was added to every time another child arrived.

At Dunvegan Yards a crane, nicknamed "The Goose," was sitting idle. Although a machinist helper and carman, Frechette had some experience with a steam shovel and he became its operator. He stockpiled hundreds of thousands of tons of coal with the indispensible machine and coaled engines and loading cars for delivery to coaling points along the line. His son recalled with some pride, and the old timers concur, "Dad could do a better job when he was 'tight' than most could do when they were sober. He worked long days and would get very dirty. ... You could scrape the grease off his overalls. When he came home at night Mother would set a basin of hot water in his lap and start to clean him up and shave him. It wasn't something he couldn't do for himself but just something she did for him."[4]

The crane was hauled around by a dinky engine, a small 0-4-0 switcher type locomotive with a saddle back water tank straddling the boiler. A small coal bunker on the side of the platform, at the rear of the firebox held fuel. Joe Frechette remembered, "Once when the dinky was taking the crane to load lumber at the Northwest sawmill, Dad blew the whistle to stop but it kept right on going. Glancing back Dad saw what looked like a body lying at the side of the track."[5] He dropped off the crane, stopped the dinky, then rushed back to where the figure lay. It was MacDonald, the operator. Because it had no back, just a coal box MacDonald must have lost his balance when adding fuel to the fire. The accident occurred near where Bill Kirkland had lost his life. "The news spread fast. Someone told my mother the crane engineer had been run over. Right away she thought it was Dad and rushed to the accident scene. Dad was there, distraught, but alive. MacDonald did not survive the accident."[6]

Harry Frechette was 63 years of age when he retired in 1943. By that time, sons Sam and Joe were well-established on the railway, eventually becoming general car foreman and general locomotive foreman respectively. Another son, Fred, worked for the railway for only three weeks as a sectionman before changing his career in favor of the Air Force.

When the government took control of the railways in 1926, young Charles Anderson was out on the line doing a three month stint as travelling auditor. A year later, he was chief clerk in the audit department. Despite his youth, Anderson already knew something about the effect of mergers. He had survived the amalgamation of the Grand Trunk Pacific and the Canadian Northern railways. That experience prompted him to join the A & GW staff in the fall of 1923. This was when he first became acquainted with John Callaghan.

blurted out, "It is simply not done your way, Mr. Callaghan." Much to his surprise Callaghan leaned back in his chair and guffawed, saying "All right, kid."[7] It was this indomitable spirit and his forte for figures that led to the diminutive Scotsman eventually becoming auditor of the railways.

Dinky Locomotive No. 1 used for switching in Dunvegan Yards. The Engineer is Con Kennedy.
Photo: CP Rail Corporate Archives, 4991

One day at lunch time when the general manager rang, Anderson was alone in the office. There was a mix-up over a train of livestock for the Edmonton stockyards and Callaghan was furious about it. As they talked Anderson tried in vain to explain that things were not quite the way Callaghan saw them. Meanwhile, the man grew angrier and angrier. Finally in exasperation Anderson

Almost the first thing that happened after the government takeover was a change in the timetable. This caused some consternation in the northern communities. An agreement for the handling of traffic off the northern lines was reached with the Canadian National Railways.[8] Passenger trains now departed from the CNR station and a dining car service was initiated.

Locomotive No. 3 and yard service crew at Dunvegan Yards. L to R:
Bert Hornbeck, Louis Peltier, Walter Crawford, Andy Heavener and Lee Card.
Photo: Courtesy of R.D.C. Comrie.

G. J. "Jimmy" McVicar watched with a skeptical eye the changes taking place with government operation of the railways. He was chief clerk in the traffic department of the ED & BC. The bespectacled, florid faced little Scot joined the railway under the McArthur regime and there was not much he did not know about the handling of traffic. John Callaghan recognized his worth and he stayed on. A number of employees, who had transferred when the CPR leased the Peace River railways, preferred to stay on with the Alberta railways. Others chose to return to the CPR, among them was E.J. Bulgin and

Alfred Gibson who was appointed auditor of the four railways.

Provision was made for the loan of CPR locomotives and rolling stock. After inspection by Car Foreman Paul Webb, several pieces were purchased. Webb was ideally suited to the railway's type of operation and his expertise was used wherever possible. Years later, when it was decided to purchase some used coaches and other equipment in the United States, Webb was the man sent to look them over. He set a precedent when he designed and executed the conversion of steel sleeper "Peace River" into a business car, which was renamed "Dunvegan," at Dunvegan Yards.[9] Besides being an expert craftsman, Webb had a talent for choosing staff who could work harmoniously together. Railroaders do not remember hearing him raise his voice. He valued the opinions and advice of fellow workers. Rather than tell someone the way they were doing something was wrong, he would say "There are a couple of ways you could handle that."

Locomotive No. 51 and trainload of ties at Lac La Biche
Photo: Courtesy of Miss Mary Watson

The railway was under new management for less than a year when it lost its competent master mechanic. George McLennan had spent most of his career in railroading. The talk of wealth had lured him west to the Cariboo gold rush in British Columbia. Although he did not return home much richer, he did have enough gold for a ring for his sweetheart. After undergoing his machinist apprenticeship with the CPR, he moved to the Grand Trunk Pacific. He was employed in their shops in Edmonton, when he decided to join McArthur's staff in 1914. Six years later, he was promoted to master mechanic

in charge of the A & GW and the L & NW railways. Sparks escaping from the smoke stack of steam locomotives, often set grass and even buildings on fire. To solve the problem, McLennan invented a spark arrester to fit over the top of the smoke stack.[10] The railway may have lost one of its best when McLennan went to work in the Sterco coal mines.

This locomotive is reputed to have been assembled by Locomotive Foreman George McLennan using parts from 3 locomotives.
Photo: Courtesy of R.D.C. Comrie

Don Turner succeeded George McLennan as master mechanic. This was a difficult position for a young man who was a boilermaker by trade. The pressure on him was eased somewhat by Locomotive Foreman Bill Gibb, a skilled machinist, who had served his apprenticeship in Scotland and gained expertise in the railway shops in Winnipeg. Unfortunately, the relationship between the two men led to such disagreement that Bill Gibb was replaced by David Brown.

Three new decapod locomotives arrived in April 1927. Numbered 52, 53 and 54, they were soon in service on the ED & BC. Engine 51 had arrived the previous year and the No. 71 was on loan from the L & NW. The shops at Dunvegan Yards and McLennan strived to meet the demand for sufficient operating equipment. Valuable work space was lost on 19 April 1927 when fire destroyed the engine house, machine shop, oil house, stores car [old boxcar] and sandhouse at McLennan. When the alarm was raised lunches were forgotten as staff and townspeople began a bucket brigade from a nearby slough. Reacting with lightning speed, employees moved four locomotives from the roundhouse through the leaping flames, but engine No.14 was badly burned.[11]

Locomotive No. 53 arrives. Back: *Art Rogers, Bob Neil, Teddy Jones, Ben Watt, Don Livingston, George Anderson, Neil Hyslop, Gus, Jim Etheridge, Joe Scott, Stein Johnson, Bill Stubbs, Joe Faulder, Jack McPhee, Sam Fee, Hugh Barker, Pat McDonald, Lloyd Arnesen, Harry Frechette, Bill Mckay, George Browman.* Front: *Jim Stevenson, George Leadbeater, Fred Harris, Bill Gibb, Stan McCloskey, Jack Ritchie, Leo Dube and Will Jones.*
Photo: Courtesy of Anne Frechette

At this time G.W.E. "Billy" Smith was in the McLennan stores department. He credited ingenuity with saving the stores. Conductor Gene McLaughlin and Fireman Red Johnstone moved some steel freight cars and positioned them between the shops and the stores car. Train Dispatcher Ernie Bromley hung blankets, soaked in the tender of an engine and draped them over the boxcar. He then climbed up and with a wet blanket over a broom swept the hot embers from the top.[12] As storekeeper, Smith's chief concern was his stock books; dodging the flying sparks, he rushed to rescue them. To his surprise he found two engineers ahead of him. They had braved the inferno to search for their "A" books. They were determined not to rewrite the examination required by all those aspiring to be engineers. The stores facilities were saved and no one had to rewrite the examination.

By that time plans were progressing for a 25 mile extension west from Wembley on the ED & BC and a 15 mile extension from Whitelaw toward Waterhole north of the Peace River on the Central Canada Railway. Rossa and Wikstrand, a railway contracting firm from Winnipeg, was awarded the contracts for both extensions.[13] Cecil Crysdale was the engineer in charge. Resident Engineer Harry Cullerne set up headquarters in a boxcar at Whitelaw from where he directed operations.

As the end of steel, Whitelaw was a busy place. It was about this time that Brakeman Wm. "Bill" Craig lost his life, when he was run over after falling from a stock car. His son, Russell Craig, was firing locomotives on the wayfreight and passenger trains into Whitelaw.[14] Despite the loss of his father, Craig retained sweet memories of Whitelaw because it was there he met the school teacher who later became his wife.

Among the grading outfits on the Whitelaw extension was Nigro and Anselmo, who had handled grading on the St. Lina line. By August 1928, track-laying was in progress under the supervision of Elmer Hagglund, foreman of extra gang 16. His father worked for the Great Northern Railway in Minnesota, and the younger Hagglund was a mere 13-years-old when he got a part-time job with the railway. He was well experienced when he joined the ED & BC in May 1922 as a sectionman and was soon promoted to foreman. But he preferred the lurch of a train and transferred to train service, eventually becoming a conductor.

Elmer Hagglund sympathized with the residents of Vanrena and Waterhole as the rails by-passed the hamlets. Waterhole had been growing for 11 years, but few owned the land their homes stood on. A new townsite sprang up on the rail line at Fairview and the residents of Waterhole moved. The railway provided land to assist the Waterhole hospital to relocate there. By the time the line was officially opened on 2 November 1928, Fairview was already a thriving community. Besides a temporary railway station, it had two large hotels, six stores, and about 15 homes in various stages of construction.

The first passenger train into the village was on schedule and was greeted by several hundred people. Celebrations that night included a free silent picture show and a dance.[15]

P.E. "Matty" Matthews opened the Fairview station.[16] Formerly a CPR agent, he had come on the ED & BC payroll in 1920. Like many of the agents, Matthews became quite involved with the community. He played

Arrival of first train at Fairview
Photo: Peace River Centennial Museum

Agent Percy Mathews, Assistant Agent Allan McDougall, Trainman Mike LaBrier, Relief Agent Holden Swift with Locomotive No. 11 at Spirit River
Photo: J. Edgar, courtesy of R.D.C. Comrie

catcher for the local baseball team in summer and hockey in winter. He always carried this enthusiasm into business and insisted that everything run smoothly and by the book.

Matthews' aggressiveness also fostered a stinging wit. The passenger train brought stationery supplies to the agents. When checking a shipment one day it was obvious to Matthews that the railway was on another stringency kick. The quantity of some items he had ordered had been halved. His temper reached a boil when he found there was one pencil rather than two. After venting his fury on his hapless assistant agent he rattled off a courteous, business-like letter, requesting guidance on how best two people should use the lone pencil. Should they cut it in half or use it in turns? The response was immediate. Another pencil arrived on the next train, along with Superintendent Deakin, demanding a written statement. Matthews insisted he had intended no disrespect, only guidance. In spite of his protests, he was awarded demerit marks, but he had made his point, never again was his order for pencils chopped in half.[17]

Because no legislation had been passed authorizing the planned construction beyond Wembley, the extension to Hythe was delayed until the Government of Canada passed Bill 57.[18] By March 1928 a location party was in the field, under the direction of Engineer R.M. "Bob" Martin. H.K. "Pat" Williams held the residency from Beaverlodge to Hythe, and recalls using smoke signals on one occasion to communicate. After the sur-

vey was complete, it was decided that revisions had to be made. Draftsman J.S. Thom secured about 20 feet of stout wrapping paper. When the calculations were made to hit a target, nine miles distant, the survey crew hacked their way through the bush to it. As a check, a bonfire of old tires was lit at an appointed time. In spite of a slight breeze, which veered the smoke a little off course, the angle reading was close to target.[19]

With the survey completed, the crew returned to stake out the right-of-way for the clearing contractors. Coming to an open field, the men found themselves held up by a farmer with a shotgun held at an angle no one was willing to argue with. It was a stand off, with Mr. Farmer refusing to lay down his weapon until the transit was safely on the ground. Bob Martin decided negotiation was the best tactic, but to be on the safe side sent for the Police. By the time the arm of the law arrived, Mr. Farmer had settled for having the line run 100 feet farther north.

Left to right: *Bill Parlee and Bob Martin of the survey crew with the unhappy farmer.*
Photo: H.K. Williams

Ideal weather conditions in June and July kept grading work progressing rapidly. Again Nigro and Anselmo was one of the grading outfits. Nick Carbone was foreman of the extra gang that laid the steel. Carbone had emigrated from Italy in 1915 and immediately began working for the ED & BC. Fred Hajek was timekeeper for the Carbone gang. The farm boy from the Viking area, had other job skills. He had taken a railway telegraphy course in Edmonton and worked briefly as an assistant agent before going out with the gang. When steel laying was complete, the gang packed up. As they were about to take the equipment into Edmonton, a wire arrived for Hajek.[20] There was a job at Spirit River as relief agent. This led to a long career as a station agent.

In September 1928, Bridge & Building Foreman Joe Hurst arrived from Fairview with his skilled carpenters, tent camp and pile driver to drive pilings for four bridges. The pile driver operator was veteran Bill Ross, who had worked on the CPR's large steel bridge near Lethbridge before coming to ED & BC.[21] One of the ballast trains was operated under the skillful hand of Locomotive Engineer Edward T. Faust. He had gained experience as a fireman on a U.S. railway before coming to Canada in 1912. He first worked for the Grand Trunk Pacific, but moved to the ED & BC two years later. The town of Faust, on the railway line, bears his name.

On the extension, Faust's train hauled gravel for ballast from Flying Shot Pit, west

Locomotive Engineer Ed Faust, c. 1941
Photo: Courtesy of D. Wakal

of Wembley. Operator Art Rupert was an expert at loading cars with a steam shovel. Work trains generally worked around the clock with the crew working in relays. The engineer operated the engine 16 hours. The fireman relieved him for eight hours and fired for another eight. The watchman fired for 16 hours. This method gave them all about eight hours "shut eye" in the bunk car attached to the train. Sleep came easy to the weary bodies in spite of clanging sounds as the cars were switched into place and loaded.

Rede Stone, 78 years old, driving last spike at Beaverlodge.
Photo: Courtesy of South Peace Centennial Museum, W.D. Albright Collection

Because the new line by-passed the settlement at Beaverlodge by over a mile, the residents moved closer to the tracks at the new townsite. The older buildings were transported there during the winter months. On 24 November 1928, Rede Stone, a well respected pioneer of the area, drove the last spike and the first train reached Beaverlodge.[22] A standard section foreman's bunk house with a lean-to kitchen was built in Dunvegan Yards as a temporary station. It opened in January 1929 with Alan B. Elliott in charge. The kitchen was so drafty that the wind could lift the tablecloth. The arrangement was less than ideal because the waiting room was located between the living-room, which also served as a bedroom and the kitchen until Jessie Elliott renovated the freight shed.

Elliott had immigrated to Canada following demobilization after World War I. The Englishman first tried homesteading in the Athabasca area, but money was scarce and he took the first job he could find, a contract for coaling engines at Smith.[23] His education stood him in good stead for he was soon working as an assistant agent and learning to telegraph. Beaverlodge was his first station agent's job and he stayed there 11 years.

The rails were 15 miles away when the new village of Hythe began to develop. The original settlement was located on the Beaver Lodge River and moved lock, stock and barrel. The streets of Hythe swarmed with people on a crisp, fall day. They had come to watch the driving of the last spike by two early settlers, Harry Fletcher and Kelly Sunderman.[24]

The temporary station was similar to that at Beaverlodge. Conveniences such as running water, sewer and electric lights were nonexistent. Glenn Kelly, son of Locomotive Engineer Hank Kelly, opened the station in January 1929. Kelly had been with the railway since 1920, but his experience had not prepared him for the large volume of work.

The stream of settlers and their effects bound
for Dawson Creek, Pouce Coupe, and Fort St.
John seemed endless. From the rail head the
goods were freighted over dirt roads to various destinations.

Passenger train at Beaverlodge.
Photo: R.E. Leake, Courtesy of South Peace Centennial Museum

15

The Pembina Valley Railway

While the government of Alberta carried on negotiations for the sale of its railways to the Canadian National and/or Canadian Pacific railways, it pressed on with plans for a new railway. Construction of the Pembina Valley Railway [PVR] began in 1926, but its roots went back to 1912. About the time McArthur acquired the charter for the ED & BC, he decided to build a rail line into the richly wooded and agricultural area northwest of Edmonton. A charter was issued by the province of Alberta to McArthur during the 1911-1912 session in the name of the Athabasca Valley Railway.[1] Hearing of the proposed railway, settlers began to pour into the district. They had visions of moving their grain to market over steel rails; but they were in for a long wait.

The railway's charter called for a 52 mile line running from Edmonton, or from a point near Independence [changed to Busby in 1915], Alberta, to a point near Fort Assiniboine on the Athabasca River. Preliminary and location surveys were handled by S.E. Reaugh during the 1916-17 winter, but the paperwork was destroyed in the fire that consumed the Dunvegan Yards headquarters building in 1918. At a directors' meeting in Edmonton on 24 February 1917, "an indenture was drawn up which provided that the Central Canada Railway would assume the payment of charter and incorporation expenses, etc." amounting to $12 thousand.[2] Extensions were granted three times, but McArthur's financial headaches with his other railways prevented further action being taken and in 1920 the charter lapsed.

In 1921, while leasing the ED & BC, the CPR briefly showed an interest in resurrecting this charter, but nothing came of it. Two years later the government of Alberta's engineering department conducted reconnaissance surveys in the area. Satisfied with the original survey, the engineers decided the railway should follow the same route, but keep west instead of turning north toward Fort Assiniboine.

There was a lull in further progress

while the government battled with the CPR about their ED & BC lease. The fact that the government did not yet own the northern lines was another snag. While ownership remained in the hands of the Union Bank and McArthur, the government could not begin construction without their approval. The engineering department used the time to reconstruct the original plans and profiles for the proposed railway from the actual notes which had been at another location at the time of the office fire.

Negotiations were close to a settlement with McArthur when John Callaghan requested incorporation of a new railway company under the name "Pembina Valley Railway." This way the railway would circumvent the jurisdiction of the Board of Railway Commissioners for Canada and avoid its interference. Although construction was approved at the 1926 session of the Legislature,[3] the company was never incorporated. To finance the construction, the government was also authorized to raise a loan of $775 thousand,[4] and Callaghan added another railway to the four he already managed.

Cecil Crysdale, engineer for the Department of Railways, was the chief engineer on construction.[5] Grading commenced in May 1926. Wet weather hindered progress. Once again, during his summer holidays University of Alberta student Pat Williams joined the location party as a rodman. He teamed up with another student, W.O. Parlee, who became a well-known Edmonton lawyer, and J.R.B. "Bob" Jones, who attained the rank of Brigadier-General in World War II. On construction they were residency No. 1 and

camped at Arvilla, which was the first siding on the new branch line.[6]

W.L. "Bill" Kelly, who became resident engineer at Manola, was also the locating engineer. Bob Martin was the resident engineer at Busby. During the summer of 1926 his wife and six-year old son, Lionel, lived in a tent. A bunk car, spurred out west of Busby, accommodated them during the winter.[7] When the students left to resume their studies, Wilf Lawton joined Martin as a rodman.

Ties were purchased from the CPR and 60 lb. rail was purchased from the Great Northern Railway at Vancouver. On 16 June 1926 the Board of Railway Commissioners authorized a junction of the PVR, with the ED & BC at Busby. Grading was sufficiently completed by the end of the year to permit the laying of track to the Pembina River crossing at Manola, under the direction of Foreman Joe Long. Not content to sit in his office and wait for reports on the progress being made, Callaghan inspected the work first-hand. Herb Dalby, who was then in the stores department, became Callaghan's chauffeur on these occasions. Soon afterwards, Dalby transferred to agency work and eventually was promoted to agent.[8]

To straddle the Pembina River, a Howe-Truss bridge was built during the winter months by Bridge & Building Foreman Jack Hudson and his crew. The material had been salvaged from a bridge at Fernie, BC, which was abandoned by the Great Northern Railway. Work progressed under the practiced eye of Bridge and Building Master John E. Deakin.

Station and section house at Busby in 1927
Photo: H.K. Williams

Steel reached Manola in January 1927. Freight for the construction department could now be hauled in by rail. The official opening of the line to Manola was held when ballasting was completed in the spring. The old-timers of the district had waited so long for the arrival of a railway; this was a cause for celebration. It was done in fine style by barbecuing a steer in a huge pit in the local picnic area. In spite of a drizzle, close to eight hundred people came to partake of the succulent meat.

Until completion of the line, trains had to back up to Busby from Manola, 18.7 miles. Manola was a logical choice as the section headquarters because the water tank was there. This was the only water supply on the Barrhead Subdivision and John Olsen was the first section foreman. Olsen spent the rest of his railway career at Manola, looking after the maintenance of the track from Busby to Barrhead. Flooding of the Paddle and Pembina Rivers often occurred in the spring. When that happened Olsen and his crew worked frantically to keep the roadbed and bridges from washing away.

By October 1927, the railway had reached its destination, Mile 26.1, in time to handle that year's grain harvest. The new town was named Barrhead. Located a few miles away from the original settlement, nature soon wiped out the telltale signs of the old townsite when its inhabitants moved to the new townsite.[9] The mushroom growth of Barrhead is a typical example of the new towns that sprang up at the end of steel. The townsite, subdivided into 60 lots, was fully sold 12 months in advance of the railway's arrival. The demand for lots was so great another 56 were put on the market. Two streets were cleared and graded, and within a year of the arrival of the railway a third subdivision of 66 lots was made. The population had increased from 50 to 250.[10]

Howe Truss Bridge at Manola
Photo: H.K. Williams

The birth of Barrhead in 1927
Photo: H.K. Williams

On 18 October 1927, the first mixed train handling freight and passengers was dispatched for Barrhead. It was scheduled to arrive at 1505.[11] The platform was crowded with spectators. Some had come long distances to witness its arrival. But they waited in vain. By 1700 there was no sign of the train. Finally the hungry and disappointed crowd dispersed. The sound of engine No. 16's whistle around 2145 prompted some of the townspeople to stumble in the darkness to the station. The crew blamed the delay on the amount of wayfreight and switching done en route.

The hand on the throttle of the first train into Barrhead was that of Locomotive Engineer Lorne Jinckle "Jinks" Frizzell, who was a resident of the village. Born on Prince Edward Island, Frizzell claimed the distinction of having been engineer on two American presidential trains before coming to the Barrhead area to homestead in 1911. Upon hearing the ED & BC railway was to be built into the Peace River country, Frizzell applied for a job. At first he filled in as master mechanic until the arrival of Bob Weir. By October 1912, he was at the throttle of locomotives in work train service, pushing the rails north.

From his experience on unionized railways in the United States, Frizzell found working conditions were a far cry from those on the U.S. roads. He was instrumental in forming the Federated Board of the ED & BC and A & GW railways. When the railways eventually became unionized, he was appointed chairman of the Brotherhood of Locomotive Engineers. Throughout his railway career, Frizzell continued to play a leading part in battling for employees' rights.

Federated Board, ED & BC and A & GW Railways c. 1914.
Back: *Al McLennan, Jinks Frizzell, Ben Martin.* Front: *Gene "Sandbar" McLaughlin and "Protestant Bill" Preston.*
Photo: Courtesy of G.W.E. Smith

Meanwhile, Frizzell developed an interest in flying. It was none other than the well-known northern flyer Wilfrid "Wop" May who inspired him. The railway engineer and the bush pilot's meeting is the stuff movies are made of. When Frizzell was on the wayfreight between Edmonton and Smith, his train was flagged down by the pilot near Picardville. Engine trouble had forced May to land his plane. Rail lines were used by bush pilots for navigation. This chance meeting was the beginning of a lengthy friendship and the start of flying lessons for Frizzell, which culminated in a pilot's licence in 1930.[12] That same year he also made his first 900 foot parachute jump.[13]

Harold Atkey, who later became expert in train handling as a locomotive engineer, was then a locomotive watchman. He rode the train to Barrhead, where his duties commenced. There he prepared the enginemen's bunkhouse for the crew, then took charge of the locomotive while the train crew slept. Occasionally in the winter an engine froze to the rails. When that happened, scrap lumber and grain doors were collected and a fire built around the locomotive to thaw the ice. Atkey discovered this could be prevented by moving the locomotive frequently during the night.

The first station agent at Barrhead was Tommy Roberts, who was transferred from the L & NW.[14] This appointment caused some controversy. According to the union agreement with management an opening such as this was required to be advertised for bid. Management skirted the rules by claiming the line was still under construction and appointed Roberts. Roberts had no idea at the time that he would spend 32 years in that station before moving to Westlock, nor that it was in Barrhead he would settle upon retirement.

Roberts worked from a temporary building while a new station was being built. A week after his wife and baby arrived, the interior of the new structure was partially gutted by fire. Only a bucket brigade by the townspeople saved the shell of the building.[15] When the station was renovated it became a social centre for the town.

The mixed train stopped overnight in Barrhead, enabling the crew to participate in the activities of the community, whether it be playing baseball, fishing, dancing or hunting. The crew needed no further urging when Tommy Roberts suggested one day they take their shotguns along on the next trip. The men rushed through their work, then set out to hunt ducks. Having difficulty moving the canoe from the marshy and muddy shore of Shoal Lake toward the reeds which would provide a blind, Roberts and Glen Barker used brute strength to push on the oars, and when they hit slack water the canoe shot forward, causing Roberts to stumble up the boat. His head hit Barker in the seat of his pants, and Barker took a dive over the edge.[16] The canoe immediately tipped over, dumping Roberts, the guns and shells into the lake. A surprised Barker sat up in the four feet of water and said, "What the hell happened?"[17] The laughter of the two trainmen on the shore still echoed in their ears as they arrived back in town, soaking wet and dishevelled.

The story grew more interesting the more it was told, but the crew members involved laughed more than anyone as their twice weekly mixed train wound its way between Dunvegan Yards and Barrhead. In 1953, Barrhead became a turn around point for trains.[18] With the trips done in one run there was no time for hunting forays or extra-curricular activities.

*The plume of smoke from a
locomotive rises in the cold air
of a winter's day at Smoky*
Photo: Courtesy of S. Deakin

Part Four

NAR and the Depression: 1930-1939

Locomotive No. 57 with Oliver Hart Parr Tractors leaving Edmonton
for Peace River, 29 January 1930. Engineer Bill Hunter,
Fireman Mark Barker and Conductor Frank Waite.
Photo: Oliver Ltd.

16

Great Expectations

All offers to purchase the northern railways were unacceptable to the government of Alberta. Premier Brownlee was anxious to sell the four railways as a package and see a joint operation with the two transcontinental railways.[1] The A & GW was the stumbling block and the Department of Railways was reluctant to operate it as a single railway. A shrewd negotiator, Brownlee intended to keep negotiating until he got the best possible deal. The newly formed Canadian National, under the leadership of President Sir Henry Thornton, was not enthusiastic about a joint operation with CPR. The first joint offer was made in January 1928. It excluded the A & GW and was declined.

The first three months of 1928 were banner ones as far as traffic on the railway was concerned. That fall Beatty took a group of CPR directors and executives from several well-known industrial and financial concerns north on the ED & BC. Another offer followed. After some adjustments the government accepted the CPR offer with the pro-

viso that the CNR could assume half the obligation. CNR consented to be the CPR's partner in the purchase in November 1928. The agreement was dated 29 January 1929 and ratified by the government of Alberta on 20 March 1929.[2] Forming a company to operate the undertakings of the ED & BC, the A & GW, the Central Canada, PVR, and The Central Canada Express Company Limited seemed a logical step. The name chosen, Northern Alberta Railways Company [NAR], was indicative of the area it traversed.

The terms of purchase were specified as $15.58 million payable in three installments and the assumption of liability for the debenture and bond indebtedness totalling $9.42 million. The two transcontinental railways agreed to complete extensions already in progress, pay the province the amount of $947 371.74 already expended and build 60 miles of additional extensions.[3] "In addition the purchasers paid the sum of $152 333.08, this being the balance of cash on hand and accounts receivable in excess of current accounts payable as at the date of transfer."[4] This brought the total purchase price to $26 099 704.82.

Sir Edward Beatty's special train crosses over Pat's Creek near Peace River, September 1928.
Photo: G.W.E. Smith

The railway was incorporated 14 June 1929 with operating offices located in Edmonton.[5] Six directors were appointed, three from each of the parent companies. The president of either CNR or CPR was also president of the NAR, alternating each successive year: "The real control was placed in the hands of an operating committee, comprising the vice-president, western region, CNR and vice-president, western lines, CPR, and a finance committee composed of a finance section and an accounting section."[6] The respective heads of the latter departments on the parent lines filled the positions on the NAR. The chairman of each section alternated every two years, and during the years in which the chairman of one section was the representative of one parent company, the chairman of the other section was the representative of the other parent company.

The property was turned over to the new management on 1 July 1929. The government of Alberta was pleased with the joint agreement. It was felt that participation of both companies would assure efficient service, provide capital for expansion and prevent duplication of rail lines.[7] When the news of the settlement with the CNR and CPR was confirmed to employees it generated excitement. Joe Frechette, then 14-years-old, recalled how at Dunvegan Yards, "everything just seemed to come awake. There were locomotives everywhere spouting steam right through the night."[8] The news was received with enthusiasm by the city of Edmonton and the northern communities. The consensus of opinion was that the CPR would never purchase a "white elephant."

More surprising was the fact that John Callaghan was to be at the helm of the new company. The appointment to general manager of the NAR required relinquishment of his duties as deputy minister of Railways. This appointment must have taken some persuasion on the part of the government of Alberta. After all, Callaghan's relationship with the CPR was less than cordial. No doubt the government wished him to look after their interests. In later years, the parent companies may have wondered about their choice when the operating committee questioned why a certain bridge had been built and Callaghan replied, "Because I said so."[9]

Retaining Callaghan as general manager ensured changes in operations were kept to a

Dunvegan Yards, 15 May 1929
Photo: Glenbow Archives, McDermid Collection, ND-3-4627

minimum. Until new stationery and forms were available, staff were issued stamps with the new name. All documents, such as bills of lading, and waybills, had to be stamped Northern Alberta Railways Company. Demerit marks were allotted to those who failed to follow this procedure.[10]

A number of special trains travelled over the railway that fall. One carried 160 delegates to the Annual Convention of the Edmonton Chamber of Commerce into the Peace River country. Another took President Beatty and the CPR directors to Waterways. Beatty was noncommittal regarding the reason for the trip up the Waterways line. But the party took the opportunity to tour the Alberta government's salt plant at Waterways and inspect the tar sand operations at Fort McMurray.

Soon afterwards, construction began from Fairview through to Hines Creek and from Hythe to Dawson Creek. Resident

Engineer Howard W. Tye was in charge of surveys, construction and maintenance work under the direction of Callaghan.[11] Together the men had made reconnaissance surveys of both routes and the previously graded line from Spirit River to Dawson Creek. The latter was abandoned in favor of the route from Hythe to Dawson Creek.

NAR Timetable No. 1 effective 1 June 1930

Settlers looked forward to the coming of the railway, but it brought changes. The original hamlet of Hines Creek had grown from the ranching area surrounding it. The rails by-passed it by three miles.[12] The first train to the newly laid out townsite arrived on 7 December 1930.

Edward "Ted" Froome opened the Hines Creek station. Prior to joining the railway in July, he had been with the CPR for ten years. His friends, Jim Holden and Joe Breau, then employed on the NAR, told him of the available opportunities. An interview with the

The crew of Passenger Train No. 6 at Hines Creek. Conductor Lee Card, Fireman Albert Morin, Engineer Bill Christian, Trainman Fred Gilpin, Express Messenger Leon Kvittem and Porter Cliff Alexander
Photo: Courtesy of Dr. Velma Gooch

Assistant to the General Manager, Mortimer E. Collins, and the offer of a job followed. It was a difficult decision to leave his wife and two young children, but they joined Froome once he had settled into the three room station at Hines Creek. The Froomes lived there for 14 years and later moved to Spirit River. When eye testing was done in 1931, it was discovered Froome was color blind. As a result, he was restricted to work in end of steel stations.[13]

Across the country Hythe was enjoying a period of prosperity as the end of steel. At the station, Agent Glenn Kelly saw large numbers of settlers unloading their belongings destined for the Rolla, Fort St. John districts and beyond. Pat Williams arrived at Hythe on Christmas Eve in 1929 to join the location party of 15. Living in tents, they used teams and sleighs for transportation.

The wooden pegs, marking the point of intersection at the end of each tangent and the start of preliminary tie lines, could not be driven into the frozen ground. Transitman Charlie Pearcy's suggestion that an eight-inch spike be used instead was considered nothing short of a brainwave.

the area had arrived in 1912. When it was discovered the steel would by-pass the old town its residents objected strenuously. But the railway company won the battle, claiming it was necessary for the town to be located a mile and a half away because of the "loss of elevation" so that the extension west

Locating party from Hythe to Dawson Creek, 1929-1930
Photo: H.K. Williams

Transitman C.W. Pearcy stands by the washtub and scrub board after hanging his clothes out to dry
Photo: H.K. Williams

With the arrival of spring, the location party went over the line to stake it out for the contractors. No reference hubs could be found. But the work was not a total loss. The spike holes had frozen up leaving nail impressions clearly visible.[14] Location of the line from Hythe to Dawson Creek was completed in April 1930 under the direction of Locating Engineer Harry Cullerne. Grading and track-laying advanced at a steady pace. Contractor John Wikstrand claimed the track-laying machine laid about two miles of track per day.[15]

Six miles farther on, Dawson Creek was waiting in anticipation. The first settlers in

could be carried on at the same grade level. Land for the terminal had been purchased from the McKeller family and Dawson Creek moved to the new townsite.

Olav Aaberg arrived from the engineering office to stake out the first 12 blocks of Dawson Creek in 1931. He also designed the large water reservoir which gathered water by cross-cut ditches on the hillside north of the railway station. Culverts carried water under the main line track to the reservoir which served as a water supply while steam locomotives were in use. It was later filled in, and the civic centre is now located on its site.[16]

H.K. Williams at Demmitt, 1930
Photo: Courtesy of H.K. Williams

L. Harry Cullerne, Locating Engineer
from Hythe to Dawson Creek, 1930
Photo: Courtesy of H.K. Williams

The first passenger train reached Dawson Creek 15 January 1931. Rudolph Lundeen, who had been with the ED & BC from its earliest days, was at the throttle of steam locomotive No. 72 as it whistled into the village. A special train with a number of dignitaries preceded the scheduled passenger train. The visiting party split up so that representation was made at both the Dawson Creek and Pouce Coupe ceremonies.

These ceremonies were anti-climactic for both villages. Steel had arrived at Pouce Coupe on 4 December 1930. At that time Mrs. P. Gauthier, the first white woman settler in the district, drove the spike at the ceremony, while her daughter, Mrs. Pat Therrien, the first white child born on the Pouce Coupe Prairie, held it.[17] At Dawson Creek, driving of the spike had been done by two early settlers, Mrs. Fanny Chase and Frank DeWetter on 29 December 1930.[19] Oddly enough, the spike used in the ceremony could not be found a couple of hours later.

The new station was opened by Agent J.K. "Jack" Hardie. It was to this town Hardie brought his young bride, Irene Squires of Grande Prairie. He was born into a railroading family and the tales told by his uncles never ceased to enthrall Hardie and his brothers as they were growing up.

At Dawson Creek the station was opened by Agent Ace Comstock, who operated it until the war years when he saw better opportunities in the real estate and insurance business. The two stall engine house at Hythe was moved to Dawson Creek and Jack Wilcox moved there as locomotive foreman. He spent the rest of his life in Dawson Creek, where he became very involved with community affairs. He was one of the first aldermen on the town council and later mayor.

While construction plans were in progress in northern Alberta, preparations were made for the expansion of NAR's telegraph service into the commercial field. Communication by telegraph was big business and NAR wanted some of the action. In Edmonton, the NAR Commercial Telegraph Office competed with the Dominion Government Telegraphs. Telegraph traffic was transferred and received from the telegraph offices of the CNR and CPR.

The NAR's commercial telegraph office in Edmonton opened on the main floor, northeast corner of the McLeod Building on 100 Street in August 1929. It was later moved to the main floor of the CPR Building on Jasper Avenue. Ralph Fullerton accepted the position of Ticket & Telegraph Agent. He was responsible for this office and others to be opened at Peace River, Grande Prairie and Dawson Creek. His jurisdiction extended to the three linemen and the booking of berths on passenger trains. After several years in the communications departments of the CPR and Canadian Northern he was well acquainted with telegraph office procedures. Fullerton had joined the ED & BC at Grande Prairie in 1921. He had worked as operator and agent prior to opening the telegraph office. When the communications department expanded in later years, he became supervisor of communications and eventually superintendent of communications.

Commercial telegraph operators and agents were paid a set salary, whereas railway agents transmitting commercial telegraph traffic received a commission. Retired Agent Gordon Waite says, "Commercial telegraphers were the elite in skill of all morse telegraphers. They handled in excess of 100 messages per day."[19] The agent and

NAR Headquarters in CPR Building,
10012 Jasper Avenue, Edmonton
Photo: Courtesy of A.M. Cruickshank

operators, nicknamed brass pounders or lightning slingers, had to have their own typewriters and bugs. The latter was a semi-automatic device to facilitate the sending of the morse code, known as a vibroplex.[20]

NAR Telegraph Office. L to R: Telegraph Messengers Clive Smith, Gordon Waite, Operators Gus Roland, Johnny Sutherland, Ticket and Telegraph Agent Ralph Fullerton
Photo: Courtesy of A. Smith, Ralph Fullerton Collection

In Edmonton, telegraph messengers were expected to supply their own uniforms and bicycles. They also looked after their maintenance and repairs. Unlike railway telegraph operators and agents, commercial telegraph personnel were not unionized at that time. Perhaps this was the reason the staff was transient. Some operators stayed less than a year.

Besides Ralph Fullerton, the Edmonton office opened with Operators W.A. "Red" MacFarlane and George Potter, Accountant Clarke McCombs and Telegraph Messengers Clive Smith and Roy Martins. Shortly afterwards, several transferred to the operating department. MacFarlane and Potter went on the line as agents. McCombs moved to McLennan as assistant agent. Smith joined the mechanical department and eventually became yardmaster. Martins transferred to the commissary department and later was promoted to manager, purchases and stores.[21]

New faces filled the vacancies. Among them was Les Robinson, whom Gordon Waite remembers as an operator with a "very carefree attitude toward life in general and used to smuggle his guitar into the office when he reported for duty. During the latter part of the evening shift when the work and daily cash balance was completed he would tune and strum the guitar.[22] It was not long before Robinson took his guitar and telegraph skills elsewhere. Cy Naylor replaced him.

In spite of his quick, irascible temper, Naylor was an excellent addition to the staff. Waite says he was "the most highly skilled of all the telegraphers I have ever known or worked with."[23] He had worked all the fast wires such as bonus [telegraphers received one cent bonus for each message over 60 in one hour], brokerage wires where the quotation board was marked up directly from the telegraph wire, Western Union and Postal telegraph companies in the United States and the CNT and CPT in Canada.

A.J.H. "Gus" Roland was a fast operator. The man with the impish smile came to the NAR from the CNR's telegraph office at Athabasca. He eventually succeeded Ralph Fullerton as Telegraph Agent. Bobby Teare succeeded Clarke McCombs. He was from the Isle of Man, and a couple of beers never failed to bring forth a heart felt rendering version of "They are hanging men and women for the wearing of the green" from this Manxman.[24] Johnny Sutherland replaced

"Red" MacFarlane. He was a former CNT commercial operator and sent the most perfect Morse. He remained with the communications department throughout his career.

Armed with a course in telegraphy taken at Alberta College, Gordon Waite felt fortunate to secure the job of telegraph messenger. He used what spare time he had to practice telegraphy. By the time he left the office, Waite's skill was sufficiently honed to enable him to work as an assistant agent, and later as agent. Before Waite transferred out on the line, one evening gale force winds toppled over a large sign on the roof of the building opposite the McLeod block. The north office windows blew in showering the NAR staff with broken glass. As it swept across the office it picked up loose paper, small office equipment and clothing in its path to the east office windows which collapsed outwards. Everything was scattered far and wide. Ralph Fullerton instructed Waite over the phone to call the general manager at the Macdonald Hotel. To his surprise the G.M.'s response was "I didn't know we had a god-damn telegraph office. Don't bother me, ask Mr. Collins for instructions."[25] Mortimer Collins arranged for the necessary temporary repairs.

With the Edmonton office working efficiently commercial telegraph offices were opened in Grande Prairie and Peace River. At Grande Prairie, Tom Lowes, who first learned Morse code in 1907, was in charge. Frederick William Radford opened the office at Peace River. He was well qualified for the position, having been with the Dominion Telegraph Service for five years before joining the ED & BC.[26] Until then the railway's communication system from Edmonton to Peace River and Grande Prairie, was used mainly for dispatching trains and railway services. The Dominion Telegraph, which had reached Peace River in 1911, handled the bulk of the public's needs. Now the railway was giving it competition with the new offices located in the downtown core.

From Edmonton NAR's telegraph lines extended to Hythe, Hines Creek and Waterways. There was also a line from Edmonton to McLennan that was usually reserved for the use of the train dispatchers located there. Every caboose was equipped with a phone. In an emergency, train crews could contact the dispatcher by using a long pole with a hook, which was hung on the telephone wires. All lines were cut into the adjacent stations, creating the communications system. The NAR and Dominion Government Telegraphs were the only communications link to the Peace River country besides the government mail, known as Royal Mail.

At McLennan, a couple of greenhorns were learning the "wire." Frank Darby's quiet, calm nature was a contrast to the eruptive disposition of Maurice Mahood. The two young men worked different shifts and shared the same single cot, on which the springs were clipped to a solid iron side frame. On the one night a week when they were both off duty, it was a different story. Fortunately, they were both slim and tired enough to sleep back to back in spite of the small space and the iron edges on the cot. Darby's musical ear helped him acquire the telegrapher's skills more rapidly than

Mahood, but eventually they both mastered it and were promoted to station agents in later years.[27]

No matter how expert the telegraphers were, it took the skill of the linemen to keep those telegraph lines buzzing. D.E. "Rory" Graeme was headquartered at Dunvegan Yards, Bill Reid at Lac La Biche, and Arthur Baker at McLennan.

The duties of the linemen included maintenance of telegraph wires along the railway's right-of-way. This they accomplished in all kinds of weather with the assistance of their open track motor cars [speeders]. When a severe storm reduced the telegraph line to a tangled mass of broken poles and wire, the linemen worked around the clock to restore communications with no machinery and few tools at their disposal. North of Lac La Biche was a desolate part of the country. One Monday morning, lineman Bill Reid set off to locate trouble with the telephone line. He had difficulty finding the source of the trouble until he came upon a line of freshly washed laundry blowing in the wind beside a section house. On closer inspection he discovered a section foreman's wife was using the telephone wire as a clothesline.

Rory Graeme was an old hand at the game of lineman. He had been with the railways since 1916 and weathered all the transitions. Toward the end of May 1930 a storm caused havoc with the communication lines. Graeme's subsequent report indicated poles had dropped like flies: "Sorry this report sounds like a calamity howl but there is a bunch of commercial telegraph business here

if we can keep the wire going, and I have run 596 miles since that storm besides propping up poles and pulling slack, and the line still looks awful."[28] After one such storm, Graeme remarked he had climbed enough poles to shake hands with God.[29]

In addition, linemen were expected to check and maintain the telegraph instruments in the various stations. The railway supplied cans of paint for the interior of stations and agents' living quarters and expected the agent to do the painting himself. The dingy interior of the office and waiting room at Morinville needed a paint job. Superintendent Deakin offered to supply cream colored paint with the stipulation that the agent apply it. The agent argued that he was no painter nor did he have any intention of becoming one. Deakin was unmoved. The railway would supply only the paint.

When the paint and brush arrived, the agent tackled the painting job. He painted until everything in the two rooms was a nice gleaming cream shade. In the meantime, the commercial telegraph office and the train dispatcher were unable to contact Morinville station by telegraph. Rory Graeme was dispatched to rectify the problem. Graeme was astounded to find the office, the waiting room and all the contents of both freshly painted. By this time the paint had dried and hardened. He had to completely dismantle all the telegraph instruments, scrape off the paint, adjust, and then assemble before the dots and dashes could be received or transmitted.

Afterwards, Graeme always referred to that particular agent as "the Painter" prefixed by a few choice adjectives. The paint was eventually scraped from the windows, but the balance of the office and waiting room remained a cream color. The coal heaters, when lit that fall, produced some very vile odors and always did retain a rather strange outward appearance. Never again was any more paint supplied to that particular agent nor did the company's paint policy change.[30]

Left to right: *Claims Investigator Nat Lynn, Agent Bert Carrick, Lineman Rory Graeme, and Ralph Fullerton, who was an operator at Dunvegan Yards in 1927.*
Photo: Courtesy of A. Smith, Ralph Fullerton Collection

Passenger train at Peace River
Photo: Peace River Centennial Museum, 71.783.11

17

Bucking the Depression

During the 1929 stock market crash, New York's Wall Street seemed light years away from the Peace River country; but its shock waves quickly engulfed Canada. Because the Northern Alberta Railways Company was in the throes of constructing extensions, the initial effect of the Depression was delayed. The decrease in the NAR's freight car loadings and passenger business began in 1930. As unemployment steadily increased the future looked bleak even to optimists.

With the completion of the extensions, NAR employees began to feel the effects of the Depression. Staff was laid off in all departments, positions abolished, and freight and passenger runs reduced to minimum service. Of 22 assistant agents on the 1932 seniority list, only eight held permanent positions. Crews did double duty to keep trains running. In the words of Olav Aaberg, "They felt they were lucky to have jobs."[1]

By July 1931, passenger service into the Peace River country was reduced to twice weekly and freight assignments were at a minimum.[2] Those with the most seniority held the few assigned runs. Among the senior engineers were Carl Gage, Hank Pentzer, Percy Brame, Lorne Nichols, Jimmy Glenton and Bill Preston. Ballasting assignments, usually available to the junior men, were curtailed.

In August 1931, employees faced a ten percent reduction in salary. This was to be the first of several salary cuts during the Depression years.[3] The effects of the Depression on farmers affected the railway. Prices for grain and livestock dropped drastically. Often the cost of freight was more than the return from a sale.[4] The railway introduced economic measures in various departments.

Agents noticed the sharp influx of settlers escaping drought stricken southern Alberta and the dust bowl of Saskatchewan's prairies. Soon it seemed people were moving from one end of Canada to the other. Money was scarce. For these men, known as hoboes, travelling seemed to offer hope for that evasive job at the next stop. Riding the rods had its risks. Often in the cities, policemen were waiting to arrest them, but this was less likely to happen in smaller towns. Locomotive Foreman Bill Kirkland recalls, "There were as many as 40 'bos' in McLennan some nights." Often he would find 20 or 30 sleeping bodies in boxcars arriving on trains. "I'd say, 'You'll have to leave. Go down by the sand house where it is warm.'"[5]

Often the firemen "turned a blind eye" to hoboes riding on the tender if they shovelled the coal ahead. Strict instructions had been issued that the trains were not to leave terminals until all the non-paying passengers were off. There is the story told of hoboes who climbed up on to the top of the locomotive tender of a train leaving Lac La Biche. The big, burly engineer told them to get off. They told him, "You're not big enough to put us off." There were too many of them to argue the point.

The conductor came up with the train orders and reminded the engineer of the instructions. The engineer replied, "I can't kick them off, one of those guys is a relative of mine." "Well, I'll kick them off," said the conductor, as he climbed up to the tender. Now the conductor had an even huskier physique than the engineer, but the rough-looking tender riders quickly surrounded him. The spring was missing from his step as he came back to the cab saying, "I can't put them off. There are some of my relations up there too."[6]

Desperate for work, job-hunters followed the extra gangs out on the line. With nothing but time on their hands, they were willing to sit and wait on the nearest fence, hoping to get a job if someone was fired by the foreman, and relying on the cook for a hand out until another freight came along.[7]

Bridge reconstruction was carried out in 1930s. This is the Swan River Bridge at Kinuso.

Agents were more acutely aware of the terrible effects of the Depression on people in their communities. The pressures to keep body and soul together often erupted in insanity. Harry Swift was working as third trick dispatcher when a man was brought in tied to a plank, screaming profanities. En route to Edmonton in a deadhead baggage car, he broke free and Conductor Wm. "Mush" Hardie used all hands available to get him back on the plank.

A passenger train with dining car 502 (formerly CP "Hazelwood") passes wagons carrying fill, 1932

In those years more calamities seemed to befall the railway than at any other time in its long history. Each spring with the break-up of ice on the rivers, flood waters often caused minor washouts of track. The spring of 1935 was to be no different from previous years. With the month of June came incessant torrential rains. This, added to rivers already swollen in flood, caused extensive damage to railway grades. Nowhere was the damage worse than at Lesser Slave Lake. Howard Tye, then resident engineer, explained why: "Lesser Slave Lake is really a large reservoir into which the waters of an extensive watershed drain and it has only one outlet, the Lesser Slave River. Particularly in seasons of heavy snow and rains the lake level rises on account of the waters flowing in faster than they can get out."[8]

"It is my opinion that Lesser Slave Lake is slowly, but surely drying up" wrote A.M. Bezanson in *The Peace River Trail*, a brochure published to promote the Peace River country in 1907.[9] This statement proved to be pure fiction. Now Lesser Slave Lake had the appearance of an inland ocean. Gale force winds dashed five feet high white-capped waves against railway tracks and bridges. The surging waves would grab a section of track, pull it out and then heave it back on to the shore. The railway was not the only target. Angry waters did not spare the provincial highway nor Slave Lake town. The whole area, flooded one to two miles in width, was covered with water.

Spike, the dog provides engine power to Foreman Bill Borty as Otto Michetti uses track jack. Lou Cyr from Chisholm Mills provides flagging protection.
Photo: Courtesy of O. Michetti

At first, trains were able to navigate through the water lapping over the grade. On 24 June, rail traffic ground to a stop. A storm had blown up overnight. In its wake it left large gaps in the railway grade between Mile 159 and 176.[10] Passenger train No. 1 was held overnight at Smith, then returned to Edmonton. The general manager was on that

At Slave Lake, an aquatic town on
29 June 1935, cars wait for a ferry ride.
Photo: South Peace Centennial Museum, W.D. Albright Collection

train and travelled from Smith to the flooded area by track motor. There Callaghan surveyed the extensive damage from the top of a boxcar on a work train. Superintendent Deakin and veteran Roadmaster Nick Hrychuk were already there evaluating the magnitude of the washouts.

Men and machines were struggling to restore the grade under the eagle eye of Section Foreman Emil Persson from Widewater.

Although it was against his better judgement, Persson followed instructions to use trees to shore up the track as a temporary measure. It was treacherous work as the water kept rising.[11]

About the time a contingent of unemployed men from British Columbia's relief camps converged on Regina inciting the Regina Riots, the NAR was hiring men by the dozen.[12] Three work trains were dispatched from Edmonton with men and equipment. The effects of the Depression had left many of these men little more than "bags of bones." Because they were undernourished they were in no physical condition to handle the hard manual labor required of them and within a couple of days many of them returned to Edmonton.

Soon afterwards, the superintendent seconded Roadmaster Charlie Erickson from the Waterways line. Erickson had prior experience with floods and a reputation for his ability to handle men. He demanded that he be given a free hand in handling the situation. His first step was to see the men on relief ate good solid "grub." Then Erickson put them to work for an hour or so in the mornings and the same in the afternoons. As they gradually hardened up he increased the hours worked until they were working full days. Very few went back to Edmonton after that, even though hip waders did little to keep them dry when they had to stand in water up to their waists tamping gravel under track ties. Erickson, who was killed in an automobile accident five years later, was

Men working in water attempt to lift track at Slave Lake, July, 1935.
Provincial Archives of Alberta, A3337

no shirker from work. He was an inspiration to the men as he worked under the water for minutes at a time fastening chains and tying timbers down.

By 26 June 1935, temporary repairs were sufficient to allow trains to run on schedule again, albeit on slow orders through flood waters. Passengers reported water covering the third step of the coaches and enginemen feared that the fire in their locomotive would be extinguished from water almost reaching the firebox.[13] It was hoped the storms that undermined the grade would cease. They did not abate.

On 10 July what management hoped to avoid happened. A train became stranded in Lesser Slave Lake. The passenger train was crossing the lake at two miles per hour as it followed Charlie Erickson, walking the track ahead. Erickson was waist deep in water checking the solidity of the roadbed. Near Wagner, south of Widewater, the train came to a halt. The engineer was backing up when the track washed out behind him. The train was cut off on all sides by the swirling waters.

The passengers made the best of a bad situation. Those willing to get their feet wet, were able to walk back to Widewater where there was a store. For passengers with small children to care for and little money, things were more difficult. Locomotive Foreman Joe Faulder's wife, Ellen, was among the passengers. She participated in the singsongs around a bonfire, the hikes in the bush and a dance at a nearby school house.[14] Two days

Passengers watch the progress of Train No. 1 through the waters of Slave Lake.
Photo: City of Edmonton Archives, EA-122-97

later the passengers were taken to Smith by automobile and horse-drawn wagon, where they boarded a train, Edmonton-bound.

While temporary repairs were in progress, Resident Engineer Howard Tye with Olav Aaberg serving as transit man and leveller, made a survey for a line revision in the flooded area. To maintain traffic was a priority and they decided to raise the existing grade above flooded levels rather than change the location.[15]

Passenger train No. 6 from Hines Creek was on its way south on 18 July when the train dispatcher received instructions to hold all trains at McLennan. At Lesser Slave Lake the track was impassable. A number of the railway's sleeping car porters found their good natures taxed when they were stranded in McLennan for three days with a train full of impatient passengers. Among them were Harley Walker and Dick Cross. Walker was a native of St.Louis who had been with the railway since his arrival in 1920. Porter Dick Cross was a favorite with staff and passengers. His talent for telling stories was enjoyed by many. He told of being a private car steward for a general manager on a United States railway. Once he served a delicacy that was an unqualified success. Eventually he had to give up serving the dish because his mother could not keep up a sufficient supply of possum to meet the demand.[16]

NAR Sleeping Car Porters Walter Zeniuk, Etein Leblanc, Lonnie Heslop, Harley Walker and Len Williams.
Photo: Courtesy of Mrs. J.B. Bowden

At McLennan passengers were not served possum but some were less than happy about their forced stay. One irate lady informed Cross, "This railway simply cannot hold me on this dreadful train another day." It took self-control to stay calm as he explained the railway was not responsible for an "Act of God" and if she insisted that the train be moved to Edmonton at once she would have to take the matter up with Him.[17] She must have taken his advice because the train was soon on its way to Edmonton.

Headquarters was in turmoil. The phone on the desk of the assistant to the general manager never stopped ringing. Once, M.E. Collins must have dialled a wrong number, for the voice at the other end said, "The Nut House here."[18] In a rare display of wit Collins replied, "Oh, no. The nut house is here." He had prior service with CPR when he joined the railway's staff in 1921. Because John Callaghan was a difficult man to deal with many railroaders preferred to take their problems to Collins. The pint consumed at the Cecil Hotel on his way home every evening was well earned.[19] The 1935 floods gave him cause to worry.

From Chisholm pit, Telegraph Operator W.J. "Bill" Donlevy, along with the bunk car that served as home and telegraph office, was moved to the gravel pit at Mile 202.[20] Three work trains hauled tons of ballast to the damaged track as water lapped at their wheels. Dispatcher Harry Swift arranged for a "call up" to Conductor Bill Yeadon, in connection with a possible eastbound move from Mile 202.

At the appointed time, Yeadon made his call using the caboose phone by hooking it to the telegraph line wire. His poor disposition was obvious as he forestalled any chit chat by yelling, "Make this snappy, dispatcher, I'm standing in water nearly up to my armpits in order to hang up this phone."[21] Without further ado he got his train orders.

Piling was driven along the worst stretch, cribbed with heavy planking on the inside, then filled with gravel for a new grade. For the next four weeks workmen struggled to tighten the track against the side hill, only to have it washed out time and time again. Henry Christoffel's crew and the Widewater extra gangs continued lifting, straightening alignment and back filling with logs. Roy Habkirk's bridge and building gang worked on raising planks and drifting [fastening] crib logs, while Paul Hudz's gang did a similar job at Mitsue.[22]

The fact that there were no major derailments was nothing short of a miracle. Near accidents were many. Seasoned locomotive engineer D.M. "Bert" Baker told of feeling his trusty "steed" begin to tip as he guided it through the water. The time span until he reached solid track and the locomotive righted itself, was only seconds, but to him it seemed like an eternity.

Where the town of Slave Lake once stood swirled muddy waters. Its inhabitants were camped two miles south near the railway in

Crib logs before planks are attached to them
Photo: Courtesy of S. Deakin

tents and shacks built from materials salvaged from the old town.[23] Besides being the station's caretaker, Katie Kirkpatrick already operated a store, restaurant and Lochvale Post Office. Nearby a new town, born of necessity, soon became a reality. Because the location of the Kirkpatrick establishment was some two city blocks from the railway station, railroaders were the heart of her business. The spare-built kindly woman had moved there from Watino with her family in 1922. She knew all the men and their backgrounds. The whole family "worked hard, but Laverne Bolster was her mother's right hand."[24] It was almost impossible that she would escape marrying a railway man.

Young Fred Gilpin had left Sudbury, Ontario, in 1929 as spring was beginning to sweep over the country. He was the last trainman hired by the ED & BC before it became part of the Northern Alberta Railways two months later.[25] The long haul over the Slave Lake subdivision seemed less wearisome with a stop at the Kirkpatrick restaurant and an eyeful of the girl he would woo and win.

While the catastrophe at Lesser Slave Lake was being tackled, the continuous rains permeating the soil caused mud slides on the east Smoky Hill. The first serious slide occurred west of Culp on 26 June. Karl Olson was section foreman for Watino West; a section he held for 34 years. When the section became available, the Swede was the only one who bid on it. In 1987 Olson recalled the reason for the decision he made 55 years earlier, "I liked this place down here, especially my woman, then we got married and raised a family. She had all her relations down here."[26]

When Olson arrived at the scene of the slide in June 1935, 100 feet of track was swinging in mid-air with ties attached. The grade had slid into the valley. Shortly afterwards, Callaghan arrived from Lesser Slave Lake to view the destruction. Henry Christoffel's extra gang was rushed to the spot to build a shoo-fly [diversion] around it.[27]

Christoffel had arrived in the Fawcett

Henry Christoffel's extra gang
tackles mud slides on Smoky Hill.
Photo: Courtesy of Mrs. Elsie Christoffel

area from Switzerland in 1914, where family members filed on homesteads.[28] After several summer seasons as a sectionman he became a permanent foreman in 1922. In the next 36 years he worked throughout the system, often with extra gangs of up to 120 men, but this was his first taste of the instability of the Smoky Hills.

Once the slides started they were continuous. Extra gangs worked around the clock trying to avert the next anticipated slide. One colossal slide was witnessed by the general manager and superintendent. A rumbling roar was the only warning to the gang of men shovelling away remnants of a previous slide. They scrambled to safety in time to see a large section of the track with ties, rails and telegraph poles slip down into the valley. Callaghan pulled his hat down over his eyes and muttered, "Too much is too much." John Deakin would not admit defeat and repairs were soon in progress with the assistance of a ditcher, but work was slow because of the constant rain.

Down in the valley, Watino was recoiling from the effects of flooding by the Smoky River. Flood waters had damaged the railway bridge partially washing out both approaches. A work train was dumping gravel from hopper cars into the washout when a mammoth slide came down a few hundred yards behind trapping it.[29]

Roadmaster Ernie Law, headquartered at Grande Prairie, had problems too. Washouts in the Grande Prairie district had cut the railway line into several sections. Law's introduction to railroading was as an itinerant preacher in railway camps during the summers when he was studying for the ministry at Wesley College, Winnipeg. Disillusioned with the ministry, he joined the CPR.[30] The staunch Social Credit supporter's upbringing in England was genteel and his interests included reading, classical music, and serious political discussions. Law's English accent was evident as he uttered his favorite exclamation "By hookey!" Few disliked this gentle man who exuded a kindly friendliness to all he came in contact with. His subordinates willingly followed his instructions at the time of the floods.

Flood water damage to the east abutment of the Smoky bridge, 1935

Flood at Waterways in 1936
Photo: Courtesy of F. Meisinger

Repairing track on Waterways Subdivision, 13 August
Photo: Provincial Archives of Alberta, A3341

John Callaghan must have wondered if it was possible for a railway to handle any more misfortune when on 30 July the track and several bridges between Mile 279 and 281 washed out on the Waterways Subdivision. He personally supervised the work of repairs.[31]

Rubber boots were essential as Section Foreman Frank Meisinger inspected the damage after the floods. One bridge had nothing but track hanging. His track motor roared as he took a run at it. The machine had scarcely reached solid ground when the track pulled apart and collapsed. From Lynton, suddenly there was a lake stretching for about three miles, slowing down the mixed train. The weight of the train navigating over the saturated muskeg made the rails sink out of sight. The caboose, which had uncoupled, was left behind. On arrival at Waterways the undercarriage of the coaches were covered with moss from the muskeg. As the end of August neared, railroaders welcomed the end of what had been nothing short of a monsoon season.

While conditions improved out on the line, changes were being made in the office which would affect train crews. Deciding the methods of bookkeeping done by conductors needed some guidelines. Auditor Fred Kavanagh circulated "Accounting Rules for Conductors" in the fall of 1935. Conductors, like Eugene McLaughlin who had a limited education, considered the making out of reports an imposition on a conductor. Writing on the table in a rolling, swaying caboose is never easy, but most become adept at it. McLaughlin did not. His writing was atrocious, but not deliberately so, as many of the office employees believed. The difficulties were compounded by his reports often being incorrect.

McLaughlin was a bachelor, a hard drinker and a man with a kind heart. He had been in the Klondike as a young lad, which earned him the nickname "Sandbar Slim." With time "Slim" was dropped, but "Sandbar" remained. Although born in the U.S., McLaughlin was of Irish heritage and possessed most of the faults and virtues that came with it. His volatile temper could flash and thunder like a summer storm, then subside as suddenly as it had started.[32] He had his own brand of swear words. "Blue Jesus" and "Holy Mary Muther of Jesus" brought many a chuckle from a colleague or passenger.

Once when McLaughlin tried to explain the disappearance of some passenger ticket stubs, the staff in the audit office scratched their heads in disbelief. It happened on a trip with Brakeman Ben Poore. After lighting his pipe, Poore tossed the match into a tobacco tin and to his astonishment its contents went on fire. McLaughlin arrived just as the blazing tin went sailing through the air out the caboose door. Poore got the full blast of McLaughlin's extensive vocabulary as he explained the tobacco tin was no ashtray, but a container for ticket stubs. A search of the location by the conductor of the eastbound freight failed to produce more than a few remnants.[33]

Shock waves rippled through the railway in November 1936 at the news of a massacre at Tieland, a flag station seven miles south of Chisholm. Carl Schwez, who had worked on the section until the previous year, went berserk, shot and killed five people then turned the gun on himself. Among those murdered were section foreman Carl Nelson, his wife, Alma, who was a daughter of Julius Ristock, section foreman at Flatbush, their young son, Edward, sectionman John Macinuk and a resident of Tieland George Reul. The carnage was discovered by Sectionman Joe Garry and Erna Ristock, Alma Nelson's sister, who narrowly escaped being shot. They left on a track motor, for Chisholm to phone the RCMP who found the gunman's body near the scene.

Wrapped in blankets the murder victims are taken from Tieland on push cars.
Photo: S/Sgt. E. Buchanan

While Tieland was the site of a tragedy in 1936, it was also the scene of joy for another section foreman some years later. The foreman's home had been replaced and Nick and Mrs. Zinko were expecting their second child. Although they were isolated from civilization, they felt no great urgency for medical attention. Their baby was not due for another week. When Mrs. Zinko began having labor pains, the train had already rolled by. Zinko bundled up his wife and young son, got them on the track motor and headed for Flatbush, where Martha Ristock was a midwife. Zinko recalls, "Finally I went up the grade and there was a train coming against me. I had to take the track motor off. We sat there on the snow like the wild prairie chickens."[34] It seemed like an eternity before they arrived at Flatbush, but reach it they did. A baby girl made her appearance in the world soon afterwards and was taken back to Tieland to live.

Meanwhile, in the corridors of power in Montreal, a decision was made by the parent companies on a replacement for John Callaghan, who was planning retirement. As he vacated his office, weather conditions in northern Alberta were the exact opposite of those in 1935. With no rain for weeks, the land was tinder dry. On 30 June 1937 a forest fire swept the Waterways subdivision destroying all in its wake, including seven railway bridges. Because the fire occurred on a weekend, the work train crew consisted of junior men. An embargo was placed on the line north of Lac La Biche making it impossible for senior men to "bump" them. The men, for whom trips had been scarce throughout the Depression, were jubilant.

restored within ten days. Complete restoration of the bridges was not achieved in that time but they were sufficiently rebuilt to allow traffic to proceed with slow orders.

Bridge at Mile 188.02, Waterways Subdivision,
destroyed by fire on 30 June 1937.
Photo: Courtesy of O. Aaberg

Superintendent Deakin assigned every available employee to a shift, including his clerk, Jim Rouse. Bridge and Building Foremen Joe Rivers and Joe Hurst worked two shifts each of ten hours per day. There were few in the bridge and building field more experienced than these two. Joe Rivers and the railway parted company the following year, but Joe Hurst stayed on. He was still a young man when he died suddenly of a heart attack.

As usual in such circumstances, Deakin worked the men hard, but he also worked alongside them. They all felt a sense of accomplishment when train service was

Deakin was at his best in this type of situation. Bridges were his field of expertise. A cabinet maker who had learned his trade in Scotland, he had begun his railway career with a bridge and building gang on the ED & BC in 1914.[35] When he was promoted to bridge and building foreman, he was nicknamed "Johnny Crosscut." His competence and dedication was acknowledged by management with a promotion in 1921 to bridge and building master. Callaghan had an affinity for the ambitious man, who lived a railway life 24 hours a day.[36] It was he who promoted Deakin to assistant superintendent in 1927 and to superintendent the following year. Like the general manager, Deakin was a very private person in his business relationships. Few got to know the man behind the steady blue eyes, who had little time for humor in his busy life.[37]

The sturdily-built Scot, with the light red hair understood the value of nickels.[38] Neglect on the part of employees was not tolerated. Nevertheless, Deakin tried to make fair and unbiased judgments when administering "brownie points" [demerits] for infractions of rules. He relished the challenge of pitting his wits against the odds when train wrecks or natural disasters occurred, such as the forest fire that burned the bridges on the Waterways subdivision.

This was the situation as James M. MacArthur stepped into the general manager's shoes in 1937. When the Waterways line was safe for traffic he made his first inspection trip. Feeling the destruction of the bridges was his responsibility, Charlie Erickson, who had been roadmaster since 1922, tendered his resignation at Lac La Biche. MacArthur refused to entertain the idea. Expecting the new general manager would want him to accompany him to Waterways, weary Superintendent Deakin was ready to go. To his surprise, MacArthur told him, "You go home and get some rest. I will see you back in Edmonton." This was the beginning of a different type of management style on the NAR.

Fireman Clarence Comrie leans out of locomotive
No.27 as new bridge nears completion on 8 July 1937.
Photo: Courtesy of O. Aaberg

Canada's Governor General, Lord Tweedsmuir,
travelled to Waterways on this train in July 1937.
Photo: Courtesy of Provincial Archives of Alberta, A4017

18
In the Shadow of War

J.M. MacArthur, General Manager, NAR, 1937-1950

On 1 July 1937 General Manager John Callaghan turned over to his successor, James Mitchell MacArthur, a railway that was just beginning to have some cohesion.[1] NAR employees soon discovered his style of management was like a breath of fresh air. There was no doubt as to exactly who was at the controls.[2]

MacArthur began his railway career when he was 16-years-old in Toronto. He rose to the position of superintendent with the CPR and was in charge of the Vancouver division at the time of his appointment to NAR. To the younger railway, he attempted to bring the discipline and efficiency of the CPR operation. Department heads were given a clear sense of their responsibilities. The chain of command established by MacArthur enabled him to be aware of everything that was happening on the railway.

Anxious to have more representation, the CNR arranged for the transfer of George

Linney to NAR.[3] Assigned to the general manager's office, Linney displaced Mortimer Collins, who was offered a position with the CPR, but refused to dislodge his family, preferring to stay in Edmonton and take a demotion. His son, Roy Collins, remembers, "This was a big crisis in the family. . . . It was finally decided that he would not go. It was a most unhappy time for him."[4] Although the office assistant position did not wield the same authority, Collins continued to have some involvement with the daily happenings of the railway.

Among MacArthur's priorities was a track rehabilitation program and upgrading of the physical appearance of the entire railway. MacArthur was a thrifty individual who would not tolerate waste. It was believed he could detect a mislaid track spike, angle bar or grain door under a foot of snow. If he noticed material lying about the yards or track he whipped off a memo to the officer responsible. Although some called him "Scrap Iron MacArthur" in jest, they would not dare do so to his face. He believed that by making an issue of minor infractions, major ones were less likely to occur.[5]

His short messages, named "butterflies," became a trademark of the man.[6] Sometimes it was a note at the end of a letter, saying "Pls spk" and signed "J.M.M." Few dared ignore the "butterflies." If they did, they heard about it in no uncertain terms. It seemed MacArthur never forgot anything.

Under the direction of "J.M.M." or "the old man," as he was often referred to, the railway began to move into the twentieth century. He soon gained a reputation for being a strict but impartially just disciplinarian. In most cases, where he felt compelled to dismiss a skilled or veteran employee for violation of a rule, such as Rule "G," he later reinstated that employee.[7] His grave manner belied the deep regard he had for family, whether it be his own or that of an employee. His concern was such that he initiated a contributory pension plan for NAR railroaders, patterned after that on the CPR.[8]

MacArthur was a knowledgeable administrator who took an interest in the details of the railway's daily operations. He also knew the surnames of the majority of his employees and addressed the men with the prefix "mister" regardless of their rank. One of his first tasks was to inspect the Dunvegan Yards facilities. At the station, his thorough inspection made his hands dusty. Apologizing profusely, Agent Bert Carrick escorted the general manager to the small washroom. To Carrick's embarrassment the water pail was empty. It was obvious, by the layer of dust on them, that neither the pail nor the hand basin had been used for some time. J.M.M. was not amused and the news of all future visits preceded him.

MacArthur had several secretaries during his tenure. Among them were Stan Morgan, Norman Howe, Jack Price and Alec Messum. On assuming the position, each was presented with a story to read, entitled "A Message to Garcia" written by Elbert Hubbard. It was about Rowan who delivered a message to General Garcia at the time of the war between the United States and Spain over Cuba. The message it contained was "when you have an assignment, follow it through no matter what the problems."

The general manager's business car was a travelling office on wheels. His secretary usually travelled with him on the line. Throughout each trip they worked. As he paced the floor, twirling his glasses in his hands, MacArthur would dictate notes or letters on observations en route. Many of the "butterflies" were the result of these trips. It was the secretary's duty to see that they were dispatched in the railway's mail bag at stations where mail was picked up. Alec Messum claims, "To miss a mail bag was nothing short of a hanging offence."[9]

MacArthur liked to keep books of statistics. Whenever he went out on a trip, he insisted his secretary take along a huge expanding briefcase, stuffed with files and statistical information. His beaver coat also had to be taken in the winter. For Messum, who was neither tall nor robust, it was a problem to carry everything. He was often so loaded down the staff fancied it was a beaver coat with legs they had seen moving across the yard.

Because MacArthur never once requested anything from the briefcase Messum decided not to take it on one trip. En route to Waterways, with several guests, MacArthur asked for a file. It was a very shamefaced Messum who admitted, "I regret I overlooked bringing it." Afterwards, MacArthur gently chided him, "Sandy, these things that I have, it is like a gun. When you want it, you want it right now. Don't ever fail to bring that briefcase again."[10] It was always taken along after that, even though MacArthur never requested anything out of it again.

"Sandy" was the general manager's nickname for Messum to differentiate him from Alex Koblanski, the steward on his private car. Previously Koblanski had been on the superintendent's business car, where he won the affection of the whole Deakin family. He was an excellent chef, who got rave reviews on his planked chicken. In his free time, the handsome steward liked to dabble in investments, termed "wheeling and dealing" by his colleagues. If MacArthur was discussing the stock market with guests while travelling on the private car, he had no hesitation in pressing the buzzer to summon Koblanski to give them the latest information.

As MacArthur settled into his new office, His Excellency Governor General Lord Tweedsmuir announced a tour of the West. The trip involved travelling via train to Waterways and then by steamship to the North West Territories. The vice-regal special train departed from Edmonton on 20 July 1937. Engineer W.C. "Bill" Hunter and Fireman J.M. "Jack" Bennett, both old rails, tried to give the esteemed passenger a smooth ride. Hunter had been an engineer with the railway since 1917 and Bennett became a fireman six months later.

Most inhabitants of the area were on the platform to meet the train on arrival the following morning. The Hudson's Bay Company had sent a stock of the finest vintage wines, and the best Scotch whiskeys, down river for the trip. What the company officials did not know was that Lord Tweedsmuir was not a drinking man and the supplies came back unopened. They were first stored in the HBC warehouse and later in a locked room at the home of the accountant. Before the navigation season was over that fall, the station staff swelled the number of guests at several parties. Unfortunately, the HBC's head office in Winnipeg eventually issued orders for return of the liquor. An audit revealed that only a portion of the original stock remained. There was quite a rumble, which died down after the accountant responsible disappeared from Waterways.

In the fall of 1937 the CPR president, who had been knighted in 1935, was again in the West on a tour of the Peace River country. On 22 September, Con Kennedy was the engineer at the controls of engine No. 102, which handled Sir Edward Beatty's special train from Edmonton to McLennan and return. MacArthur and Deakin accompanied the special party. Wild duck was on the menu and quickly became a favorite with the visitors. The first consignment was from Chief Dispatcher L.W. "Sandy" Saunders at McLennan, where the train switched to engine No. 58 and the crew was changed. Engineer Carl Gage took the train on to Dawson Creek. A second shipment of duck was received at Watino when Assistant Resident Engineer Wilf Lawton, who was an excellent shot, placed 40 ducks on board. On return to McLennan engine No. 102 with Hank Kelly at the controls took the train to Peace River.

*Locomotive No. 102 looked its best for
Sir Edward Beatty's tour in September 1937.*
Photo: W. Wishart

Unlike his predecessor, MacArthur had no engineering background, and in November 1937 he promoted Howard Tye to the top engineering position as engineer, maintenance of way and structures. He had been a teacher before changing careers and joining the CPR. Subsequently, he graduated from the University of Toronto in 1906. When war broke out, Tye was with the CPR's engineering department. He enlisted and returned to the CPR after demobilization. When work petered out, he joined Alberta's Department of Railways and went to work on the L & NW until its sale to the CPR in 1928.[11] Although he was of serious countenance, his colleagues found Tye to be a kindly man, who was frugal with the railway's money. This earned him the nickname "Hardwood." Stations were not redecorated on a regular basis, but rather on the request of the agent. On one occasion, when a request for repainting was received Tye informed the agent that since the passenger trains passed his station in the dead of night, it was in no urgent need of a coat of paint.[12]

By 1938, Tye had a continuing program in place for replacement of 60 lb. rail with heavier rail, and installation of creosoted ties. A half yard Dominion dragline was purchased and a concentrated effort made to stabilize roadbed and handle ditching for drainage.[13] Jack Kelly was hired as the operator when the railway purchased its first dragline. He insisted on having his wife live with him in the bunk car. Prior to that the men were parted from their spouses when they were out on the line. It was a concession of which many others took advantage. To while away the time, Mrs. Kelly occasionally wrote rhyme – some of it about the railway men.[14] Kelly had operated a dragline at the Abasand plant, near Draper [old Waterways].[15] On the NAR he was soon nicknamed "Dragline" Kelly.

At that time, the hamlet of Waterways was still a frontier town. Roy Ellstock, Bill's son, wondered if he had entered a B grade western when he was shot at shortly after his arrival. The handsome city lad had come to work in the station and was taking a stroll along the only road leading to Fort McMur-ray, when a man came rushing down a hill, with another in hot pursuit. There was a crack and a "ping" as a bullet went flying past young Ellstock. He did not stop to ask questions. Rumor decreed the rifleman was a trapper who had come home to find another man in bed with his wife.

It was at Waterways that Ellstock met "Goldfields Rosie" as she was boarding the train for Edmonton. Ellstock told her she would have to pay a couple of dollars extra on her excess baggage. Without further ado, Rosie hitched up her skirt and went digging in her stocking for the money, as the red-faced young man watched. In spite of the hazards of the job, Ellstock remained with the railway, eventually becoming transportation supervisor and chief train dispatcher.[16]

Besides regular freight, the railway transported some unusual cargo south from Waterways. Salt was one of the first industries of the area. It had been discovered in the Fort McMurray region in 1907. Several attempts were made to produce and market the product over the years. The Alberta Salt Company built the first plant, which went into operation in 1925.[17] Even with government intervention it was not a financial success. Industrial Minerals Limited, controlled by the Dominion Tar and Chemical Company, was the last company to make salt production a viable operation. Early in 1936, a well was drilled and a salt plant built near the railway tracks at Waterways. Two years later shipments commenced. By July 1939 a total of 304 carloads had been forwarded.

The railway continued transporting the product until the plant closed in 1950 when salt beds were developed northeast of Edmonton.[18]

In the fall of 1938, gold bullion was added to the commodities shipped south from Waterways. Consolidated Mining and Smelting Company had begun production of gold bricks in Yellowknife, Northwest Territories.[19] In October 1938 Mill Superintendent Fred Walton packed the first gold shipment in a wooden crate. At the Yellowknife post office Otto Thibert stood guard over it with a shotgun all night.[20] Gold was transported south by plane in winter and by barge from Yellowknife to Waterways in the summer.

At Waterways station gold shipments received no better treatment than any other commodity. The locals knew Agent Bert Viney ate his meals at the Boisvert Hotel. One evening the drayman stopped at the hotel to tell Viney he had left a gold brick on the platform for shipping. It was still there when Bert finished his meal and returned to his station.[21]

On one occasion, the wooden crates containing a shipment of five gold bars were too large to fit in the strong box. On train day there were more passengers than seats and the overflow was accommodated in the express car. Shortly before departure, the agent loaded the gold into the express car and stashed it under the desk. The train was met in Edmonton by railway constables reinforced by City Police. They were astounded to see about 25 passengers jumping out of the express car. The CNR management was not impressed by this casual handling of the gold and soon afterwards larger safes were installed in the Waterways' station and NAR express cars.[22]

When a gold brick every fortnight became a regular shipment, the railway issued special handling instructions. In the express car it was to be carried "in the burglar proof chest. This requires the presence of the agent and one member of his staff, to load, as each hold one combination only. The same procedure is followed in opening at Edmonton. Mr. Dominy [NAR's traffic supervisor] has the upper combination while Mr. Dean, the terminal agent of the CNR has the lower one."[23] In Edmonton, NAR and CNR railway police met trains carrying the valuable commodity and accompanied the shipments to the CPR station for transporting to Ottawa, Ontario, or Trail, British Columbia.

Gold was not a strategic metal and production petered out during the war years, but resumed again in 1946.[24] In later years the shipment of gold was a yearly affair. In these larger quantities it would not fit in the strong box. Instead, they were transported in wooden crates which occasionally served as a seat for employees riding in the express car. At Lac La Biche the passengers and crew trooped over to the cafe without giving a thought to protection of the gold. Upon reaching Edmonton on one occasion, Conductor Gerald Whiteman swung off the train to register at the CNR station. When he returned to his train he was accosted by a contingent of railway and city police, who insisted on checking his bag before allowing him to leave.[25]

Left to right: *Metro Kochan, Section Foreman Mike Legoda and Frank Pisatcky make track repairs at Mile 239, Lac La Biche Subdivision in July 1939.*
Photo: Courtesy of F. Pisatcky

*U.S. Army troops returning on rotation to U.S.
wait to board NAR train.*
Photo: U.S. Army

Extra 58 West leaving Dunvegan Yards in August 1943
Photo: Courtesy of J.G. Rouse

Part Five

The War Years: 1940-1945

Congestion at Dunvegan Yards during W.W.I
Photo: Provincial Archives of Alberta,
A. Blyth Collection, BL50214

19

Important Defence Link

A world trembling on the brink of war seemed far removed from the population of northern Alberta, who were still battling the effects of the Depression. The outbreak of war in the fall of 1939 reached the north by radio. It stirred the patriotism of Albertans and railroaders alike. Feeling their duty lay in defending their country, they began enlisting in droves.

In Canada, railways were designated "an essential service" during World War II. While a large segment of the population was away at war, on the NAR railroaders had battles of their own to win. The railway was undergoing a metamorphosis as a result of hostilities. The almost super-human efforts of personnel made the NAR a railway to which the war heroes were proud to return.

On 7 December 1941 the Japanese attack on Pearl Harbour catapulted the United States into the war. This blow was compounded five months later when the Japanese overran the islands of Kiska and Attu, part of the Aleutians, in southwestern Alaska.[1] Their presence so close to the unprotected north was a threat to all of North America. The problem was discussed at the next meeting of the Permanent Joint Board of Defence, which had been formed the previous year. Its members included representatives of both the U.S. and Canada. In a boardroom in Washington, D.C., the joint chiefs of staff of the U.S. military grappled with the problem of how to protect the continent. The only highway to Alaska was the Pacific Ocean and it was vulnerable. The string of air bases, known as the Northwest Staging Route, stretching from Edmonton to Fairbanks, Alaska, could only handle the movement of aircraft and some supplies.[2] Another way to transport troops and armaments to the north had to be found.

A little known railway ran into Dawson Creek, 500 miles northwest of Edmonton, but there were close to 1 600 miles of untamed bushland from there to Fairbanks, Alaska.

Few seated around the table in Washington had heard of the railway that was then Canada's third largest.[3] Transcontinental railways, Canadian Pacific and Canadian National, were not household names in the U.S., but they were known. Reservations diminished somewhat upon hearing these two companies jointly owned the smaller railway and their resources were available to the NAR.

Conductor Wm. "Mush" Hardie and Harry Chausse chat in a caboose, summer 1941.
Photo: G.W.E. Smith

In mid-February 1942, taking for granted Canada's concurrence, the U.S. decided to build an all-weather highway along the route of the air bases.[4] U.S. troops were already en route to Canada by the time the recommendation of the Permanent Joint Board on Defence reached the Cabinet War Committee on 5 March 1942.[5] The Canadian government was more than willing to do everything within its power to assist the U.S. The simple agreement between the two countries was

executed with a minimum of delay.[6] With the stroke of a pen NAR became an important defence link. Given top priority among North American railways, it was called upon to handle the equivalent of main line transcontinental railway traffic.[7]

This was the same railway which, less than two years earlier, had been informed by Major-General George R. Pearkes, V.C., officer commanding the Pacific Coast Command for the Canadian Army, that it was not considered to be of national importance. Ignoring NAR, discussions had been held with Canada's two major railways and plans had been made for protection of their bridges against attacks. In a telephone call NAR's general manager indignantly drew the Major-General's attention to the fact that "the NAR had approximately ten million bushels of wheat to bring out of the Peace River country and if this is not considered of national importance from a food supply standpoint then we have nothing more to say."[8] MacArthur made his own arrangements for watchmen to guard the Athabasca, Smoky, Heart and Peace River bridges.

The horror of the Nazi rampage in Europe manifested itself in strange ways in Canada. Arrests were made under the War Measures Act and thousands herded into internment camps. Fearful that Nazism might get a foothold in their country, Canadians became suspicious of fellow Canadians. NAR employees whose opinions were construed as sympathetic towards the Nazis were occasionally reported to management by colleagues. Because the railway needed them and the RCMP preferred to know where they were, nothing further was done. One conductor found himself the subject of an embarrassing investigation because of a chance remark overheard by an extra gang cook as the train crew ate breakfast. In a discussion about the war, he was asked what he thought Canada should do if Hitler invaded. Cantankerous at that early hour, he said, "Let him have the God damn country." He kept his opinions to himself after that.

There was no time to worry about "subversive" remarks for several years after that. There was a job to be done – a big one. With a nine month deadline in which to build a military highway to Alaska, the U.S. and Canadian governments showed their solidarity by keeping "red tape" to a minimum. The building of the Alcan Highway commenced from both ends and work was carried out in several sections.

In March 1942, in minus 30 degrees weather, the first Pullman cars carrying U.S. troops arrived in Dawson Creek. Engineer Frank Lepine, who had been with the railway since 1914, was at the controls.[9] The Americans he carried north were the vanguard quartermasters' troops with Lt. Colonel E.A. Mueller, as sector quartermaster. Anxious to maintain a good relationship between his men and residents of Dawson Creek, the colonel ran a tight ship. These men prepared the camp for the arrival of thousands of soldiers from the United States Army Corps of Engineers. Bell tents and portable quonset

huts became a common sight. Others were shipped by sea, rail and truck to Whitehorse, Yukon, and Fairbanks, Alaska.

U.S. Army soldiers arriving in Dawson Creek in 1942.
Photo: Courtesy of D. Baker

Time was of the essence and no one knew that better than railway employees. Relieving Section Foreman Jerry Wowk was transferred from Grande Prairie to Dawson Creek where he supervised the building of storage tracks and installation of switches. Jimmy Prasses and Don Baker were among those who worked on the installation. Baker, Section Foreman Bob Baker's son, recalls: "The ground was still frozen. In order to lay our switches, we had to pick loose the ballast so we could get ties in place between those already in service. Once we got past the frog, we could just lay the ties on top of the frozen ground for ballasting later."[10] Some of the new trackage was in the U.S. Army yard, west of the village. To speed up the movement of supplies the army temporarily operated a diesel switch engine between the new army classification yard and the quartermaster's spur tracks. [11]

Equipment for building the Alaska Highway arrives in Dawson Creek.
Photo: Courtesy of D. Baker

Coaches filled with raw recruits and experienced soldiers arrived in Dawson Creek to tackle dense wilderness, extreme cold in winter and swarms of mosquitoes in summer. Chief Dispatcher George Thompson and his staff at McLennan faced an enormous challenge. Standing on the platform with the ever present cigar in his mouth he shook his head as troop train after troop train rolled past. He had been with the railway from 1919 and never had it been so busy.

The small station at McLennan was too cramped. To accommodate the dispatching office and yard office facilities, a second storey was added. The battle had just begun for NAR. To keep trains moving, the parent companies provided what staff they could spare. A number of experienced retired people were enticed back to work. Among them was Ira Leigh Boomer, a retiree from the CNR, who had been superintendent of transportation. Conductor George Stephenson says of Boomer, "He was a great dispatcher. He always knew where everyone was on the line and where they were going. He could keep it all in his head."[12] There were the occasions when Boomer resorted to unorthodox methods to keep trains moving at a time when every minute counted.

Assistant Agent Rex Lambert and Chief Dispatcher George Thompson at McLennan.
Photo: Courtesy of Velma Gooch

Trains passing the dispatching office on their way north, had U.S. Pullman coaches but the diners belonged to NAR. The railway's dining cars had class in the days before the Alcan Highway. The waiters looked impeccable in their pressed white jackets. Passengers wrote their orders on the meal check. This method eliminated disputes as to whether the correct order was received and prevented any dishonesty on the part of staff. Tables were elegantly set with damask tablecloths and napkins. With trains packed to overflowing it was decided to dispense with traditions such as finger bowls on the tables because some customers drank their contents.

Dick Cross was steward on Diner 600, but found prejudice reared its ugly head when the Americans came to dine. Feeling the smart of racial slurs he eventually requested the position of porter. Once when some American and Canadian porters began arguing over which lived in the better country, Cross told them, "I do not get paid as much as you, but I can sit down with the conductor and other white people, but you can't do that in the U.S."[13]

Jack Graham replaced Cross as steward and remembers the hectic pace in the tiny kitchen. "We served 1 165 meals on one trip from Edmonton to Dawson Creek in three sittings. . . . We had 17 sleepers and everybody had a meal ticket."[14] The construction workers were at the entrance to the dining car as soon as the train left Edmonton. This would continue all the way to Dawson Creek. Although the dining car closed its doors at 0100 to allow the staff some "shut-eye," by 0300 there would be pounding on it. Hungry men wanted breakfast.

Liquor was rationed. Located at Pouce Coupe was the only liquor outlet between the Peace River Block and Whitehorse, in the Yukon. The monthly limit was a 26 ounce bottle allotment, later reduced to 12 ounce. Usually the line-ups were long. Protection at the entrance was provided by a swaggering U.S. Army military policeman, with a gun strapped to the hip. For a price, his pals could jump the queue.

The top brass of the major contracting companies in the area made a point of being on friendly terms with Agent Jack Hardie. Irene Hardie remembers, "Jack had many fake telegrams to deliver to the liquor store manager to save the VIP's from having to stand in line for their quota."[15] Some of the telegrams were addressed to Jack Hardie. Bill Donlevy recalls many a coded message read, "Reserve a room at Hart House [name of hotel in Pouce Coupe]. Prefer room 26, if possible." Hardie knew the telegram translated to "Pick me up a 26 of Lemon Hart Rum, if available." Hardie's friendship with the liquor vendor enabled him to obtain the better brands from under the counter.[16]

Bootleggers took advantage of the numerous passenger trains passing through. There were those who sold cold tea or water for a dollar an ounce. The scam was pulled off by topping off the bottle with a little liquor.[17] Just as the train was ready to leave, the con man pretended to be drinking. The buyer would smell it, pay the price, jump on the train and be well on his way before discovering he had been hoodwinked.

On another occasion, an enterprising fellow was at the train looking for a sale, with a bottle stashed in his pocket. The local RCMP officer strode up with his billy club dangling at his side. As he passed the would-be salesman it accidentally hit the pocket, shattering the bottle. The bootlegger had a difficult time nonchalantly walking away as the "licker" trickled down his leg into his boot.

As troops, workmen and equipment continued to pour into the Peace River country, three or four sections of train No. 1 became a regular occurrence. Retired Roadmaster Otto Michetti, who was then section foreman, recalls the effect of the increased volume of traffic on the NAR: "I dare say no greater demands have ever been placed on any railway in North America than the demands made towards and fulfilled by the NAR between 1942-45, considering the increased percentage of traffic on its then prevailing facilities. The extraordinary demands of this unexpected volume of traffic created havoc to the physical resources of railway facilities and of employees in all departments."[18]

Within a short time, over 10 thousand American soldiers and some 6 thousand civilian workers from the U.S. Public Roads Administration were stationed at intervals along the 1 523 mile Alcan route, stretching from Mile 0 at Dawson Creek through to Fairbanks. For a railway not built to move such massive quantities of traffic, the handling difficulties were unbelievable. Built with light rail, tracks and sidings were insufficient. Facilities were inadequate, money was scarce and manpower in short supply.

The newly appointed road foreman of engines wondered how long inadequate equipment could stand up under the vastly increased train movements. Ed Faust, nicknamed "Soft Exhaust" and "The Westinghouse Kid," claimed to know more about air brakes than any engineer in NAR service. He had worked on railways before coming to Canada in 1912. After two years as air brake instructor with the GTP railway, he became an engineer on an ED & BC work train laying track into the Peace River country. His name was immortalized by naming the village of Faust after him.

Master Mechanic Charles Stewart had the headache of securing sufficient equipment. When he transferred four years previously, he had brought 26 years of railway experience to NAR. Much of it was gained on the CNR. But nothing could have prepared him for the problems he now faced. The parent lines came to the rescue by supplying whatever locomotives and equipment could be spared. Experienced staff were also loaned or transferred to the subsidiary railway. Charlie McElheran was among them. He transferred from CNR's car service department in Winnipeg as car accountant.[19] John Christie had handled that end of the business for 11 years, but had just been pro-

Car Accountant Charlie McElheran
Photo: Courtesy of Jack Christie

Traffic Supervisor Jack Christie
Photo: Courtesy of Jack Christie

moted to traffic supervisor. In spite of his experience, business was so brisk McElheran and his staff had a difficult time keeping tabs on the interchange of cars and the demurrage that accrued.

Light rail bent beneath the weight of heavy freight trains carrying road building machinery north. At strategic points on the line, the 60 lb. rail was replaced. Track crews worked long hours laying 80 lb. and 100 lb. rail, installing water supplies, coaling plants, wyes, new sidings and renewing old ones.

Besides passenger and freights, there were stock trains, which usually ran on weekends. In those days stock train crews could be on duty for up to 16 hours, occasionally for 24 hours.[20] Conductor Jim Winter-

mute recalls, "Stock days were always miserable."[21] On one trip he worked with two of his brothers; Frank was the engineer and Bill the brakeman. At Belloy the whole crew assisted with the unloading of a carload of cattle into a boxcar. There was some difficulty directing an angry bull toward the doorway of the car. This was accomplished by using a partition from a boxcar, but all of them knew that if the bull hit it they were in trouble.

The traffic department was extremely overtaxed. Although his title was chief clerk, James G. McVicar had been running the department from 1917. It was not until its expansion in 1942 that he received the deserved title of traffic assistant and Girvin Walker replaced him as chief clerk.

*Locomotive No. 101 pulls the
eastbound stock train by Pibroch.*
Photo: Courtesy of D. Baker

McVicar had lost his wife in the flu epidemic of 1918 and became a single parent. Although he could swear like a trooper, he was kind to his staff and they remember him with affection. His short stature did not apply to his Scottish burr, which needed no amplification to be heard the other side of the office. Shirley Hunter [nee Murphy] was a member of McVicar's staff during the early part of the war years and recalls, "Jimmy McVicar was a nice man to work for. He would come into the office in the mornings looking immaculate but it only took one cigarette before there were ashes everywhere. He smoked like a chimney."[22]

Margaret Nix [nee Latter] was also in that department and recalls those hectic years for the traffic people: "We didn't have enough rolling stock and the Americans didn't understand our little 'toonerville' railway. Jimmy McVicar worked so hard to try and get those trains through. . . . He would be at the station when the trains were going out at all hours of the day or night. Everything was an emergency."[23]

Girvin Walker was the antithesis to McVicar. He had come to the A & GW as an office boy in 1924 and three years later he moved to a clerical position in the traffic department where he remained. Quiet and unassuming he seemed to move at a snail's pace. Nevertheless, he accomplished more in a day than some did in a week.[24]

In an unprecedented move, a quiet spoken gentleman, who had spent most of his career in the office, was appointed assistant superintendent in March 1942. Charles G. Dominy travelled with the first troop train to Dawson Creek expecting to return to Edmonton. Except for a bundle of dirty clothes that arrived at regular intervals, that was the last his family saw of him until the middle of May. His wife and children moved to Dawson Creek for the summer and Lillian Dominy assisted with the car checking: "They were just unloading stuff all over the place. There were tremendous stocks of material piled up and covered with tarpaulins."[25]

Railroading seemed a natural choice of career for Dominy, and his brother Jack.

Their grandfather, father and brother all worked for the CPR. When their father was transferred to Regina, Charles Dominy got a job in the CPR offices there in 1912. On 1 July that year a cyclone devastated the city. The Dominy home was among those destroyed. Shortly afterwards the family, except for Jack, moved to Edmonton.[26] Dominy worked for the CPR and the ED & BC when it was on lease to the CPR. In 1929 he joined the newly formed NAR as traffic supervisor, with responsibility for the handling of express, mail and baggage.

Charles Dominy had no idea when General Manager MacArthur suggested he become assistant superintendent for six months, that it would become a two year term. He was responsible for the north end of the railway. With trains running at all hours of the day and night, he seldom got a full night's sleep. Nevertheless, Dominy appreciated the pressures placed on his fellow railroaders. His kindness and understanding during this time are well remembered by those he supervised. When he returned to headquarters in 1944, it was as office assistant to the general manager.

Because of the acute shortage of labor in McLennan, employees' relatives took up the slack. Lillian Dominy joined the locomotive foreman's office staff. She had come to Canada with her family as a young girl and the years did little to diminish her English accent. Marge Bodnaruk, wife of Walter, also worked in the office. The language of train crews booking in at the wicket was often enough to make a preacher blush. If the men swore in front of his female staff Locomotive Foreman Joe Faulder meted out their penance, "Bring back two big chocolate bars from Dawson Creek for these girls." Soon there were boxes filled with bars, some of which found their way to a friend in the Air Force.[27]

Faulder was among those feeling the strain of overwork. He had moved his family from Edmonton to McLennan when promoted to the foreman position in 1930. During the war years it was imperative that maximum effort with minimum down time be extracted from each locomotive. A new four-stall engine house was built increasing the work area. Keeping the old and often antiquated equipment operating was a difficult job. Faulder ended up in hospital and there decided his railroading days were over. After several moves, the Faulders settled in Jasper with the majestic beauty of the Rocky Mountains as a backdrop.[28]

It was during the war years that railways across Canada dispensed with tradition and hired hundreds of women to fill jobs traditionally held by men--NAR was no exception. There had always been women on the railway in office jobs, but few made it their career. Usually their employment was severed upon marriage. Isabel Paul had joined the NAR's accounting section in 1937. She was one of a number of women, who were just beginning their careers and eventually would retire from the railway.

Back: *Engineering staff Maureen O'Byrne, Susan Colville and Freddie Henry.* Front: *Secretary Express Department, Gwen Vigus, Chief Clerk, Engineering Department, Bill Harris, Boarding Car Inspector, Art Williams.* Photo: Courtesy of J. Christie

Muriel Rose became a member of general office staff in 1939 and although she married, changing her name to Callfas, she never broke her service. She spent almost her entire career as staff records clerk where her prodigious memory for details was put to the test. Dixie Wright, who joined the NAR in 1941, was among those who served in the Air Force during World War II and returned to resume her career. Lola Pucci first joined the staff in the station at Peace River, then moved to Grande Prairie.[29] Gwen Vigus first joined the general office staff and later moved into the express and traffic departments. Among the newcomers to the audit office during those years were Vera Wriglesworth, Margaret Huston and Faye Suddaby. During her tenure, Miss Huston

was secretary to four of the railways' auditors. Thirty years later, Miss Wriglesworth had the distinction of being the first woman to retire from the NAR and the others gradually followed.

Master Mechanic Charles Stewart took the first step in hiring women to work in the shops. David Brown, who was then locomotive foreman at Dunvegan Yards, was agreeable. He needed reliable workers. Whether they were men or women was of no consequence. Two young women started work in the locomotive shop during the summer of 1943. Former General Locomotive Foreman Joe Frechette recalled: "Their work consisted of sweeping floors and wiping locomotives. . . . Their willingness to work opened the door for those who followed."[30] When they resigned, the women who replaced them ranged in age from the teens to the early forties.

The car and stores departments also hired women.[31] There was no discrimination as far as wages were concerned. The women were paid on a par with the men. To their surprise, the men found them to be pleasant, willing and industrious workers in spite of the grimy surroundings. Gradually, the women won their respect and when a new five stall engine house was built, a lunch room, with benches, a table and wash basin, was made available to the women. They even got their own private privy. It was not the Ritz, but washing facilities were most welcome to clean off the accumulated grease and grime.

Over the next few years, 11 or 12 women

laborers worked in the shops. Few were overwhelmed by the number of males they worked with. In fact, their presence tended to modify the language used. This was no place for *haute couture* fashion, instead overalls, jeans, caps and thick gloves were more in order. There were a couple of young women who stood out from the crowd. Annie Bzita [now Mrs. Marshall], daughter of Coach Cleaner Harry Bzita, was only 16 when she began working in the shops. Joe Frechette says, "For a very young girl in that environment she was a very good worker."

Female laborers at Dunvegan Yards in 1943. Left to Right: *Ann Zotack, Annie Bzita, Margaret White-house, Beulah Caron, Olga Ursuliak, and Clara Frost*
Photo: Courtesy of Mrs. Olga Steele

Olga Ursuliak [now Mrs. Steele] was the daughter of Mike Ursuliak, foreman in the stores department. But Miss Ursuliak was not destined to remain a shop laborer. At night school she took secretarial training. Soon she was calling crews, but at reduced pay. When the locomotive foreman's clerk moved on, leaving a vacancy, she applied for it, causing much controversy. Never before

in the railway's history had a woman sought to invade the inner sanctum of the locomotive foreman's office but times were changing. Locomotive Foreman David Harper, who had replaced David Brown, asked for the opportunity to allow Ursuliak to prove herself, and she did.[32]

Meanwhile, supplies were not reaching the Alcan Highway fast enough. While the ground was still frozen army truck convoys transported supplies northwest overland from Edmonton. With the arrival of spring, trucks became mired in mud. Often the railway equipment came to their rescue.[33] During the summer months, it was left to the railway to take all tonnage north.

The two yard tracks at Smith were unable to handle the increase in traffic. Otto Michetti recalls arriving there with an extra gang to construct two additional tracks. He had released one track for service and begun construction on the other when he was awakened one night by operator D.R.B. "Dick" Macnaughton requesting permission to use the second track to clear the main line for train No.2. Michetti says, "I told him he could use one half only, as the rest of it was spiked to gauge only every fifth tie and rails joined with only one bolt. When I arrived at work the following morning I had to wait until an eastward train cleared it as the whole track was occupied with cars. . . . What kept the wheels on the rails is beyond me."[34]

At Smith, George Bisson was locomotive foreman and Charles Passmore was night foreman. The two men had worked together from 1923. Billy Smith recalled, "Bisson was from France. He spent a lot of his own money to buy tools the railway should have provided, but did not."[35] Bisson had been with the railway since its construction days. His greasy overalls belied the fact that he was a well read man. Passmore recalled that if he did not understand Bisson's instructions, "he would get a piece of chalk and start to draw the diagrams out on the floor. . . . He was a good machinist. I could do a master job, but I could not compete with him, he'd do a better job."[36]

About the time his son lost his life when his ship was torpedoed, Bisson moved his family to Edmonton where he worked in the shops at Dunvegan Yards. Passmore stepped into the vacancy and Jack Darvill took over the duties of night foreman. Because it was an intermediate terminal and served equipment, Smith was very busy. Freight trains laid over and their crews had to be called. Heated cars were attended to or their contents would freeze. Cars with fish from Slave Lake had to be kept cool. Between them, Agent Fred Hajek and Telegraph Operator Macnaughton worked 12 hour shifts, to keep traffic moving in and out of Smith. All train orders were transmitted by telegraph.[37] Macnaughton moved on the following year to take over the station at Chisholm. Later, he became a train dispatcher, but the war years were the busiest he ever experienced on the NAR.

Train No. 1 derails one mile east of Hythe on 29 June 1943.
Photo: Courtesy of R.D.C. Comrie

20

Wartime Workhorse

Dawson Creek was a tranquil farming community, with a population of about 600, when fame was thrust upon it. Building of the highway to Alaska galvanized the British Columbia village into activity, and stimulated its economy and that of the surrounding area. Its streets and high wooden sidewalks, swarmed with soldiers and civilian construction workers. Tent cities mushroomed. Shacks sprung up overnight. The quiet, peaceful existence of its inhabitants was being rapidly shattered.

With the sudden influx of people into Dawson Creek came the inherent problems of a boom town. Construction accidents caused injury and death. Fights were common on the streets or in the bars, where beer was sold in quart bottles. The criminal element became noticeable. Incidents of robberies and break-ins soared in the village where few previously locked their doors. The small Dawson Creek detachment of the British Columbia Provincial Police was unable to cope. With the thousands of men and scarcity of female companionship it was expected that incidents of assault and rape would escalate. Nevertheless, the balance of life prevailed and many wonderful friendships were made. Besides, there were the joys brought by the union of Dawson Creek girls with U.S. soldiers in marriage. Never would this north village return to the pastoral contentment it had enjoyed.

Suddenly, Dawson Creek was the stepping stone to Alaska. Its facilities were insufficient to meet the demands of the population, which had increased four fold, excluding employees from the construction companies and the U.S. Army.[1] Inadequate sanitation facilities, water supply, and police and fire protection were among the many problems the village commissioners had to face. It was not until the spring of 1944 that Dawson Creek had a water and sewer system.

There were more annoying problems.

There seemed to be line-ups for everything. The hotel and rooming houses were filled to overflowing. The small cafes and restaurants could not cope with the patronage. When they ran out of food a sign was placed in a window reading "No more food" and the doors closed.

Unlike the restaurants, E.T. "Jack" Swift could not hang up a sign saying "Yard Full." Although he was agent, he also handled the duties of yardmaster. Railway facilities were totally inadequate. The congested yards were expected to handle freight trains that increased to four a day.[2] W.J. "Bill" Donlevy moved to Dawson Creek temporarily. Besides Swift, there were Assistant Agents Roscoe Comer and Edward Black, Telegraph Operator Harry E. Korsmo and Express Clerk Clifford E. Townsend. Donlevy recalls, "It was an impossible situation with not near enough staff to handle the work."[3] Soon afterwards, Swift departed for Lac La Biche.

The express department was a shambles. In spite of years of experience, Townsend had difficulty keeping control. Every available space was used to store shipments. Theft was rampant. In an effort to curtail the many claims, a uniformed policeman was hired to patrol the property. Jock Thompson's physical strength was a match for most men. Although a quiet man by nature, he had a delightful sense of humor. Many a consignment, containing a favorite liquid refreshment from Quebec, where liquor rationing did not apply, arrived for a highway worker. Thompson had an instinct for finding the brew no matter how well concealed.

Donlevy's father William C. Donlevy, who had retired in 1940 from agency work on the CNR, was persuaded to tackle the reorganization of the express department. He was joined by Leon R. Kvittem, who had accounting experience. The senior Donlevy's remarkable mathematical ability came to the fore and assisted in the clearance of a backlog of shipments in double quick time.

As traffic and demands on its staff continued to increase, Conductor W.J.A. "Jack" McArthur came from McLennan and temporarily took over the duties of yardmaster. Dawson Creek station was extended, a new freight shed, express office, and waiting rooms were built, and still it was not enough.

Daily passenger train service to Dawson Creek heralded in the new year in 1943. George Potter, then agent at Rycroft, spoke for many when he said, "Those were the days when railroading was fun. We worked hard and had very little time for ourselves, but it was exciting and we enjoyed every minute of it. We were happy in the thought that we were doing something worthwhile and accomplishing much to be proud of."[4]

Shortly before the railway inaugurated a daily passenger service to Dawson Creek, Allan Elliott transferred from High Prairie to take charge of the station in November 1942. Bill Donlevy became accounting agent and got his first experience with a million dollar balance sheet. Two experienced railway accountants, Bill Porterfield and Bill Taylor, and Cashier Earl Hallman from Vancouver, were welcome additions to the staff complement, which had increased tenfold. The railway erected four cottages, three bunkhouses, and a frame cook house to serve meals 24 hours a day to accommodate additional personnel.

Elliott's wife, Jessie, thought she was having a nightmare. The station staff had increased but few were trained. Because of the heavy workload, bags of money were stashed away in every available hiding place in the station living quarters, until there was time to bank it.[5] Sleeping with $100 thousand in cash and bonds tucked into the pillowcase was a common occurrence.

In the Edmonton office, Treasurer A.R. Curran was having money troubles too. The system of collecting outstanding accounts from the U.S. Army was fraught with red tape. When the amounts owing ran into six figures NAR began to experience cash flow problems and Curran took drastic action. Stan Morgan, who was a member of his staff, says, "We were operating on a shoe string; had no money. I recall Curran cutting off the credit of the United States . . . because he had no money to pay his people. . . . He wired both CN and CP in Montreal, and as usual they would have to get together to make a decision. . . .Montreal [location of CN and CP headquarters] did not know what was going on out here."[6]

Curran's bold move was akin to slap-ping the hand of God. In no time flat the telephone lines between Washington, Montreal and Edmonton were humming. Curran's actions had the desired effect. Bill Donlevy recalls, "Accomplished bills of lading, buried for months in red tape, suddenly arrived at the audit office in Edmonton. Many large items of long standing were finally cleared but many still remained, especially in the express department."[7]

The audit department was outside the jurisdiction of the general manager. Retired Auditor Fred Kavanagh explained how it worked, "The Accounting Department reported to the Board of Directors [in Montreal] and there were certain rules."[8] The rules of the Administrative Council Commission had to be followed. In Montreal, four people controlled NAR's purse strings. There was a chairman of the accounting committee and a chairman of the finance committee and two members. One chairman was from the CNR and the other from the CPR.

During this time, Charles Anderson, who was assistant auditor of revenues, recalls working "up to 98 hours a week at the height of it, seven days a week, every night, except Sunday."[9] The computer era had not arrived and everything was done by hand. The billing system, involving exchange rates, interest and land grant rates, "was enormously complex. It took 18 years to clear up the accounting and financial end of it."[10]

Jack Dominy was brought into the office as senior revenue clerk. He had been travelling auditor for 15 years and the bane of the station agents' existence. The auditor played cat to the agent's mouse. His arrival was unannounced, but the news usually reached the agents before he did. On the occasions when it did not, the sight of him stepping off the train had a strange effect on some agents. In one case, the agent could be seen sprinting for his office, where he emptied his pockets into the cash drawer. Dominy, a quiet bachelor, was an industrious, methodical worker, who liked to pause now and then, pull out his pipe and tobacco pouch, then go back to work on the figures puffing contentedly. During the war years, his accounting skills, along with those of the entire department, were tested.

At the end of September 1942, construction equipment from both sections of the Alcan Highway met at Contact Creek.[11] Although the official opening was held in November, the highway was no more than a 24 foot wide tote road. It was the responsibility of civilian contractors to turn it into a highway and the olive green army machinery was quickly replaced by the bright yellow of the Public Roads Administration.

Prior to 1942, communication north of Edmonton was limited to mail, the NAR and Dominion Government telegraphs. Because the existing telegraph line was of insufficient capacity to meet its needs, the U.S. Army asked the NAR to build a new system to Alaska. The railway declined. It had neither the staff nor the resources and the U.S. Army Signals tackled the job themselves.[12] In the

summer of 1942, construction began on the two thousand miles of pole-line between Edmonton and Fairbanks, Alaska.[13] NAR transported the materials and assisted by providing a work train. Railway right-of-way was used for many sections of the Alaskan communication system – a privilege for which NAR charged a yearly rental fee of $1 800.[14]

Section Foreman Carl Luh used this speeder to transport U.S. Army personnel during the building of the Northwest Communications line.
Photo: C.J. Swanson

As the deadline for a hook up between Dawson Creek and Washington neared, the line was a long way from completion. The worst blizzard in memory slowed the work to a crawl. Jimmy Holden, who was then agent at Hythe, recalls the men used ingenuity to get the line operating in time. By nailing wires to trees and stringing it along fence posts as a temporary measure, they managed to have it operational by the deadline.[15] Adjustments were made later and the

Agent Jimmy Holden's office in Hythe station
Photo: C.J. Swanson

line was in full operation by the winter of 1943-44.[16]

At the end of the war, the U.S. Government turned this system over to the Government of Canada. The telegraph and teletype portion became part of the CNR communications system. Alberta Government Telephones [AGT] was alloted a channel to provide long distance telephone service. NAR protested loudly. The railway wanted compensation for loss of telegraph revenue and was paid $9 thousand for one year by the Dominion government. But it was a battle that was won by AGT.

The U.S. communications system was in the throes of construction when Henry P. Briggs left CPR's communications department in September 1942. As NAR's supervi-

sor of communications, the quiet, easy-going man set about overhauling the railway's system. The expansion and improvement was carried out gradually. A big advancement was the *H carrier system*, purchased as army surplus after the war and installed from Edmonton to Peace River. Unfortunately, ill health forced Briggs to retire in November 1949; but the department continued to modernize under the hand of Walter McNalley. Communications was a very integral part of the railway's operations, in times of peace and war.

During the war, the communications systems were an important link to the rest of the world for residents of Dawson Creek. When disaster struck on the evening of Saturday, 13 February 1943, NAR's telegraph was the sole link to the outside, because the Dominion government telegraph office was demolished. That evening as station staff worked overtime, in an attempt to lessen the backlog at the busy terminal, they heard the wail of the fire siren. A fire was blazing a short distance away. A string of boxcars on the team track blocked the view from the station windows.

Pulling on their coats, Bill Donlevy and Secretary Connie Langfeldt went outside to get a better view. As they neared the point where the way cars were split for the crossing someone yelled "dynamite" and there was an earth-shaking explosion. They dove for the shelter of a boxcar as burning debris, sparks, bales of copper wire, crossarms and picaroons showered around them. When they saw a cap and scalp stuck to a boxcar, they knew how fortunate they were to find themselves unhurt.[17] The deathly silence that followed the blast was soon broken by cries of pain and terror. Ticket Agent Harry Newton was not so fortunate. Flying debris damaged his wrist but he was soon back at work nursing it in a sling.

Switch Foreman Spike Sullivan and helpers Bill Howe and Charlie Burns were switching in the yards when they noticed the flames belching out of a livery barn. In an attempt to move the boxcars spotted on the team track away from the burning material, Howe climbed up to release the hand brakes on the cars. He was walking over the top of a car, when he heard someone yell "dynamite." Then he had a brief interlude as an

angel: "The next thing I was sailing through the air like a bird, but being young and agile I landed on my feet unhurt."[18]

When they recovered from the initial shock, station staff worked against time to prevent the whole station from going up in flames. They had no time to watch the flames that were rapidly engulfing the main business section of the town. Inside, filing cabinets lay with their contents spewing out onto the floor, office equipment, desks and typewriters were up ended, thousands of fragments from shattered glass and papers were everywhere. The fuel oil heaters with chimneys awry were dangerous until righted and their chimneys reconnected.

It began as a fire in the livery barn of a contractor constructing the telegraph line down the Alcan Highway. The wooden structure, in which 60 cases of dynamite and 20 cases of detonating caps were stored, caught fire.[19] Fire trucks from the town and the U.S. Army had it under control when without warning there was an explosion. The wind whipped the flames into a frenzy as they swept through the block on their path of destruction. Buildings within a six-block radius were destroyed or damaged. The U.S. Army took charge of the situation. A large firefighting force augmented the efforts of the residents. While U.S. tank trucks hauled precious water from Pouce Coupe, 8 miles away, the water from an NAR engine was used for the fire hose.

Nick Moskalyk, then pump repairman,

rushed by track motor to the scene. On arrival at the pump house, he found the cylinder head on the engine broken. He recalls, "They needed 40 thousand gallons right now and no fooling."[20] Superintendent Deakin had arrived before Moskalyk. Together they travelled in the Studebaker rail car back to Tupper to get a cylinder head from the pump engine at that water tank. Back in Dawson Creek, Moskalyk soon had water pumping like there was no tomorrow. Breakfast on the superintendent's business car was welcome the following morning after 24 hours without a meal.

Flying glass injured people in the streets, in stores, in restaurants and in their homes. Express Messenger Charlie Wilton was enjoying dinner at the home of his niece in Dawson Creek when the explosion shook the house and shattered the windows. Glass splattered across the food on the table ending the meal and leaving Wilton with a gash in his forehead.[21] Seated with his back to a window W.C. Donlevy was dining with the Elliotts in the station living quarters at the time. The back of his head, neck and arms were a mass of cuts caused by the shards of flying glass as the window imploded.[22] Jessie Elliott escaped injury by a stroke of luck. She was in the kitchen and returned to find her chair at the table covered with glass. She spent the rest of the evening treating cuts and burns and worrying about the money stashed in the living-room.

Not all the injuries were treated at the railway station. The hospitals were overflowing with injured. The railway's medical officer, Dr. Leo Giroux, was on his evening rounds at the village hospital when the disaster occurred. The blast had knocked out the power plant, but resourceful hospital staff used candles until electricity was restored. Extra staff came by plane from Fort St. John and landed on the airfield lit by flares and automobile headlights.

Had the explosion occurred later, Saturday night crowds would have thronged the streets and the loss of life might have been greater. Most of the U.S. soldiers were having dinner at the time. The more seriously injured were flown to Edmonton. But for five people there was no recovery.[23] Four civilians and a soldier died trying to stop the fire from spreading.[24] Two were on the roof of an adjacent building, vainly spraying water from an U.S. Army tanker when the explosion came. To the onlookers, it seemed as if they vaporized before their very eyes.[25]

By 10:00 p.m. Saturday, the fire was under control. Soldiers patrolling the streets of the town kept honest men honest. On Sunday night, there were still fires smoldering. If it were not for the people milling through its streets Dawson Creek with its boarded up windows would have looked like an abandoned town. Everyone wanted to have a look at the disaster area. U.S. Army police kept the area cordoned off. The damage was estimated to be $350 thousand.

At the railway station, staff were swamped with a deluge of incoming and outgoing telegrams, as well as press releases.

Every telegraph operator was pressed into service, working in shifts. To handle the overflow the railway opened a second telegraph office to manage the commercial telegraph business.

The following week an inquest was held into the deaths of the five people. Allan Elliott was a member of the jury. The verdict reached was gross negligence in the method of storage of dynamite in the possession of a sub-contractor of the Miller Construction Co. Miller Construction Co. was found guilty and fined $10 thousand, but the conviction was appealed, and quashed.[26] By this time,

the burned out block in Dawson Creek had new, modern buildings in various stages of construction.

The road that was such a remarkable achievement was renamed in June 1943. "The Alaska Military Highway" was to replace "Alcan" Brigadier General, J.A. O'Connor announced. The Canadian government did not react to that announcement until a month later when it was decided "Alaska Highway" was the most suitable.[27] The original name had been chosen to pay tribute to Canada's involvement in the project, but apparently Canadians disliked it.

An entire block of Dawson Creek's business section burned in 1943.
Photo: Provincial Archives of Alberta,
H. Pollard Collection, P6856

Work on the Alaska Highway began winding down. By 1944, gravel surfacing was completed. All that remained to be done was the construction of some permanent bridges. The process of shipping out machinery, trucks, army huts and material from Dawson Creek began in 1944 and continued throughout 1945. A great deal of surplus material was taken to the local dump and bulldozed under. Through War Assets Corporation sales, Canadian companies and organizations bought some surplus equipment.

In proportion to the amount of tonnage that moved over the NAR during the war years there were relatively few derailments. An accident that occurred on 18 January 1944 stood out in Glen Barker's memory. A poor joint between 60 lb. rail and 90 lb. rail caused train No. 1 to derail. Locomotive CP 5104 and a mail car overturned. The mail car caught fire and Mail Clerk A.R. Osterman suffered an injured back, but the staff managed to save the mail. Fireman Eugene Toutant escaped injury by jumping clear as the engine ploughed a furrow and came to rest by a fence.[28] He gave up his firing rights after that and returned to the safer occupation of watchman. Rather than jump and risk being hit by the tender, Locomotive Engineer Glen Barker stayed with the locomotive. He climbed out in one piece. Instructions from Master Mechanic Stewart told Barker to go to Smith and take Train No. 2 into Edmonton. Stewart knew that if Barker did not get back on the engine immediately, there was the

possibility that he never would.

Derailment near Kinuso on 18 January 1944
Photo: T.K. McConkey

Although no equipment was damaged, Orville Willis had a hair-raising experience on News Year's Day 1945. It was his second trip as conductor and the temperature was at least minus 35 degrees. No one seemed too anxious to work that night, including the engineer who had been celebrating the dawn of a new year. The men in the caboose commented on the bitterly cold, clear night as the train climbed the hill up from Watino. Was that a shout? A cry of distress? No one lived along the stretch of track enveloped in the eerie half light. Willis pulled the air, the train stopped and he walked back down the track. To his surprise he found the engineer lying in the ditch with a broken ankle. Fireman Tony Bussieres had been running the engine while the engineer loosened up some frozen coal in the tender. He had lost his balance and the fireman had not noticed he was missing.[29]

By the end of 1945, the Alaska Highway maintenance operations had been transferred to Canada, roads had been improved and constructed throughout the Peace River country, and Dawson Creek had grown up. It was now a town with a permanent population of 3 200, and the Alaska Highway was a transportation artery in North America that would continue to grow in importance.

21

Rails to Riches

The dust surrounding the agreement to build the Alaska Highway was scarcely settled when other decisions affecting NAR were made in Washington. With the threat of invasion by the Japanese imminent, the U.S. turned to Canada to ensure a supply of oil to Alaska.[1] At this time Canada also became a supplier of pitchblende to its southern neighbor.

In 1942 the Canol agreement, an abbreviation for Canadian Oil, was signed between the U.S. and Canada, and arrangements made with Imperial Oil to use its oil fields at Fort Norman, in the Northwest Territories.[2] The first well was drilled there by Imperial Oil in 1920.[3] Now the U.S. planned a $135 million oil pipeline that would straddle the mountains of the Yukon.[4] This decision increased the volume of traffic to Waterways, the gateway to navigation on the MacKenzie River system.

Originally, the American plan was to bury the pipeline but U.S. officials knew nothing about the muskeg and permafrost to be tamed. They were incredulous when told by Fort McMurray freighters Mickey and Pat Ryan that the permafrost could be as deep as 90 feet in the territory to be crossed.[5] The plans were quickly reversed and the pipeline built over the ground.

Coinciding with the opening of the navigation season in May 1942, the railway began transporting carloads of steel pipe, supplies and machinery to Waterways. The substandard track was Roadmaster Ernie Law's responsibility. The poor condition of the roadbed was the result of lack of funds for the necessary improvements rather than neglect.[6]

Because the original ballasting material used on the northern part of the line was obtained from sandhills close by, maintenance crews continued to use sand from sand cuts. Otto Michetti recalls, "Eventually the supply receded further and further away from the track, at which time wooden rails were placed to allow a push car closer to the receded supply. A contraption turnstile was invented by Foreman Mike Havrikeska to balance the loaded car and turn it on to the track to be taken where required."[7]

Many of the section foremen and section-men were Indians and Metis from the surrounding area. The majority were good workers, but understanding the pay cheque system was a problem for some. When they were paid they disappeared for about four days. Once the money had dwindled they returned to their jobs, resulting in four days' pay being deducted from the next pay cheque. They demanded to know why the amounts on the pay cheques kept reducing and the foreman had difficulty explaining the process to their satisfaction.[8]

A small, wiry section foreman, who had been with the railway since 1927, knew how to solve the problem. Besides his railway job, Walter Buchkowski ran a cattle ranch, along with a grocery and dry goods store. He took out contracts for ties with the railways, hired local people to manufacture them, then paid them in trade from his store. His success in business caused some envy. One Lac La Biche businessman was so bold as to charge that Buchkowski was neglecting his railway duties in favor of his business enterprises. An investigation by the railway found otherwise. In fact, Buchkowski's section at Mile 149 was the best kept on the Waterways subdivision. Otto Michetti recalls that in the 10 years he was roadmaster in that area, "He never gave me an opportunity to delegate

Sand over the rails caused Locomotive No.54 to roll near Mile 27.5, Lac La Biche Subdivision, July, 1942. Brakeman Latimer and Engineer Con Kennedy were not seriously injured.
Photo: Courtesy of R.D.C. Comrie

work to him. It was always done before I could say so and always done in a satisfactory manner."[9]

The section foremen and their crews worked long hours to keep the track operational. During the first nine days of June 1942, 10 special trains carried some 2 200 U.S. soldiers in 113 passenger cars to Waterways.[10] Their arrival caused mass confusion in Waterways. A sea of tents were soon erected on Little Prairie, between the railway terminal and Fort McMurray. Army contractors also erected a hotel, with the luxury of hot and cold running water. From Fort McMurray a large number of the soldiers were transported by air to Fort Norman.

Len Williams was a sleeping car porter on trains taking the soldiers north. Usually the highest ranking U.S. Army personnel and citizens of note were accommodated in Williams's car. He had come from Mississippi, before the railway was built and settled in the Amber Valley area of Alberta, where a number of other black immigrants homesteaded. He became a permanent employee of the railway in 1928, and a well-known personality along the 385 miles between Edmonton and Fort McMurray. Tales are told of Williams' friendliness. Like other railway employees he often spent his layover time in Edmonton shopping for the people along the Waterways line or doing their banking. When children from Fort McMurray travelled alone on the train he took care of them.[11] By the time Williams reached retirement age in 1957, the golden age of passenger travel was on the wane, but he enjoyed its heyday during the war years.

Sleeping Car Porter Len Williams
Photo: Provincial Archives of Alberta, PA20115

Harry Gough was a dining-sleeping car conductor on the Waterways run. On one trip Bishop Breynat was among the passengers and produced a bottle of well-aged brandy to share a nightcap with the crew and his fellow travellers. Gough was stopped by a friend on his way back to the smoking lounge to partake of the brandy. A little irritated by the delay, he said, "Don't stop me now. Bishop Breynat has offered me a drink of 40-year-old brandy, and I want to get there before it becomes 41-years old."[12]

Sydney Bradburn had little time for socializing, his responsibilities were increased in June 1942 with his appointment to assistant superintendent. He had represented his colleagues in the Brotherhood of Railway Trainmen for many years. In this capacity, he and Superintendent Deakin had locked horns, like two old rams, on numerous occasions.

That summer, Tom LaBrier got a job as a trainman and made a trip to Waterways. It was a lot different from his memories of his first trip at the age of five. Of that time he wrote, "I don't know how to express myself other than it was complete love. The environment stimulated all of my senses to such a degree that I can still see the people that were there, and the smell of oil, steam and the movement of the train has stayed with me all of my life."[13] Railroading had been the career of many of his relatives and LaBrier had grown up on a steady diet of railway yarns. His great grandfather, John Charles McLeod, had worked for the Intercolonial Railway and the CPR. His aunt, Becky, had married the ED & BC's Chief Dispatcher Reg Lee. His grandfather, Fred McLeod, had worked for the CPR and the ED & BC, and his father, Michael LaBrier, had been an early conductor. The blood of a railroader ran in Tom LaBrier's veins and in time, he too became a conductor.

The influx of Americans into Fort McMurray in 1942 gave the town a financial boost. The work load of the railway's engineering department also increased. At Waterways the railway rearranged and extended the yard tracks to accommodate the extra business. Wilf Lawton, who was then assistant engineer, supervised the laying of an additional 9 155 feet of trackage in the U.S. Army yard. Section Foreman Frank Meisinger and his section crew at Waterways handled the laying of steel. It was at that time that a bridge, financed by the U.S. Army, was built over the Hangingstone Creek and the track extended 1.5 miles. The railway finally reached Little Prairie but the Waterways station remained where it was. By the beginning of July, 934 car loads of material for the Canol project had reached the rail head. [The extra trackage has long since been removed.]

The sturdily built Meisinger is Austrian by birth and had been with the railway since 1930. His remarkable ability to handle large numbers of men was soon evident. Consequently, he often supervised extra gangs all over the railway system. It was not unusual for Mary Schmidek [now Hryniuk] to feed 70 – 100 men on Meisinger's gangs.[14] Not many tangled with Meisinger. He expected his men to produce but he was no shrinking violet himself when it came to work. His great physical strength became legendary on the railway. Sectionman Wm. "Bill Banko" Bence was also not afraid of work. He was a powerful man who liked to compare his strength with Meisinger's. Banko would lift one tie on

U.S. Army troops arrive at Waterways.
Photo: Provincial Archives of Alberta, A14441

his shoulder, then Meisinger would lift two. Banko would then lift three to win the contest.[15]

Paul Sawin, who later became section foreman, relieved on the Waterways line and recalls that Banko "could lift 660 lbs. of rail" alone. "We had to drive steel. . . . I unhooked the push car to put one end of the steel on it and one end on the track motor. Bill said, 'Move the push car away.' He walked up, picked up the rail and put it on the car."[16] Because of the shortage of men during the war years, Banko moved to Waterways. There he did the work of at least three sectionmen.[17] Locomotive tenders, with a capacity for 16 to 20 tons of coal, often arrived almost empty. With a large scoop he threw the coal five or six feet up into the tender. If

there was a west wind blowing coal dust made him unrecognizable. After completion of the Canol project Banko returned to the section crew. [In 1980 Mile 14.3 Edmonton Subdivision was named Banko Junction in his honor.]

From Waterways, cargo for the Canol pipeline was shipped down the Mackenzie River by barge to Fort Fitzgerald, then taken along the Ryan Brothers' portage to Fort Smith. The transportation companies already plying the waters of the Mackenzie River could only handle a small portion of the cargo. The U.S. Army had to build barges to get their supplies to destination.[18] The first oil began to flow in the pipeline in late 1943.

Every year at Waterways, the opening of

the navigation season meant a sharp increase in the work load of station staff. Shipments for the Canol project soon had the railway yards full. Agent Bert Viney had seven trains in the yard one day. Engineer Glen Barker had to hold his train out of the terminal for three hours while Conductor Amos Slack got his train assembled to move south.

Wilf Lawton, Engineer Maintenance of Way and Structures, 1949-1965
Photo: Courtesy of Mrs. Kay Lawton

Viney handled all the station work alone, working long hours. It was not until his health broke down that an assistant and an operator joined him. This was later increased to a staff of 13. Happy to have the help, the kindly man took his young staff under his wing. Pressure caused hemorrhaging of his inner ear, temporarily disabling him in 1944. Evacuation of the U.S. Army from Norman Wells was just beginning and Maurice Mahood's guiding hand took over the running of the station.

Waterways was Mahood's favorite agency, although he worked hardest there and did not have the finest of housing. During the busy season from April through October, from 1936 until 1940 he worked as operator. During that time, he and his wife lived in tents with built-up wooden sides. In the fall, he was laid off and scrounged around for spare board jobs all winter.

The production of oil at Norman Wells far exceeded expectations. After the Japanese vacated the Aleutian Islands the urgent need for the oil, the pipeline and refinery dissipated. By May 1945, the U.S. Army had shipped the last of its personnel and equipment south from Waterways. Some years later the pipeline was dismantled.[19]

There were other activities besides the Canol pipeline to keep the Waterways branch busy. During this time NAR became a pawn in the race to create an atomic bomb before the Germans did. The U.S. wanted uranium with its energy producing qualities to further its atomic research. The nearest source was Eldorado Gold Mines Limited at Port Radium on Great Bear Lake, in the Northwest Territories.[20] There the landscape about the mine was dotted with piles of pitchblende, from which valuable uranium could be extracted. In covert negotiations with the LaBine brothers, ownership of Eldorado and its subsidiary the Northern Transportation Company Ltd. changed hands and became Crown corporations.[21]

At Waterways, NAR stood poised on the

threshold of the atomic age. Packed in bags, the ore was transported to the rail head via the northern waterways during the shipping season.[22] There the heavy sacks were loaded into gondola and boxcars for transporting to Edmonton. A shocked world learned of the use of uranium when Hiroshima, in southwestern Japan, was devastated by an atomic bomb on 6 August 1945. Fifteen years later the bottom dropped out of the uranium market and Port Radium became a ghost town soon afterwards.[23]

Left to right: *General Manager J.A. MacArthur, Assistant Superintendent Syd Bradburn and Yardmaster Jack Vollans inspect loads at Dunvegan Yards.*
Photo: Provincial Archives of Alberta, A. Blyth Collection, BL502/1

Diesel engine 208
Photo: Nicholas Morant
CP Rail Corporate Archives

Train No. 8 on main line near Dunvegan Yards. Locomotive No. 161 was purchased from C.P.R. in June 1947.

Part Six

The Final Years: 1946-1980

Engineer Frank Lapine at the controls of steam locomotive
Photo: Courtesy of R.D.C. Comrie

22

The Bubble Bursts

In the aftermath of the war, railway traffic began to settle into more normal patterns. Upgrading and improvements necessitated by heavy traffic during the war years continued. Railway employees who had enlisted, returned to protected or guaranteed jobs. This resulted in quite a reshuffling of personnel due to seniority regulations affecting certain positions.

Highway building and grading in the Peace River country was at its zenith.[1] In co-operation with the Canadian government the highway running north from Grimshaw to Hay River, NWT, was built. The Whitecourt-Valleyview cutoff was completed. As major all-weather highways began to give rapid access to areas served by the main line of the railway, competition from highway transport intensified. The increasing popularity of the private automobile made train travel less attractive. Curtailment of dining and sleeping car service followed.

In July 1945, the entire train dispatching staff was moved to headquarters in the CPR building in Edmonton. Upgrading of the communications system prompted the centralization of operations. The move caused a great upheaval for dispatchers and their families. Chief Dispatcher George Thompson, who had been in the office in McLennan for 25 years, was among those who left a lot of memories behind.

At that time, Lee Halasa, who was destined to become NAR's chief engineer and gain the unqualified respect of his peers on the parent lines, was a building inspector with the CPR. In the fall of 1946, a notice was circulated regarding a vacancy for an instrumentman on the NAR. He applied for the job. Some two weeks later Halasa was on his way to Waterways to meet C.J.L. "Sandy" Sanderson, whom he was replacing. Sanderson, who was billeted in an old bunk car, invited him for breakfast at 7:00 a.m. the following morning. To Halasa's astonishment the table was beautifully set with a white tablecloth and crystal.

Sanderson was short in stature, but every inch an Englishman. The bachelor attempted to maintain a semblance of gentility while working in conditions that shunned it. If a train with the general manager's business car passed by while he was out on a job, he always stopped to wave. Once, while on a ditching survey, a train came by with the business car. As Sanderson began to wave the tip of his snowshoe caught in a fence spinning him in a cartwheel. He did not find the scenario nearly as amusing as the officials in the private car.[2]

Lillian Dominy remembers him as "a very charming man . . . he had been a captain in the First World War."[3] Prior to joining the NAR as a seasonal instrumentman, he had spent 22 years with the CPR on engineering work and four years with the Dominion government locating air fields. Now he was 65-years-old, going to the west coast to retire and leaving an opening for a younger man.

As Lee Halasa settled into his new job, he also settled into his new home in Edmonton. He had found it by answering an advertisement offering room and board. On arrival at the house he explained he was a newcomer to Edmonton and had just begun working for the NAR. At the mention of the railway, the lady of the house immediately invited him in and introduced herself as Nellie Prest.[4] He had stumbled on the home of Ben Prest, who had left the railway some 15 years earlier. Prest and Halasa became firm friends, whose favorite topic of conversation was engineering.

Gradually, Halasa became acquainted with the roadmasters and their territories. Among them was George Natale, an Italian immigrant whom everyone called "Tony." The World War I veteran worked for the CPR before coming to the ED & BC in 1921. He kept a close watch on the speed of trains. If they were running late, engineers often exceeded the speed limit to make up time. Once when the roadmaster was riding the passenger train, Johnny Scott's hand was heavy on the throttle. At Rycroft, Natale walked up to the engine to lecture the engineer on the dangers of excessive speed. Scott was using his oil feeder on his locomotive at the time. With every, "Yes, George. Yes, George" he squirted oil onto Natale's shoes. By the time the roadmaster discovered what was happening his shoes were a mess.[5] The train crews revelled in teasing the rotund bachelor, who enjoyed it and often turned the joke on them. If anyone dared play such tricks on any other official of the railway it would not have been tolerated.

In the agents' offices, strung out along the line, life was not dull either. C.J. "Swany" Swanson was in Peace River relieving the agent. As he prepared to meet the challenge of another day on 30 December 1947 darkness still shrouded the station. Despite the minus 30 degrees temperature, he expected nothing more than a routine day. A train crew had left for Judah with the first cut of cars of a double. [The hill was so steep 2.6

percent tonnage had to be reduced and several trips made. This is known as doubling.] At the summit Brakeman Wm. "Bill" Lee uncoupled caboose 13002. The unoccupied caboose had different plans and rolled backward on the descending grade. Conductor W.C. "Scotty" Hall gaped as his caboose careened toward Peace River. Watching it negotiate the first curve on the seven mile route he believed it unlikely he would ever see it in one piece again.

In the station the sound of screeching wheel flanges was familiar, but a train-less caboose flashing past the window at about 60 mph meant trouble. By the time Swanson grabbed his jacket and a lantern, the caboose had crossed the Peace River bridge and was climbing the ascending grade toward Roma. He rushed to warn traffic on the bridge, which shared railway, highway and pedestrian traffic. He stood helpless as the caboose used the grades like a seesaw, moving too fast to permit boarding. On its third run by the station it slowed down enough for Swanson to jump aboard and set the handbrake.[6]

The anxious crew was in hot pursuit with the engine in reverse. Around every curve the men expected to see the remains of the caboose on the hillside. They arrived at the station to find it waiting for them. The commotion had caused little more than a startled horse as it pulled the milk wagon toward the bridge. Since the only damage was overheated wheels and a burned mattress it was agreed not to report the incident.

All involved thought they had the best kept secret on the railway until six weeks later when a lady blew the whistle on them. At a Board of Trade meeting in Peace River, the chatty lady complimented General Manager MacArthur on his railway before mentioning, "It was sure funny what happened to the caboose."[7] That was the first MacArthur had heard about the incident. In no time flat one of his famous "butterflies" was winging its way to Superintendent Deakin. After a full investigation, discipline was meted out to all involved, including Swanson. He was the recipient of 15 merit marks for getting the runaway caboose under control. In the same envelope bearing the good tidings was another memorandum assessing his record with 10 demerit marks for not reporting the event.[8]

That was one of many an averted crisis, but some happened in spite of the best efforts of railway workers. The summer of 1949 was hot and dry. In the Assineau River Valley a lightning strike touched off a forest fire, that was soon out of control and making short work of the railway bridge at Assineau.[9] Before Train No. 1 was due at Slave Lake, Agent Gordon Waite alerted all vehicle owners in the area, asking them to remain on standby. When the southbound passenger train arrived at Kinuso Agent Dave Myron held it there. Passengers from both trains were transferred using the vehicles on the highway to circumvent the damaged bridge. Superintendent Deakin happened to be on the northbound train and he stayed to direct

Edmonton Chamber of Commerce members toured northern Alberta via the "Friendship Train."
Left to Right: Superintendent J.E. Deakin, Traffic Assistant G.J. McVicar, Trainmen George
Kopf and Wilbur Wintermute, Road Foreman of Engines R.D.C. Comrie, Engineer Tom Lycan,
Fireman Jack Griffith, Conductor Claus Turninga and General Manager J.M. McArthur.
Photo: McDermid Studios

the rebuilding of the bridge. When work began there were officials in plenty. The men who got the work done were also there. Archie McKillop, with a bridge and building gang, was moved in from Pouce Coupe to rebuild the west end of the bridge, while David Little's crew worked on the Edmonton side under the eagle eye of Bridge and Building Master George McCracken.

Operating one of the pile drivers was young Stan Hryniuk. As the son of Section Foreman Paul Hryniuk he had grown up on the railway at Ellscott. To work for the NAR was then his ambition, but ambitions change and he eventually became an official in the provincial government's public works department. He first became acquainted with the pile driver in 1946 as fireman for

Washday for Pile Driver Operator Stan Hryniuk
Photo: Courtesy of S. Hryniuk

*Cook Mary Schmidek toils over a
hot stove to feed extra gang crews.*
Photo: Courtesy of S. Hryniuk

Hoist Engineer Bill Ross. Ross had only been retired for a few months when Hryniuk's skill on the machine was put to the test at Assineau.[10] The men worked almost continuously for two days and nights, often with the superintendent alongside them, until the bridge was opened to traffic.

It was while working with the bridge and building department that Hryniuk met the pretty girl who would become his wife, Mary Schmidek. Margaret Crawford, who was an experienced cook on the big gangs, taught the younger woman the ropes. All the cooking was done on two big coal stoves and she recalls baking 20 to 25 loaves of bread a day. A bull cook kept the cooks and cookees supplied with coal, wood and water. There were no refrigerators and meat was stored in a pantry with blocks of ice. The facility had to be washed regularly with baking soda. If the lockers were dirty, the meat crawled with maggots. Mary Hryniuk remembers one such incident, "I had to clean the whole thing out. It was alive. We had to take all that meat and bury it. . . .Those ice boxes were good if people kept them clean."[11]

All supplies were ordered from Boarding Car Inspector Arthur Williams, who was located at Dunvegan Yards. Williams had worked in the CNR's boarding car department for two years before joining NAR as a cook. He cooked on the bridge and building and extra gangs before enlisting in the Canadian Army in World War II. Upon his return, his seniority was such that he was in a position to "bump" Harry Gough, who had been promoted to boarding car inspector in his absence.

Ingenuity was a trade mark of NAR's railroaders. In 1949 it was much needed when a steel water tank was moved from Clairmont to Grande Prairie where the water supply was more suitable for locomotives. The steel tank was raised and tracks built beneath it. Then General Car Foreman Paul Webb directed its loading. It was quite a sight as it straddled a gondola car. En route to Grande Prairie the curves had to be negotiated by using jacks to control the centre of gravity and keep the tank upright. Engineer Jack Tullock gladly turned the locomotive controls over to Road Foreman of Engines Clarence Comrie. It was a slow process travelling the eight miles in eight hours.

Water tank enroute to its new destination
Photo: Courtesy of R.D.C. Comrie

A strike in August 1950 crippled railway service in North America. During the disruption tracks had to be patrolled by management staff before trains could run. Otto Michetti was among those patrolling the track and recalls, "the men were legislated to return to work by the federal government, which appointed Justice Emmett Hall to arbitrate the dispute and he awarded them everything they had struck for, arguing that their standards had been neglected since World War II."[12] The strike resulted in increased wages and a 40 hour work week.[13]

The settlement of the nine-day strike spawned a competition to see which railway could get the first freight train on the move. In Dunvegan Yards a locomotive was at the ready. After the "back to work" order reached union strikers in Edmonton, Yardmaster Norman McCrum summoned a crew immediately. A train was assembled and on its way in short order. Engineer H.W. "Harry" Dyer and Fireman J.D. "Jim" Ewart chuckled at the thought that they might beat CNR and CPR as their 42 car freight train left Dunvegan Yards for Dawson Creek. *The Edmonton Journal* of 31 August trumpeted the outcome, "NAR Freight Train First Out of City as Strike Ends." Operations were barely back to normal when the running crews went on strike and traffic was once again briefly interrupted.

J.M. MacArthur, who had steered NAR toward modernization, retired at the end of 1950, and John F. Cooper from the CNR stepped into his shoes. The Scotsman had immigrated to Canada with his parents at the age of 10 and settled in Winnipeg where his father was employed by the Grand Trunk Pacific Railway. At age 16 Cooper became a clerk with the CPR, but left them two years later to take up a similar position with the GTP. The desire to defend his country lured him to enlist in 1918. Following discharge and some business training, he joined a livestock company, but railroading still held his imagination. He rejoined the GTP as a draftsman and was soon climbing the ladder of success. When the GTP was taken over by CNR, he was successively roadmaster, assistant superintendent, and superintendent. In 1950, he was general superintendent of the Alberta district and in line for a promotion to a senior position in Winnipeg. This did not materialize. Instead he was appointed general manager of NAR – a crushing blow from which he found it difficult to recover.

The mustachioed, soft spoken Cooper was not as dynamic an individual as his predecessor. Recognizing he had inherited a well organized railway, he relied heavily on the expertise of his management team. When mid-management vacancies occurred he made appointments from within the company. In his leisure hours he enjoyed sports, particularly curling. At least once a year he took his curling rink into the Peace River country to play in bonspiels. He was the skip and a good one.

As with all switches in management, changes were inevitable. One change that occasioned comment was the building of a

J.F Cooper, General Manager, NAR, 1951-1964

separate entrance and passage to the general manager's office. The regular inspection trips that were a trademark of MacArthur's tenure also dwindled. But there was plenty of activity in other departments. In an attempt to standardize the rules, the Board of Railway Commissioners instructed the NAR to adopt the Uniform Code of Operating Rules, which replaced the General Train and Interlocking Rules. Superintendent Deakin and Kenneth R. Perry, assistant to the general manager, were sent to Montreal to familiarize themselves with the new rules so that they might instruct NAR officers upon their return. Several officers were delegated the task of instructing employees in the new rules and supervising examinations.

Section crews repair washed out track near Mile 199.3, Waterways Subdivision, May 1951.
Photo: O. Michetti

It was during this time that oil became the fuel used to power locomotives. The program of conversion was carried out, under the direction of Archie Wotherspoon, who had succeeded Charles Stewart as master mechanic in 1946. The tall, easy-going man had served his apprenticeship on the CNR, before transferring to NAR. He broke his service to try his hand in the business world, but returned to the railway as machinist and became locomotive foreman at McLennan during the war years. A smoker, he battled lung cancer before succumbing to the disease at 56 years of age.

Others also died while in service. A heart attack was to blame in the death of Conductor Leander "Lee" Card at Chisholm in 1942. A native of Nebraska, Card came north to visit relatives in the Sexsmith area. There he could pursue his love of horses, but it did not put bread and butter on the table and he joined the railway in 1919. Card was alone in the caboose at the time of his death. He had fallen from the cupola, striking his head and died 30 hours later in hospital. His son, Trainman Robert "Bob" Card, was overseas fighting for his country at the time, but returned to NAR and followed in his father's footsteps by becoming a conductor.

Four years after Card's death, a call boy found W.E. "Bill" Bell dead in his caboose. Conductor Jack Cole found his brakeman, dressed in his heavy Stanfields underwear, sitting up in bed, stiff as a board. Worried he might be accused of murder when police arrived, he told them, "Look him over. I didn't choke him." He need not have worried, the older man had died from a heart attack.

Heart attacks were not the only killer. The railway spur line to the Chisholm lumber mill was every bit as lethal. When setting cars off westbound, train crews often resorted to dropping cars into the spur. This practice was against the rules and caused the accidental death of Conductor Bill Yeadon in 1944 and Conductor Jens "Swede" Hansen in 1956. Although of German extraction, Yeadon was born in England. He joined the ED & BC in November 1918, but had little opportunity to use his fluent German. His cheerful outlook on life was welcomed by the way-freight crew with whom he worked for quite some time before the accident.[14] Hansen was Danish by birth and had come into

*Master Mechanic Archie Wotherspoon
in steam shop at Dunvegan Yards.*
Photo: McDermid Studios

the Peace River country prior to the arrival of the railway. He tried homesteading in the Sexsmith area in 1913 before becoming a permanent railway employee in 1928.

In a similar type of accident at Mitsue in 1951, Conductor Glen Kirkland lived to tell the tale but lost a leg. Remembered as the best baseball and hockey player in the Peace River country before the accident, he will only say, "I was in good shape." He was working as a brakeman the day of the mishap. In the process of dropping off a water car for Charlie McCormick's bridge and building outfit, he lost his balance. He says, "I was sure I had control of it, but I lost it and down I went. Gee, did I make love to those ties. . . .The brake rigging [beneath the car] tore my clothes right off. I went to get up and said 'Oh, that's my foot' and reached over." He remembers the trip to McLennan as pain racked in spite of the ministrations of the Slave Lake district nurse and Dr. Harvey Fish from McLennan, who broke all speed records driving to meet the train at High Prairie.

Conductor Jack Sissons and the rest of the crew were certain Kirkland would never skate again, but he proved them wrong. He was on skates the following winter, but he did miss the fun of participating in hockey games. He has had about 25 artificial legs over the years and some of the first ones got him into some embarrassing situations. Once he slipped in an Edmonton store knocking himself out and his prosthesis sideways. When he revived a little old lady was by him saying, "Look, he broke his leg too." He replied, "It's all right. I'll fix that" and proceeded to adjust his leg as the lady visibly blanched.[15]

Alfred "Sheep Herder" Emery also lost his life on the railway, but not at Chisholm. The brakeman was riding the pilot of the engine, which had no footboards. While attempting to pull his hood over his head to ward off the chill of the night air, he lost his footing and tumbled beneath the train.[16] In the engine cab Russell "Smiler" Hadley waited in vain for the brakeman's signals. Upon checking, he found the body in pieces on the main track.

For Clarence Comrie it was one of the most difficult investigations he ever undertook. He recalls, "I felt so sorry for Smiler. There was nothing he could do." Hadley was so distraught; his voice was little more than a whisper. He had been with the railway since 1913 and running engines since 1919. The investigation was a terrible strain on the naturally reserved man, who was a low-key conversationalist at the best of times. The customary smile was missing from the tortured face as he tried to explain what could have happened. Although it was not his fault the farm boy from Winterburn, Alberta, spent many a sleepless night reliving the events of that day.

Sleeping Car Porter Jack Panteluk also was among those who lost their lives on the railway. He was on his last trip before retiring in August 1958. Shortly after departure of the train from Peace River, he was found unconscious lying on the tracks with both legs and an arm severed. He died in hospital the following day. Thirty years later his colleagues still wonder how the accident could have happened. Perhaps he was running to get on the train, slipped and fell between the tracks.[17]

Panteluk was no rookie. He had been with NAR since 1930. As a news agent he was a slick operator, who loved to outwit his clientele. When a passenger asked, "How much are the oranges?" He would sometimes reply, "15 cents each, three for 50 cents." The passenger invariably responded, "I'll take three." *The NAR Buffet and Sleeping Car Department News Bulletin* recognized Panteluk's salesman abilities in its June 1949 issue. "News Agent Jack Panteluk continues to lead the field in the matter of average sales. Is there no one to give Jack a little competition in this regard?" It also reported, "A genius is a man who can buy from Mr. Panteluk and sell to Mr. Walker at a profit." [We met the Sleeping Car Porter Harley Walker earlier].

The revenues from the dining car operations continued to plummet. Better roads for automobile traffic and air service were prime competition for passenger traffic. During the war years, dining car staff had been severely overworked, which initiated their organization in 1944. With J.P.D. Morin as chairman of the NAR committee, they were represented by a Calgary branch of the Brotherhood of Railway Trainmen. Criteria for membership included being over 21 and white. This caused some difficulties for NAR, whose dining car crews were mostly under 21 and some were black.

A veteran of World War I, Percy Morin had been a cigar maker before learning the news agent business on the CNR. His closest brush with fame was when he rolled a special order of cigars for the Duke of Windsor. He transferred to the NAR dining cars in 1930 and during the busy war years he and his wife, Eva, served meals on car "McKay," followed by car "Fort McMurray," and later Dining Car 1856 on the Edmonton to Waterways runs. When he needed extra help he employed his daughters. As a side line, he also ran the Capital Cafe with his friend Jack Panteluk. By the time of his promotion to boarding car inspector in 1952 business was dwindling on the dining cars.

A survey of the dining car service was undertaken by the parent lines in 1953. To curtail losses, dining car crews and service were pared to the bone, and service on the McLennan to Hines Creek tri-weekly run was eliminated. Effective with the new timetable in April 1955 diningcar service on Trains Nos. 1 and 2 was also discontinued and their staff laid off. A news agent from the company servicing CNR and CPR took over the route, but even this was dispensed with when sales continued to drop.

Among the casualties were the sleeping cars on the main line and their porters. Porter Johnny Bowden did not look his age when he joined the railway during the busy war years. He was a tall, handsome black man, who held himself very erect. The dapper dresser, who also sported a pencil thin moustache and smoked cigars, was nicknamed "Clark Gable" by the staff.[18] Bowden assisted with the organization of his colleagues and became chairman of the Brotherhood of Sleeping Car Porters on the NAR.[19] The porter's lot was not always an easy one. It was his duty to regulate heat in the sleeping cars, using a coal stove as the only source of heat and a shovelful of coal as the regulator.

Bowden worked the Edmonton to Dawson Creek run. There was no time allotted for sleep until they reached their destination. No thought was given to obtaining a birth certificate from Bowden until some 14 years later. Then it was discovered it could not be recovered. The government eventually fixed his birth date at 1889 and he was obligated to retire. By that time, he had actually worked two years beyond the retirement age of 65 years.

When John Deakin went on preretirement vacation in 1953, after almost 40 years of railway service, L.W. "Sandy" Saunders succeeded him as superintendent. Born in Springfield, Nova Scotia, the affable man was a favorite with his colleagues. His connection with railroading, began with the CPR in 1912, and was lengthy. Said to have originally started as a trainman in Alberta on J.D. McArthur's logging trains in 1918, he later turned up as cashier in the audit office.[20] After a short stint as agent at Peace River, he transferred to the dispatching office at McLennan. There his avid interest in sports stimulated the formation of baseball and hockey teams. Saunders enjoyed a drink and the Order of Railway Telegrapher's yearly meetings always generated good fellowship. What was probably the first meeting was held in the summer of 1927 at Charlie Wing's restaurant at Waterhole. Saunders improved the taste of the soup with the addition of a generous drop from a bottle of Scotch. Local Chairman Bill Reid drily observed that it was a criminal waste of good "licker."[21]

Shortly before Saunders became super-intendent, General Motors carried out a study on the possibility of introducing diesel locomotives to NAR. Nothing further happened until 1954 when the question of dieselization was paramount again. Although NAR had 15 steam locomotives of its own, it was forced to rent eight locomotives from the CPR and six from the CNR to supplement its power needs.[22] A new day dawned when the first four GP-9 diesel units arrived between Christmas and New Year's Day in 1957. Because the master mechanic was on vacation, it became Road Foreman of Engines Clarence Comrie's responsibility to get them into service immediately. He recalls, "I went for three nights and four days without taking my clothes off." William "Bill" Gilchrist, then shop foreman, says, "I was there day and night to. . . .There were great arguments when the diesels came between Dave Harper, Archie Wotherspoon and I."[23] Everyone knew something about the diesels, but no-one knew enough. In spite of the arguments, Wotherspoon and Gilchrist, who had undertaken their machinist apprenticeship together, remained good friends.

Locomotive Engineer Tom Lycan, who was a 27 year veteran, was proud to be at the throttle of the first diesel locomotive on its initial run to Smith on 2 January 1958. He knew the diesel engine was far more efficient than the steam engine and reputed to be trouble-free, but he felt a little insecure without the familiar tool box and oil can with its long spout.

Engineer Tom Lycan at the controls of a new diesel locomotive.
Photo: Courtesy of J.H. Laurie

That summer, changes in middle management caused a shuffle in the superintendent's department. Upon his retirement in August 1958, Saunders was succeeded as superintendent by Jack Vollans. During the early part of the war, Vollans had transferred to the railway from the CPR as yardmaster at Dawson Creek. A month after his appointment to superintendent, Vollans was back in Dawson Creek to celebrate the arrival of the Pacific Great Eastern Railway. The wet, blustering day did not mar the celebration as the golden spike on the PGE was driven by Wes Harper, a businessman who owned one of the larger stores in the town. The provincially-owned PGE was later renamed the British Columbia Railway.

On a windy morning in November 1959, as the first rays of sunlight brightened the sky, four people died in the worst tragedy in the history of the NAR. It happened at Carbondale Junction, 13.6 miles north of Dunvegan Yards. Passenger train No. 2 was bound for Edmonton when it collided head-on with northbound freight train No. 31.

That morning Harry Dyer looked forward to the feel of the new peppy diesel units responding to his touch as Train No. 31

NAR passenger train No. 1 and No. 2 at the CNR Station in Edmonton on 1 August 1958. Trains consist of baggage cars, mail cars and passenger coaches.
Photo: Provincial Archives of Alberta, Wells Studio Collection, WS19512

with 119 cars pulled slowly out of Dunvegan Yards. John "Snoose" Edmundson, son of Roadmaster Teddy, was conductor and had 33 years of NAR service. He expected his train to reach Carbondale in time to clear passenger train No. 2. Relieving Section Foreman Paul Pilip was on his way to the tool house across from Carbondale station as the freight train arrived shortly before 0800.[24] The train stopped, backed up, and stopped again. As it started forward once more Pilip heard a bang and the brakes apply. Looking west he noticed smoke and watched the passenger train come around the bend with veteran Engineer I.T. "Buck" McLeod at the controls of steam engine CN 5115. He remained rooted to the spot as it sped by him, ramming into the stationary freight train. Later he described the loud crash, "just like atomic," then watched in horror as the station burst into flames.

The remains of station after the collision of two trains at Carbondale
Photo: Courtesy of R.D.C. Comrie

The sudden impact ruptured a tank car immediately behind the two diesel engines. Its cargo of gasoline gushed forth and ignited, engulfing the station building, a garage and three automobiles parked near the platform. Trapped in the inferno, Agent Arthur Fraser, his wife, Alice, and their son, attempted to flee the flames. Their charred bodies, burned beyond recognition, were later recovered from the rear of the station.[25]

Albert Villeneuve, fireman on train No. 2, was crushed in the cab doorway of the locomotive as he attempted to jump to safety. It took four hours to cut the body of the 32-year-old man from the wreckage. By rolling out of his cab window Engineer McLeod survived and only sustained a fractured leg. The leaping flames destroyed the station and diesel unit 208. The steam locomotive was damaged beyond repair. In the mishap, communication lines were severed, cutting contact with headquarters. Passenger Conductor Harry Chausse picked himself up from where he had been hurled to the floor. Satisfied his 31 passengers were alive, he left Train Baggageman Barney Finley checking their injuries, while he set about establishing communications with headquarters from a farm house in the vicinity.

The collision was Bill Donlevy's unexpected introduction to the world of the chief dispatcher. W.T. "Bill" Turner had retired from that position two days previously and had been succeeded by Donlevy. His instinctive common sense helped him keep calm as he gave instructions for ambulances and the fire department, while mourning the untimely death of his friend Art Fraser.

Born in Drumheller, Art Fraser had moved to Dawson Creek with his parents. There he joined Agent Ace Comstock in the station and did other odd jobs to help support his family.[26] To make some extra cash, he competed in boxing matches, appearing at work the following day often with visible signs of the fight. He was also an active Jehovah Witness in the communities in which he worked. He lived his faith in his day-to-day dealings with people, gaining the respect of his peers. The Frasers had been in Carbondale for four years. Art Fraser had often spoken of his belief that the end of the world would come by fire. It turned out to be a true prophesy as far as his world was concerned.

Passengers on the train were more fortunate, only 13 were injured. The two most severely injured were taken to hospital by ambulance along with employees Engineer McLeod and News Agent John Chrunyk. Conductor Chausse accompanied the rest of the passengers by bus to the CNR depot, where they were examined by a company doctor. Chausse's father, Peter, and three brothers, Ed, Charles and Jim had all worked on the railway for varying periods of time and Chausse knew the accident was the worst disaster any of them had experienced.[27]

By that time, every officer who could be spared was at Carbondale. General Manager Cooper's face was etched with sorrow as he viewed the devastation. He declared, "It is the most gruesome railway accident I have ever experienced."[28] Left standing was the office safe and the lone brick chimney of the station, which looked desolate amidst the ashes. Stan Morgan from the treasury department was there to open the safe: "We should have waited until it had cooled off. It was roasting hot but the money inside was okay."[29]

Working in bitterly cold winds, restringing wires, Walter McNalley and his crew from the communications department had service restored within three hours. The wreckage took longer to move and delayed all trains. There was little sleep for Assistant Superintendent Pat Storms as crews with aching hearts worked through the night under powerful spotlights clearing the wreck. The track was opened for traffic by 1500 the following day.[30]

The railway's investigation revealed rules had been violated. The entire train and engine crews of train No. 31 were dismissed and the engineer on train No. 2 was assessed 30 demerit marks. At the coroner's inquest, the jury's findings were that the crash was the result of a "series of unfortunate circumstances."[31] The pall caused by the tragedy still hovered over the railway as the New Year ousted the old.

Agent Charles Torrey holds mail hoop with order for conductor
Photo: Courtesy of Mrs. P. Munro

23

The Romance of Steam Ends

Progress has its casualties and modernization is not without its flaws, and so it was with NAR as the winds of change reached all departments. With the introduction of diesel locomotives, more efficient methods of operation and mechanization of track work, there was a gradual drop in the number of personnel required to operate and maintain the railway.

About this time the staff from the stores department in McLennan moved to Dunvegan Yards, where G.W.E. "Billy" Smith was storekeeper. When he became supply car storekeeper in 1928, he had moved his family to Edmonton.[1] For over ten years, with the exception of the Waterways line, he travelled over the system on the supply car distributing supplies to section crews and stations. The feisty little Welshman, known as "Smithy," was a veteran of the First World War, having enlisted in the Royal Welsh Fusiliers and fought in the Dardanelles.[2] Although he came back alive, he found peace eluded him in Wales and so left for the Peace River country in 1919.

Smith worked on a farm before getting a permanent job in the stores at McLennan where he spent 35 years. He was popular with railroaders in all departments and his pixie face with its infectious smile was always a welcome sight. When he retired in 1959, as head of the stores department he joined the Corps of Commissionaires. Notwithstanding his pleasant disposition, he fought for what he believed in. At his prodding, the city of Edmonton moved the cenotaph, honoring First World War veterans, to Sir Winston Churchill Square in front of Edmonton's City Hall. In his ninetieth year, along with neighbors, he battled city hall and won the right to keep a marigold patch they had planted on a city boulevard. He took pride in his prodigious memory, and loved to talk of his early days on the railway. When he fought his last battle in August 1987 it was against cancer. Behind, he left a host of friends, many of whom were recipients of his generosity and his wit.

Smith was retired when the era of passenger service into Peace River town came quietly to an end in May 1960. A mixed train, carrying passengers and freight replaced the regular service to Hines Creek, linking at McLennan with the twice-weekly Edmonton-Dawson Creek passenger service. Simultaneously, the Post Office inaugurated mail delivery by truck and the railway lost its last source of revenue on the passenger trains. No mail cars operated between Edmonton and Waterways. Royal mail was handled in the express car with a portable mail box in the doorway to post letters. At flag stops a willow wand fashioned into a loop, called a "hoop," was held up with a package of mail attached to it. The express messenger or trainman "reached out from the baggage car, slipped his arm through the ring and the mail was on board."[3]

The end of an era for steam locomotives was also on the horizon. In a ceremony at Dawson Creek on 14 May 1960, Mayor Jack Wilcox recalled being locomotive foreman

Left to right: *Engineer Neil Doherty, Porter George Dalton, Conductor Ed Chausse, Locomotive Foreman Francis Schenk, Fireman W.S. "Slim" Wearmouth, Trainman George Kopf and Express Messenger Nick Krawchuk*
Photo: Courtesy of Peace River Block News

Sorting letters in mail car
Photo: Courtesy of CN Visual Communications

when the first passenger train rolled into town.[4] Engineer Neil "Doc" Doherty's feelings were mixed as he piloted engine CN 5104 on its way. He had hired on with the NAR toward the end of the Depression and the railway had been good to him. Although the lot of the fireman had not been an easy one, Fireman J.S. "Slim" Wearmouth felt some regret. Firing a locomotive was darned hard work and he would not miss the cinders in his eyes, but he still had a fondness for steam power.

Locomotive Foreman Francis Schenk's face had a sadness about it as he watched the last plume of smoke disappear into the distance. He had come to Canada with his folks from Minnesota in 1907 and into the Grande Prairie district 10 years later. He spent some rough years farming before becoming locomotive watchman on the railway in 1923. Schenk knew he would miss those clanking, hissing steam monsters. He had watched the evolution from coal shovelled by hand to stokers, followed by oil. The modern, no-nonsense diesels did not require the same care and attention. The useful days of the roundhouse, water tank and reservoir, which stored water for the locomotives, were drawing to a close.

With the demolition of water tanks Nick Moskalyk found himself jobless. He had travelled all over the railway system as

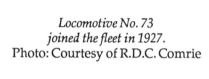

*Locomotive No. 73
joined the fleet in 1927.*
Photo: Courtesy of R.D.C. Comrie

pump repairman for 21 years, keeping the water pipelines and the old pump units, some of them dating from 1912, in operating condition. His motto was "if things had to be done, they just had to be done." A crisis, a quick phone call and Moskalyk was on his way, treating his track motor like a race horse. When asked how he arranged his hours Moskalyk chuckled, "I had no hours, I was paid by the month."[5]

Moskalyk was not without a job for long. His promotion to travelling electrician kept him out on the line rewiring section houses and stations. Riding a track motor, Moskalyk became known as a "fast runner." He claims he sometimes travelled at 50 miles per hour on the track motor but those who rode with him swear it was faster. They always checked to see if they were in one piece upon arrival at their destination. Moskalyk seldom took a tumble. He knew every square inch of the roadbed, since he had started as a seasonal sectionman at age 14. When he retired as shop supervisor at Dunvegan Yards in 1974, he had the longest service of anyone on NAR with over 51 years in railroading.

Other changes were taking place on the NAR. On 1 March 1961 two promotions occurred in the mechanical department. Clarence Comrie, who had been with the railway since 1927, was promoted to master mechanic after the untimely death of Archie Wotherspoon, and William Gilchrist to general locomotive foreman, succeeding Dave Harper. Comrie was not replaced as road foreman of engines. Although short in stature, he had the stamina and staying power of his Scottish ancestry. Revelling in the new challenge, he tackled the dual position with a vigor and enthusiasm few possess. Conductor Tom LaBrier summed up the essence of the man, "[He] did more than any other to give the men on the NAR a sense of pride by his example. . . .I don't think there was a man who worked with him or for him, who cannot have a kind word to say about him."[6] Even though he is in his eighties, Comrie's boundless energy continues to amaze people.

About this time, seeking ways to improve its efficiency, the audit department came under the scrutiny of the parent lines. The department was under the control of Charles Anderson, who had succeeded Fred Kavanagh as auditor, and Treasurer Christopher Cobb. The result was the integration of the finance and accounting sections of the NAR under the jurisdiction of the auditor and the early retirement of the treasurer.

North of the railway, development of the rich lead and zinc deposits at Pine Point, on the shores of Great Slave Lake, Northwest Territories, had accelerated. In 1960 the announcement in the throne speech at Ottawa that Grimshaw was to be the southern terminal for a proposed railway to Great Slave Lake could only benefit the NAR. Construction of the GSL railway by CNR on behalf of the Government of Canada, commenced at Roma Junction, 8 miles west of Peace River.[7] The movement of construction material over NAR stopped with its completion in 1965, but the ore traffic generated by this new line put NAR in the black financially. With the exception of the war years, the railway had operated with a deficit and was subsidized by the parent companies.[8]

The retirement of General Manager John Cooper in February 1964 meant more changes in managerial style for the railway. He was succeeded by a man who left his mark on the NAR as sure as if it had been done with a branding iron. Kenneth Russell Perry burst onto the railway like a human dynamo. As a person, he was an enigma, but to the NAR he brought high standards and a progressive outlook honed on the CPR.

Perry was the son of a CPR station agent at Mowbray, Manitoba. During the Depression he worked on a CPR section gang and later moved to the station office until that job petered out. With typing and shorthand skills, the ambitious young man arrived in Montreal in 1935. Paying jobs were unavailable, but he would not be deterred. He offered to work for experience and the CPR accepted his offer. It was not long before his abilities were recognized and he was moving up the corporate ladder with a salary. He was secretary to President Sir Edward Beatty in 1942 when he went overseas with the Royal Canadian Engineers. On his return to the CPR he became assistant superintendent at Moose Jaw, and later at Bassano, then followed over two years in Edmonton as assistant to the general manager of the NAR. Back on the CPR, he rose rapidly to the position of superintendent before returning to the NAR as general manager.

K.R. Perry, General Manager, NAR, 1964-1977

Shortly after the arrival of Perry, Superintendent Jack Vollans retired. The general manager used the opportunity to reorganize the department. He assumed the superintendent duties and appointed two supervisors of operations. For R.V. "Pat" Storms and J.G. "Jim" Rouse it was merely a change in title.

Storms had begun his railway career on the L & NW and continued it with the NAR.[9] He acquired experience in various positions before becoming a well respected official. Storms had been assistant superintendent since 1950 and had headquarters at McLennan and at Edmonton from 1958.[10] Rouse, who was in a similar position, was located in McLennan. He moved to Edmonton after Storms' retirement and was replaced by Conductor Ken Mitchell at McLennan.

During his first months in Edmonton, Perry made numerous trips over the railway. He found little to his liking. Few departments escaped his displeasure. He had a temper, which when unleashed could reduce an employee to a shivering lump of jelly. In his dealings with people, he was ruthless if they did not measure up to his expectations. Yet, this same man was moved to tears of sorrow as he told his secretary of the loss of a brother to cancer and again on the sudden death of a dear friend.

Perry was a strong-willed manager who found it difficult to accept advice from his subordinates. He liked to say, "I run a one man show." A booklet he had written while on the CPR on how to conduct an investigation was used. Investigations, carried out in the case of some infringement of rules, were often conducted by himself. He would confuse the hapless suspect so hopelessly that the individual would agree to almost anything to bring the interrogation to a conclusion.

Every morning, Perry scrutinized the

reports for the previous day's operations. Then Chief Dispatcher Bill Donlevy was treated to what the general manager referred to as the "hour of charm." Donlevy remembers it as anything but that "[Perry] refused to accept any reasonable explanation of train delay, even bitterly cold weather, the possibility of engine failure or over heated journal. . . .He kept saying, 'Such delays are intolerable on the CPR.' To myself I would say, 'Damn the CPR' and I meant it."[11]

As staff responded to his direction, Perry's attitude changed. He began a program of upgrading to bring the NAR up to the standards of Canada's major railways. He delegated more authority to department heads, and the "hour of charm" vanished. He had come to respect the dedication, versatility and resourcefulness of his staff. He insisted on economical operation of "his" railway and he got it. Retired Track and Equipment Supervisor Sam Rouleau remarked, "He was as tough as nails. He had to have the last word, but he was a good railroader."[12]

In his quest to improve the railway's image, Perry became a one-man public relations department. He travelled the 923 miles whenever possible, making his presence known in the communities. On his business car "Peace River", he was an excellent host who often enlivened a conversation with a witticism. The steward on the private car was Jack Graham. Perry liked to choose the menu and to serve his guests himself from the head of the table. One of his favorite meals was liver and onions. If Graham knew a guest detested liver he would cook a steak and quietly do a switch at the table. Fortunately for Graham, Perry never noticed, or if he did he chose to ignore it.

Determined to upgrade the railway's plant, Perry tapped every source for funds. As he built up the capital works of the company, NAR was able to apply depreciation funds to the financing of the much needed capital programs on the NAR.[13] He initiated a concentrated program, which included embankment widening, ballasting, siding extensions, ditching and relaying with heavy rail. As soon as the frost was out of the ground, draglines were dispersed to load gravel, then handle ditching. They worked until freeze up, then came to Dunvegan Yards for the winter, during which the crews overhauled their machines in the maintenance of way shop. Consequently, there was little an operator did not know about his machine.

Frank Loewen was foreman in the maintenance of way shop at Dunvegan Yards. He had started with the railway in the early 1930s as a bridge and building helper and had become a highly skilled workman over the years. In 1971, he was promoted to bridge and building foreman. Anxious to see workers were treated fairly, he served as local and later general chairman of the Brotherhood of Maintenance of Way Employees.

Upgrading of the Waterways line, which had begun in 1959, continued. Sam Rouleau, then roadmaster, supervised 11 draglines lowering culverts at one time. Some of the equipment was leased and the operators were inexperienced with dredging spongy muskeg. A wrong move and one contract operator found his machine slowly sinking into the morass before another dragline pulled it to safety. Experienced railway dragline operators like Bill Woodley, George Kuziw, Gene Bachand and Ted Deynaka had no such difficulties.[14] The muskeg was so deep in places that timber pads, bolted together in threes, were used like rafts to keep draglines from sinking. Ditching was always done backing up and the oiler would attach cables to hoist the pads and swing them around behind him.[15]

E. "Gene" Bachand was the first operator of the new Weldon crane the railway bought. During the Depression his family moved north to Joussard, where as a youngster Bachand climbed onto many an NAR train. Bachand worked on a section crew for two years, before enlisting in the Canadian army in 1942. After his discharge, he was oiler for master Dragline Operator Bud Ott. When Ott quit Bachand replaced him. Bachand's knowledge of his machine's capabilities showed in his expert handling of it, particularly at wrecks. He handled rerailing of cars expediently and safely.

Ditching on the branch to Waterways was memorable for Bachand. His wife and children joined him in the outfit car during the summer holidays. Bachand says, "The first thing to be erected was a clothesline. . .

.On washdays the train crew passing would fill the gas [operated] washing machine, often with warm water, and we'd go to the nearest creek for drinking water. The passenger train would bring supplies and a block of ice once a week. We had no light plant just kerosene lamps and an ice box. But we liked it, even the kids."[16]

Bachand was among those who rejoiced as tonnage moved by the NAR increased with the development of oil and gas in the Slave Lake region and the building of a huge Great Canadian Oil Sands Co.[GCOS] plant, 24 miles north of Fort McMurray. Management hoped the Waterways line, which so many said would never earn its axle grease, might now become the jewel in NAR's crown. GCOS had won the race to develop the Athabasca oil sands. The venture brought prosperity and expansion to the isolated town of Fort McMurray. With no highway link to the rest of Alberta, freight and passengers were handled by the NAR and Pacific Western Airlines. The opening of the plant and a highway to Edmonton occurred almost simultaneously.[17] As an experiment, in 1966 a dayliner had replaced passenger trains to Waterways, but with highway competition for the same number of travellers the venture was unsuccessful and the NAR substituted mixed trains.

About this time, a dispute developed regarding the handling of NAR express shipments at the CNR facilities in downtown Edmonton. The result was NAR moved its operation to Dunvegan Yards. When Agent

Social Credit Party's Whistle Stop Tour in 1968. Left to right:
Dr. Boisvert MLA, Conductor Bill Simmons, Premier of Alberta Ernest
Manning, Engineer Lee Sebastian, Supervisor Operations Jim Rouse,
Locomotive Foreman Roland Dube, and Ray Speaker MLA.
Photo: Government of Alberta

Gordon Waite took over the agency he found "utter chaos." To restore order, he resorted to a training program for the entire staff. Waite says, "Shed Foreman Ross McIlveen soon had his staff handling 2 800 pounds per man per hour compared to 1 800 pounds on CPR and 1 300 pounds on CNR."[18] To alleviate the cramped quarters, new station and freight facilities were built at Dunvegan Yards in 1965. That same year, all passenger trains originated and terminated there, and NAR entered the trucking field. An overnight service to the Peace River country for less-than-carload freight, and express replaced the service once supplied by wayfreight and passenger trains. By November 1968 expansion had taken place and a 6 000 foot warehouse was added to the Dunvegan Yards terminal to handle freight and express.

The death sentence was passed on the profession of telegraphers with the arrival of teletype service and telex. It was an evolution that gradually edged out those who "pounded brass" and the use of Morse code. Commercial Telegraph Agent Walter Johnson says, "The only thing we had left was to handle cables."[19] The teletype machines hooked up a company's branch office with its

Dayliner CP9023 on last trip, 29 April 1967.
Last crew: Conductor Bill Simmons, Brakeman
Ken Mitchell and Engineer Buck McLeod
Photo: Courtesy of Wm. Simmons

engineer, commercial telegraphs, McNalley liked the idea of working for a small company. He arrived in April 1951 to find the system had not kept pace with progress elsewhere, but the staff was dedicated and hard working.[20]

Superintendent Communications Ralph Fullerton
stands behind Agent Tom Lowes while Equipment
Mechanic Gerry Ballantyne is on the telephone.
Photo: Courtesy of W.W. McNalley

head office or other branches. With the advent of telex a company could reach another tied into the worldwide network. Railways got the franchise for telex in Canada and it was an economical system that made money for them. The first four machines installed by NAR's communications staff were in Peace River in March 1962. That the equipment had been manufactured in Germany did not faze Plant Supervisor Walter McNalley until he discovered the instruction books were all written in German and had to be translated into English to be understood.

An Albertan by birth, McNalley had gained experience in railway communications with Canadian National Telecommunications and Alberta Government Telephones [AGT]. When NAR offered the job of

It was soon obvious that the enthusiasm and cheerful nature of Ralph Fullerton, then supervisor of communications, buoyed his staff even when things were not going right. Sometimes they went really wrong. In 1964, a fire in the J.D. Levesque building in Peace River sent the communications equipment crashing into the basement. The team worked steadily without sleep to get the essential circuits operating. To lend his support, Fullerton came from Edmonton and worked alongside his men. When he retired at the end of 1966, McNalley succeeded him.

Recognizing his limited knowledge of the advances made in communications, because his background was mainly telegraphs, Fullerton hired young men, like McNalley and G.A. "Al" Smith, who had the experience he lacked. Smith joined the department by a twist of fate in 1956. He had been a teacher with an avid interest in radio communications when World War II broke out. He enlisted in the Navy where he was taught basic communications and international morse. On discharge, he joined Alberta Forest Service Communications [AFS].

Dissatisfied with low wages, the AFS field staff decided to check rates at other companies to have ammunition for their claims for higher wages. Smith was delegated to investigate an NAR advertisement for an assistant to the communications engineer. Smith enjoys regaling friends with the story of what happened next. "Ralph Fullerton interviewed me. Caught up in his enthusiasm about communications into the north country, I found myself accepting the job which offered $325 a month, $10 more than I was already making."[21] Smith was soon designing communications systems and working long hours alongside the rest of the staff when a crisis occurred or a major installation had to be made. Eventually, upon McNalley's retirement, he became superintendent of communications.

Agent Maurice Mahood operates the obsolete "Bug"- once a mainstay of the telegraph office.
Photo: Herald Tribune

Engineer Tom Gregg in the cab of Locomotive No. 202 in Grande Prairie Yards.
Photo: J.F. Seath

24
Coming of Age

By the mid-sixties Soviet and American astronauts were floating and walking in space, but in northern Alberta NAR's troubles were more of the earthly variety. In the Peace River Block, competition for grain traffic handled by the railway loomed on the horizon. The government of Alberta had enlisted the assistance of CNR to build the Alberta Resources Railway in 1965. Built amid controversy, the 234 mile ARR, extending north to Grande Prairie from the CNR main line west of Hinton, was completed in May 1969.[1] It provided a shorter transportation route to the Pacific Coast and a saving in freight rates. Under lease from the Alberta Resources Railway Corporation, it is operated as the Grande Cache subdivision of CN Rail with its Managing Director Charles Anderson, whose stewardship is as effective as when he was NAR's auditor.

In the car control office, Mel Hauer, who succeeded Charles McElheran as car accountant in 1969, and his assistant Dixie Wright noticed a decline in the demand for grain cars. Nevertheless, NAR continued to carry a large percentage of grain from the Peace River country, but never again would the quantities reach the unprecedented 43 381 236 bushels carried in the 1961-62 crop year.

Disturbed by the number of injuries sustained by employees on the job, General Manager Perry saw the necessity for a program in safety education. Safety Supervisor Jack McLean came from Vancouver to inaugurate the railway's first accident prevention program in 1966. Soon afterwards, a booklet titled "Code of Safety Rules and Safe Practices" was distributed to employees. McLean's cheerful nature and his penchant for telling jokes made safety education a pleasant experience. With his belief that safety is everybody's business, incidents of personal injuries began to decrease. The railway encouraged the decrease by awarding yearly safety certificates to individuals and a system trophy in recognition of excellence in safety performance. Employees were divided into five groupings – Maintenance of Way; Motive Power and Car; Communications; Other Transportation and Trainmen, Enginemen and Yardmen. By 1972, the company had reduced its ranking injury ratio from 50.5 to 23.2 in 1965.[2] This ratio gave "a true picture of the number of injuries in relation to employees' total exposure to injury."[3]

The future of the railway's agencies came into jeopardy with the appointment of a committee in 1968 to study plans for a Centralized Agency Service[CAS] based on plans formulated by the parent companies.[4] A number of small stations on the NAR had been closed over the years. The fate of others was sealed with an announcement from the general manager on 20 October 1969: "The Railway Transport Committee of the Canadian Transport Commission has approved Northern Alberta Railways' application to withdraw 34 line agents and 12 caretakers from its stations in the Peace River country, northern Alberta and British Columbia and to implement its plan to provide service through a Centralized Agency located in Edmonton." The days of the station agent were numbered.

On 1 February 1969, a technological, operational and organizational changes agreement, signed with the labor organizations, went into effect.[5] It was an attempt to minimize the effect on employees. This agreement provided for retraining, relocation expenses and maintenance of earnings. Nevertheless, a number of highly skilled agents and assistant agents opted for early retirement allowances.

Prior to that, committee chairman Jim Rouse, with members Jim Dove from the audit department and Clarence Price from the traffic department, criss crossed northern Alberta spreading the CAS doctrine. In each community they interviewed residents and every customer to assess their needs. Opposition to the railway's plan voiced at meetings was quickly withdrawn. When details of the plan were worked out, a submission was made to the Canadian Transport Commission, and the NAR committee temporarily disbanded, only to be later reassembled to approach each community involved for a letter of support. Jim Dove says, "None of us thought it was possible, but we did it. The result was we got a board order to proceed without a hearing."[6] This was a real coup.

As a member of the committee, Jim Rouse was an excellent choice. He was genuinely concerned about the people in the areas affected. Besides, he knew most of those on the town councils and their families: "We spoke to every chamber of commerce and town council in the towns served by the railway."[7] Rouse had first made the acquaintance of northerners in 1929 when he joined the railway as clerk to Superintendent Deakin. As the son of Bridge and Building Foreman Jack Rouse, it was unthinkable that he would not choose railroading as his career. With the exception of six years in the Canadian Armed Forces, he later travelled the length and breadth of the railway as trainman, conductor and local chairman of the Brotherhood of Railroad Trainmen.

When Rouse was promoted to assistant superintendent at McLennan in 1958, he and his wife, Marion, quickly became integrated into the community. While he served on the board of McLennan's Sacred Heart Hospital, she indulged her interest in the arts by volunteering to train a figure skating troupe and teach dancing. Rouse was operations manager when he became involved with CAS. He knew its implementation would be unpopular. By the time he moved to Edmonton early in 1971, upon Storms' retirement, the savings generated by the CAS system were mounting.

Jim Dove was the "figure man" on the CAS. He had been tallying figures in the audit office for some years. A course in computer programming opened his eyes to what the future held for accounting offices where all the paper work was done by hand. Soon after making a proposal to Auditor Charles Anderson that would improve the system, he was winging his way to Montreal to see firsthand the computer applications and car accounting systems in effect on the parent lines. Those companies were at that time also experimenting with systems similar to the CAS, which Dove would later help develop. A second trip to Montreal with Bill Donlevy, then chief train dispatcher, convinced Dove that a CAS system should be developed and computerization was imperative and the general manager agreed. The chairman of the operating committee approved the

implementation of the CAS system, but quashed the computer idea. Instead, keypunch machines were installed and staff trained in their operation. Dove remarks, "For a while some kept doing books as well, but I knew we had succeeded when I got a call in the middle of the night some time afterwards. The machines had broken down and no one knew what to do."[8]

The CAS plan went into effect on 1 February 1970. Operators and terminal operating staff were established at Dawson Creek, Grande Prairie, McLennan, Peace River, Smith, Lac La Biche and Waterways. On-hand depots were set up at 22 locations. Travelling representatives handled customer contact, complaints, and collection of overdue accounts. H.G. "Harry" Miseck was responsible for the area from Edmonton to McLennan, with headquarters at Westlock. Neil Pinkham looked after Hines Creek, Grande Prairie and Dawson Creek and Noel Boisvert's territory stretched from McLennan to Peace River and Smoky subdivision.

The on-hand agents, local contractors and highway carriers, came under the jurisdiction of Clarence Price when he was promoted early in 1972, to supervisor, express & highway services in charge of all noncarload traffic and freight. Price was well experienced for the job. He had spent close to 30 years handling express, starting off as helper to the express messenger. Price found himself with expanded duties in August 1972 when the railway inaugurated pick-up and delivery of express, and less than carload freight. Dawson Creek and Grande Prairie were each supplied with two trucks and Peace River with one for local deliveries.

Cream and trucks did not take kindly to each other. Shippers took the cream to the station in cans. The railway issued a waybill, which was later changed to "cream tickets" to alleviate paper work. Inside a truck, cream cans were like dancers who lay over in exhaustion after the performance. The only problem was the toppling over spilled their contents. For a while the railway was buying more cream than the dairies. When the price for shipping cream was raised this traffic declined.[9]

NAR enters trucking field

In the meantime, modernization of the plant at Dunvegan Yards continued. A seven thousand square foot maintenance of way equipment repair shop was opened in 1971. The purchasing and stores departments were amalgamated under the direction of Roy Martins. Shortly afterwards, a new 14 thousand square foot modern stores building

was opened at Dunvegan Yards replacing antiquated facilities.[10] The original stores building was built in the 1920s and added to in 1944. The stores department supplied the entire railway with materials ranging from safety pins to locomotive axles.

Roy Martins had come a long way from the day in 1929 when he had fibbed about his age to get a job as telegraph messenger on the NAR. In later years he worked on the dining cars, as store supply car man, commissary agent and purchasing agent. During World War II, after joining the Royal Canadian Air Force as a navigator, Martins voluntarily became a member of the Pathfinders group. Pathfinders located the enemy target and marked it for the bombers following. By the end of the war he had flown 37 dangerous missions. He was decommissioned with the rank of Flight Lieutenant and returned to the railway. His experience prepared him well for the challenges to be faced as manager, purchases and stores.

John A. King expected to step into Martins's shoes upon his retirement, but the general manager had him earmarked for another department. In October 1970, he took over the management of real estate. Feeling inadequate in an arena with which he was unfamiliar, he immediately enrolled in several courses, including property management. He says, "I decided I had to educate myself if I was going to do the job properly."[11] As he became more knowledgeable, King was able to save the railway money on property taxes and bring in extra revenue by increasing rents on leased property which were still at 1920s rates.

While the real estate department was moving into the 1970s, the NAR story was being captured on film. A circular from the Edmonton Chamber of Commerce that appeared on the general manager's desk in the autumn of 1970 sparked the idea of a film on the railway. The Metropolitan Edmonton Educational Television Association, known as MEETA, was in the process of making a number of industrial studies for their "Portfolio" series.[12] Always anxious to improve the image of the railway, Perry found the money to produce the movie on a cost-sharing basis. Getting the exact shots needed was no easy matter. When it came to the "on film" dialogue, the film crew was surprised to find amateur "actors." Conductor Gordon McArthur and Engineer John Kalyta were perfect on the first take.

Shortly after this, a competition was held to find a name for a proposed in-house newspaper as a means of communication between the railway and its employees, both active and retired. From 300 entries the name submitted by S.E. Nelson, a retired sectionman, and R.K. Cook, chief clerk in the general manager's office, was chosen. The first edition of *The Headlight* was launched in September 1971. Lionel Cordingley was the newspaper's first editor. He took on the responsibility when he retired from the position of office assistant to the general manager and secretary, pension committee. He had

transferred to the NAR from the CNR as disbursement accountant during the hectic war years and remained with the NAR. Succeeding Charles Dominy as the general manager's right hand in 1958, he had worked closely with two general managers.

With his military bearing some made the mistake of thinking Cordingley was unapproachable, but once the initial contact was made employees found him to be a fair supervisor. The impression he gave was one of never making a decision without thinking it through. This quality and his background knowledge of the railway gained from his administrative position made him a good candidate for editor. When the Cordingleys decided the Alberta winters were a trifle too cold and took to spending them in warmer climates, Perry took over the function of editor himself with the assistance of Secretary Janet Strong and later Ena Byrne [now Schneider].

By May 1972, ground had been broken at Dunvegan Yards for the erection of an L-shaped, 24 thousand square foot, split-level building as headquarters for the NAR.[13] The architectural work was carried out by CNR's department of architecture in Montreal. In Edmonton, Assistant Engineer Doug Wong supervised the work of the general contractor. To facilitate organization of personnel for the move to the new building Alec Messum, who had filled the vacancy left by Cordingley's retirement, was appointed office manager in July 1972. He was succeeded by Walter Arason as office assistant to the general manager and secretary, pension committee.

Arason's railroading career had begun as a roadmaster's clerk on the CNR. At the time of his appointment to NAR, he held the position of special reports assistant, vice-president and general manager, mountain region. At NAR, he gained a reputation for his sensitive handling of negotiations with the numerous railway organizations and in 1974 his title was changed to administrative assistant to the general manager, which was more in keeping with his duties. His compassionate nature became evident in his dealings with NAR's pensioners. Alarmed at how unprepared retirement age employees were for the big change in their lives, he assembled an information package for those nearing age 65. Each individual received notice six months prior to the actual retirement date and was invited into the office to discuss details. When a death occurred, he personally visited the bereaved widow or widower, explained entitlements with regard to the spouse's pension, and assisted with the completion of government forms. Often widows had no idea of their spouse's financial standing and he caught the brunt of their anger. Nevertheless, Arason remained philosophical and continued to provide assistance and an escape valve to those who needed it.

While work was progressing rapidly on the new headquarters building, an exceptionally heavy rainfall on the 10th and 11th of June, 1972 caused flood conditions on the Smoky River which shut down the railway west of Watino. Peaking at 23 feet above normal three days later, 220 feet of grade was washed away, leaving swinging track in its wake.[14] The force of the water was so great the upstream wing, weighing 240 thousand lbs., of the east bridge abutment was sheared off and carried away before the level began to drop.[15] Unable to cross the Smoky to restore telecommunications, the ingenious communications department tied wires to a push car and pulled it across the suspended track. By 22 September, the water had receded somewhat and tons of fill were poured into the gaping hole. The earth filling, track-laying and ballasting went rapidly after that. The line was restored to traffic before month end.

On the afternoon of 9 December 1972, a special train left Dunvegan Yards for Busby, picked up two red-suited passengers, and returned. The crew consisted of Conductor Glen Kirkland, Engineer John Scott, Fireman Bob Coffin, Trainmen Carl and Gerald Whiteman. No one was making money.[16] It was the first NAR Santa Claus train and the brainchild of the Social Club Committee, headed by Chairperson Doreen Kohlruss. Employees had always participated in social activities such as curling and bowling. The social club had been in operation for several decades. Its members organized events throughout the year, and usually the children's Christmas event was a party at a local hall. Club members were jubilant when General Manager Perry proved he was not Mr.

Scrooge, by agreeing to supply the equipment for a Santa Claus train if crews would volunteer their time. That was no problem. There were more volunteers than jobs, but they came along to help anyway.

Everyone entered into the spirit of the event. Ken Craik, from the traffic department, stood in for the busy man as he had done at the children's party for many years. This time he was accompanied by Mrs. Claus [Ena Byrne]. Expectant little faces were pressed to the train windows as a horse drawn cutter carried the red suited couple to the train at Busby. Bill Donlevy's doubting grandson was heard to say, "Santa is really alive after all." This event was to be repeated regularly afterwards with the same success.

Mr. and Mrs. Claus wave from caboose No. 13020 as the train leaves Busby for Dunvegan Yards
Photo: K.R. Perry

The following February, NAR staff vacated the CPR building in Edmonton's downtown core and took up residence in the new headquarters building at 13025 St. Albert Trail. Alec Messum had done his planning well. "The move itself had to be planned like a cross-channel invasion," remarked the general manager.[17] By Friday afternoon, office staff had emptied their desks into marked boxes ready for the movers. At Dunvegan Yards, Mary Arseniuk, cook on Extra Gang 12, assisted by Aubrey Arthur, boarding car inspector, kept the hungry volunteers fed throughout the night.

Dunvegan Yards – Headquarters building in centre with express sheds and station on right.
Photo: E.G. Holtner

There was no time for communications staff to admire the foyer's feature wall of 60 lb. rails, rolled in 1912 and 1914, nor the brightly colored carpets and drapes in the new building. There was an eleventh hour crisis to be solved. Al Smith had everything organized well in advance for the move when a hitch developed in the plans. Datek Industries had installed a new dispatchers' control system and on the afternoon of the move it was discovered the equipment was malfunctioning.[18] While loaded moving vans were heading for Dunvegan Yards at midnight, the communications staff was tearing out the old system to install at Dunvegan Yards. The railway was without a dispatcher for a few hours but some dedicated telephone systems helped keep them in touch with essential points.

Train No. 76 near Venice on Lac La Biche Subdivision
Photo: J.B. Armstrong

25
End of the Line for Blue Train

NAR's staff was nicely settled into the new headquarters building in the summer of 1973 when rail traffic ground to a halt at the end of July for 66 hours. Nonoperating railway employees wanted higher wages. A series of rotating strikes began backed by sympathetic operating employees. It took a return to work order of Parliament to get trains moving again.

Shortly after this, Bill Donlevy hung up his hat in his office for the last time and Samuel Mickelson replaced him as supervisor, transportation and chief train dispatcher. The native of Winnipeg, Manitoba, had been with the railway since 1927 and had worked in agencies across the system prior to his promotion to station agent in 1935. The slim man with the ready smile had been at the train dispatcher's desk since 1950.

As Mickelson took over the chief dispatcher's chair, Alberta's liquid gold at Fort McMurray was making headlines in newspapers across Canada. Syncrude Can-

ada Ltd. was constructing an oil extraction plant at Mildred Lake, 5 miles north of GCOS, near Fort McMurray.[1] NAR intended to get a large slice of the action.

While railway management kept an eye on Syncrude's progress, work began on an intermodal transportation package for NAR, involving rail and truck transportation for on-site delivery of construction material for the plant. In formulating the intermodal proposal, NAR enlisted the expertise of the parent companies, as well as CP Transport and Midland Superior Express.[2] The proposal was accepted by Syncrude and Canadian Bechtel Limited, the company building the plant. NAR hoped the increase in tonnage would be the key to making the Waterways line profitable. The only flaw was the 60 lb. rail on the subdivision, which would cause some difficulties, until the program of replacement with 100 lb. rail was completed.

It was first planned that an intermodal transfer yard would be built at Draper, where the railway owned 740 acres of land. The Department of Highways discovered that water seepage, soil instability, muskeg and grades in the vicinity made the building of a road impractical.[3] Instead, it was decided to develop 290 acres of Crown land at Lynton, 10 miles south of Fort McMurray. 10 miles of track were installed in the yard and a truck road built to the plant site.

The on-going intermodal road haul from Lynton to the construction site was contracted to Pe Ben Industries Company Ltd. This new dimension to railway services necessitated some intermodal expertise. E.E. "Ted" Kent, who had extensive experience in the trucking and heavy hauling industry, was hired as manager, intermodal services. His sojourn with NAR was short and Harry Miseck stepped into Kent's shoes, upon his departure. The area was familiar territory for the congenial Miseck. It was in the Waterways station that he began his career in agency service in 1942. He returned to that station in 1965. Now he was back once again, as manager, intermodal services. He had worked as travelling representative for six years prior to his appointment. When the intermodal position was abolished in 1977 Miseck moved to McLennan as operations manager, replacing R.A. "Bob" Lloyd, who moved to Edmonton in the same capacity.

Bill Donlevy found himself coming out of retirement to accept the contract position of traffic coordinator, intermodal services. His background in dispatching was invaluable in dealing with clearance matters arising

Operations Manager Bob Lloyd accepts the Annual System Safety Award from Harold Stepney on behalf of "Other Transportation."
Photo: E.G. Holtner

from the movement of heavy and oversized vessels to the Syncrude project.[4] In coordinating an orderly flow of construction materials, he worked closely with the traffic department headed by Jim Dove. To handle the extra duties, traffic personnel was reshuffled when the assistant traffic manager's position was split in two, leaving W.C. "Mac" McCumber solely responsible for rates and divisions, and George Mather in charge of marketing and sales.

Political involvement almost caused the collapse of the Syncrude consortium. Shipments by rail came to a halt in late 1974, and only resumed after Syncrude struck an agreement with the governments involved.[5]

Oil fever had taken Alberta by storm, but on the NAR, train day was still the highlight of the week for the communities along the Waterways line. The "Muskeg Mixed" continued to provide the only ground transportation link to the outside world. While few passengers travelled between Edmonton and Lac La Biche on the twice weekly train, north of Lac La Biche little had changed. As always the scheduled timetable was elastic, but there were no complaints as the antiquated combination coach-cabooses continued to haul passengers, freight and mail northward. The largely Indian and Métis population depended on the train and the assistance provided by the train crews. Many of the people in villages, such as Conklin, trapped for a living in winter and worked on the railway's section gangs or maintenance of way crews in the summer. Although the coaches were ancient, radio-telephone communications with the engineer ahead was a modern luxury train crews enjoyed.

Even in the 1970s, train crews on the Waterways subdivision were still a compassionate lot. Like their predecessors, they provided the human touch, by passing along newspapers, shopping, cashing cheques and picking up and delivering medication. On one occasion the duties even extended to delivering a baby. The expectant mother entrained at Chard. Conductor James Walsh wondered if the train would reach Waterways in time. He told Engineer Bob Coffin, "If you see a red fusee sticking out of the caboose, do not stop anywhere else just high-tail it to Waterways."[6] When labor began en route the midwives were none other than Jim Walsh and Trainman Elmer Dodds.[7]

Train No. 76, "The Muskeg Mixed" leaving Lac La Biche
Photo: J.B. Armstrong

*Conductor Jim Walsh drops off
supplies to Oscar Olson at Margie.*
Photo: Courtesy of Jim Walsh

In 1974, Carl Whiteman was conductor on the Sunday train and his brother Gerry on the Thursday run. Their affinity for railroading came from their father Albert Whiteman, whom we have already met. Carl worked on the NAR dining cars before falling in love with Audrey Kirkland, whose father, Bill Kirkland, stepfather Tom McCombs and brothers Bill, Walter and Glen were all NAR railroaders. Although Audrey's brother Cecil only briefly joined the railroad, he did marry railroader Jens Hansen's daughter, Marjory. With a wife to support, Whiteman transferred to the operating department where there were more opportunities for advancement. When he became a conductor on the Waterways run in 1956 he, too, provided a special service to the people whose main street was the NAR.

Sound judgement was a trademark of the Whitemans, but sometimes strictly adhering to the rules was next to impossible. Once a group of 100 native firefighters, who had been battling flames north of Fort McMurray, arrived at Waterways station. With insufficient passenger accommodation Carl Whiteman had a spare gondola car switched next to the coaches and they climbed in. As the train was rolling along it hit a sun kink in the rails, causing 22 cars to derail. When Whiteman reached the gondola, like Mother Hubbard's cupboard it was bare. In the confusion, the frightened men had jumped out and disappeared.[8]

*Mosquito netting helps Gerald Whiteman, the
conductor on the work train, get some sleep.*
Photo: Stan Hryniuk

Like his brother, Gerald Whiteman was on the dining cars before transferring to train service. For many years he also served as general chairman of the Brotherhood of Railway Trainmen and was highly regarded by management and colleagues for his competence in handling negotiations.

In train service, Whiteman discovered there were tricks to the trade that only experience could teach. He remembers, "Every time I opened a [way] car I'd put a new seal on. I used to get out and reseal every car opened at a stop; a lot of unnecessary work. Later on I found out that the 'proper way' [against the rules, but easier] to do it was to break the first seal, register it, then sit in the caboose and do all the sealing in the caboose."[9] The unused seals were destroyed.

It was on Gerald Whiteman's train that a cold day in early January 1974 got an unusual warming up. As was his habit, Whiteman walked up to inspect the train at Egremont. He then climbed into the cab with Engineer Wilf Wishart as they proceeded to Thorhild. Just as the train reached the village, the voice of Wally Bristow, the brakeman at the rear end, came over the radio shouting, "The express car is on fire."

To save the rest of the train, Whiteman gave instructions for the burning car to be set out. With the car in the siding, he sprinted over to the hotel to ask someone to call the fire department. The beer parlor's occupants said, "Consider the fire department called, that's us." Within minutes the fire siren was wailing. Thirty-five thousand dollars worth of liquor sat on the floor, beneath which the fire was confined. Whiteman directed the rapidly gathering crowd "to form a human chain to move the cases of liquor."[10] Despite their best efforts, some of the water-soaked cardboard cases fell apart, crashing to the ground, shattering the bottles. Many a bottle found its way into a snow bank. Thorhild residents remember the incident as the jolliest start to the New Year they had ever experienced.[11]

While there was no question of dispensing with the mixed train to Waterways, passenger service to Dawson Creek was a severe drain on the company's revenues. The railway had been trying for some years to drop the service. In 1972 the Canadian Transport Commission held hearings in Edmonton, and on 11 April 1974 board order R-18508 authorized the termination of main line passenger trains 1 and 2. The end of the line had come for the "Blue Train," christened by Ken Liddell of the *Calgary Herald* because of its royal blue color.

A mood of melancholy, tinged with nostalgia, affected the crew that took the last passenger train from Dunvegan Yards to McLennan. Conductor Glen Kirkland, Engineer Bill Fee, Fireman Harold Stepney and Baggageman Metro Goriniuk were all long service employees. They knew the passenger service was no longer viable, but seeing it disappear was like swallowing a bitter pill. At McLennan, the crew was replaced by Conductor George Stephenson,

Engineer Mel MacFarlane, Trainman Roland Dube and Baggageman Herb Cobb.

Conductor George Stephenson on the last passenger train.
Photo: Courtesy of G. Stephenson

Last passenger train arriving at Dunvegan Yards, 1 June 1974. L to R: Baggageman Metro Goriniuk, Conductor Glen Kirkland, Fireman Harold Stepney and Engineer Bill Fee

Retired Conductor Dick Coulman tagged along for old times sake and assisted Conductor Stephenson, whose face glowed as bright as the polished buttons on his uniform. Although he had been 36 years with the railway, he still was proud to wear that old uniform and the memories it evoked were many. The Depression was at its depth when Stephenson rode the rods to Alberta from Saskatchewan in 1935. He made his way to McLennan to visit his sister, Elsie, who was married to Frank Donovan, a conductor nicknamed "Tilly the Toiler" after a comic strip character. Donovan used his influence to get his brother-in-law a job on the NAR at a time when they were scarce. In time, Stephenson became very involved in the McLennan community where he stayed until retirement.

At Grande Prairie, members of that city's Chamber of Commerce draped the front of engine No. 302 with a banner announcing the last run, then 40 members climbed aboard for the trip to Dawson Creek. It was a ride down memory lane for Jessie Elliott, who was a young girl when she rode the first passenger train into Grande Prairie in 1916. On the outskirts of Beaverlodge, the trip took a theatrical turn when 12 masked bandits thundered up on horseback, firing blanks from their pistols. The desperadoes kidnapped President Denis Bryan and Past President Clem Collins of the Grande Prairie Chamber. Abandoning their trusty steeds, they hustled the captives into a waiting station wagon and headed north. A red uniformed RCMP officer took off in hot pursuit. As in all the good movies, the Mountie "got his man." The prisoners were released and returned to the train at Hythe, which continued on to Dawson Creek.

Operating the NAR's telegraph in the station at Dawson Creek was Donna Porada, who was the railway's first female telegraph agent. Porada had succeeded A.E. "Jim" Chilton upon his untimely death the previous year.[12] When she joined the telegraph office staff in 1960, the office was located on 10th Street in Dawson Creek, but was later moved to the station. Porada had seen the telex and direct dial long distance telephone diminish the role of the telegraph office, and she knew the end of passenger service would kill the dwindling business.

While the telegraph business limped along in the 1970s, other problems were becoming evident. Vandalism had been on the increase and danger lurked in the most unexpected places. Equipment damage, smashed windows in vacant buildings, rocks piled on tracks, unlocked switches, rock throwing and pot shots taken at trains as they rolled by made crews feel as if they were indeed in the Wild West. When a small-bore bullet smashed through the window of an engine cab east of High Prairie, narrowly missing Engineer Trainee Robert Penner, the railway organizations sought protection for their members. NAR responded by establishing a quick radio link with the RCMP.[13]

At Dawson Creek vandals sent seven BC Rail boxcars on a Sunday jaunt toward the Alberta border in February 1974. As Agent Operator-Machine Clerk Gordon Waite and his wife, Lona, sat down to lunch they saw a string of boxcars rush by the station. Lunch was forgotten as Waite gave chase in his car. He reached the second highway crossing ahead of the runaways, but they were moving too fast to board. At the next highway crossing, Waite managed to climb aboard and set the brakes 3.5 miles from where the cars had taken flight. They had passed over six public crossings before they were stopped.[14]

This time no accident occurred at the crossings, but such was not always the case. The following month, Don Clark was engineer and Jim Gauvreau trainman on Train No. 52 when it ploughed into a heavy-duty truck loaded with logs at the Wapiti road crossing in Grande Prairie. The engine was hauling 31 loads, six empties and a flanger, operated by Sectionman Ed Heft, when it derailed. Fortunately, it was only the equipment that sustained damage.[15] With its head smashed in, engine No. 207 was not a pretty sight when it finally derailed.

Although the Dunvegan Yards shops were not designed or equipped to tackle such major repair work, the mechanical department soon had the badly damaged engine back on the rails looking like new.[16] Master Mechanic John Fraser's staff had risen to the challenge. Fraser had been raised surrounded by railroaders in McLennan, where his father, Duncan, was the railway's pump man and his mother, Jessie, worked as road-masters' clerk. The elder Fraser also had been among the organizers of the Brotherhood of Maintenance of Way Employees on the railway. Like many a railroader's son, John Fraser saw the railway as a career choice. He was ambitious and studied to further his advancement. It paid off. He was mechanical supervisor at the time of his appointment to master mechanic in 1972. Fraser was younger than many of the men he supervised, but in his 20 years with the railway he had seen them tackle many a similar type of repair job with equal success.

Locomotive No. 207 after collision with logging truck at Wapiti Crossing in Grande Prairie, 5 March 1974.

Toward the end of 1975, NAR's hunger for heavier diesel power was satisfied with the arrival of four SD 38-2 type 2000 horsepower diesel locomotives. At a cost of $2.1 million they were the cadillac in locomotives and the first of their design to be built in Canada by General Motors [Diesel] at their plant in London, Ontario. Designed to haul heavy loads on steep grades at low speeds, the units were expected to be better able to subdue the Peace and Smoky River hills. Phil Dickinson, who handled the first train out of Dunvegan Yards pulled by one of the new diesels, had seen a lot of changes in his 38 years with the railway. With retirement looming on the horizon, Dickinson knew there would not be many more "firsts" for him, as he handled the controls of the powerful locomotive.

NAR was handling bigger loads than ever before to the Syncrude plant. The movement of the heavier pieces was done during the winter months when frost penetration of the muskeg was at its greatest. In mid-January 1976, a special train left Dunvegan Yards with the heaviest load ever carried on the NAR. The reactor, destined for Syncrude, "had a gross weight of 1 110 600 lbs. or 555 tons."[17] The equipment was moved on two 12-axle cars borrowed from an U.S. railway. It was decided that the 60 lb. rail and the

Locomotive No. 401 was one of four new SD32-8 diesels that arrived to augment the fleet in January 1976.

bridges should be travelled at a speed of 10 mph. To provide continuous surveillance during the night, an observation caboose with wing floodlights was placed behind and a flat car idler in front of the load. Conductors Ted Stewart and Don Boake each had a train crew to make continuous movement possible. Along with Locomotive Engineers Ron Dempsey and Phil Dickinson, they knew successful handling of this big load would set the standards for others to come.

Gofiner reactor on route to Waterways.
Photo: Courtesy of E.G. Holtner

With a converted boxcar as the dining room, Cook Anne Bowman served man-sized meals. Cooking on a moving train was not a new experience for Bowman. For 13 years she had cooked for extra gangs using a similar big, black monster of a stove with its rail around the circumference to keep the saucepans in place. The general manager was among the officials who enjoyed her hearty meals on the long, tedious journey. The only crisis occurred when the pipe-

smoking Perry found himself in the cab of the trailing unit with his pipe and matches but no tobacco. Phil Dickinson, who was well supplied with both tobacco and cigarettes, responded to an SOS call over the radio. There was a noticeable sigh of relief when the load was spotted on Bechtel's spur. The trip had been made with no mishaps. In the following months there were some mighty heavy loads but none equalled the challenge of the first one.

Tumbler rings on specially designed well cars were four inches above the rails.
Photo: Courtesy of A.J. Dove

After the Christmas holidays in December 1976, the general manager called a meeting of the officers. Not a man to couch his words in frivolous trappings, he told them matter of factly that he was dying. What words did Ken Perry use? No one remembers exactly. It was the shortest meeting ever held in the boardroom. Numb with sorrow, no one felt very talkative. Manager, Purchases and Stores J.H. "Jim"

Laurie, who had succeeded Roy Martins in 1974, was at that meeting. He remembers the shock experienced by him and the other officers, "Who could believe that this vibrant man, who drove himself as hard as he drove his staff, was dying?"[18] Only two weeks previously he had been contemplating what career move he would make when he retired in less than two years time. Perry was 63 years of age when he died of cancer on 6 February 1977.

J.O. Pitts, General Manager, NAR, 1977-1981
Photo: Provincial Archives of Alberta
Edmonton Journal Collection, J4539

26

Golden Years

The railway was like a ship without a rudder in the weeks following Ken Perry's death. The rumor mill was busy. It was 15 February 1977 before the empty chair behind the general manager's desk was filled. James Orest Pitts' personality and appearance were the exact opposite of his predecessor. His modest style was anything but flamboyant and his unflappable temperament was a welcome change. As he quietly educated himself on the railway operation he won the respect of NAR personnel with his acknowledgement of their expertise.

Jim Pitts was CN Rail's regional manager of administrative and technical services prior to his appointment to NAR. Raised in Saskatchewan, Pitts became acquainted with railroading at a tender age – his father was a CNR section foreman. He joined that railway as an operator and train dispatcher in 1945. Four years later he was studying electrical engineering at the University of Saskatchewan. To finance his

education, he "socked" away wages earned by working for the CNR during his vacations. Following graduation, he spent two years in England on an industrial scholarship.

Pitts returned to the CNR in 1956 as assistant regional transportation engineer in Winnipeg. Appointments followed at intervals and in 1969 he became CN Rail's manager for the province of Alberta. The Great Slave Lake Railway and the Alberta Resources Railway came under his jurisdiction. In this position, he developed a rapport with NAR personnel that was to continue when he became its general manager. He was aware of the closeness, akin to that of a family, of NAR employees – a family in which he soon became immersed. Nevertheless, he knew the railway could not live in a time vacuum and technological changes already begun would continue.

A week after his appointment, Jim Pitts took his first trip to Waterways. On arrival at

Lac La Biche he was startled to see bullet holes in the station door. Agent Operator Stu McGregor hastened to explain the incident had occurred without any provocation on his part. A man brandishing a gun had commanded McGregor's attention in the wee hours of the morning on 23 February. As he quickly shut the door he heard the ping of bullets ricochetting off it. Earlier that morning Mechanical Supervisor Tom McVeigh had received minor injuries when shot and wounded in the left leg as he approached the station. A 17-year-old assailant was later arrested in connection with the incidents.

By spring, Pitts saw first-hand how NAR staff handled emergency situations. The trouble began in mid-April 1977 with an ice jam on the Clearwater River. The angry waters surged through Waterways and the lower townsite of Fort McMurray. A hole blasted in the ice the following day permitted flood waters to recede, leaving more than $2 million worth of damage. A state of emergency was declared. Bars and liquor outlets were closed until 7:00 p.m. on 16 April – a tragedy in itself for some. At Waterways, flood waters partly submerged eight railway bunk cars and tore away at the roadbed. This territory had been under the jurisdiction of Roadmaster Norman Dziwenka since 1972. He recalls, "Five or six washouts occurred, to a depth of four feet in places where the railway track parallelled the Clearwater channel, between Draper and Waterways."[1] As the water receded, sectionmen moved in to repair the damage and the track was restored

for traffic by 22 April.

Mother Nature was not about to let the railway off so lightly. There followed a series of disruptions when three derailments occurred within 24 hours. On 24 April, train No. 40, with a consist of 74 loads and 18 empties, derailed at Mile 32 on the Edmonton subdivision. Spring rains had softened the track, causing derailment of the fifty-second car in the consist. The following 11 cars followed, tearing up 325 feet of track. Two hours later, Engineer John Glowinski found himself in a similar predicament. Train Extra 303 East was travelling toward Busby. He hoped the train would stay on the spongy track, but Lady Luck had withdrawn her favors. The fourteenth car derailed at Mile 8.5 on the Barrhead Subdivision, causing six cars to derail ripping up 230 feet of track in the process.

General Manager Pitts and Chief Engineer Halasa were at the scene the following day with Roadmaster Peter Semenchuk. They admired the speed and efficiency with which General Car Foreman Bud McLean directed the cleaning up of the wreck. As they watched, news arrived of another derailment at Mile 222.7 on the Waterways subdivision. Pitts remembers, "Lee Halasa's usually calm demeanor was shaken by the news."[2] Nine cars, including one depressed six-axle flat dimensional load and eight loaded tank cars derailed on mixed Train No. 75, when the load shifted.[3] Conductor Jim Walsh and Engineer John Kalyta viewed with dismay the 625 feet of damaged track, including the deck of the bridge.

Although their trucks were deeply buried in the grade, the cars remained upright. Norman Dziwenka had a work gang and some others working in the area brought to the scene. Mechanical Supervisor and Road Foreman of Engines Frank Dove, Assistant Chief Engineer Rene Lessard and Bridge and Building Master John Brunetta arrived to assist. The train crew worked alongside the men rerailing the cars using the engine that was there. The track was restored without the assistance of auxiliary or other equipment and was opened by 28 April.

Things were beginning to settle down, but the rain continued and by mid-May slides began on the saturated Smoky River hills. The track moved several feet out of alignment in some areas and in others slumped, causing cracks. Section Foremen Arvad Anderson from Watino and Bill Bremner from Girouxville worked long hours along with their crews. Once traffic was moving again additional earth work, pile driving, and ditching was done in the following weeks to stabilize the embankments in the extensively damaged area.[4]

Damp weather did not deter Barrhead from pressing ahead with its plans for a fiftieth anniversary celebration. On 30 June 1977 business car "Peace River" carried dignitaries and railway officials to Barrhead for the occasion. To add to the excitement, the train was ambushed by two masked bandits at Manola. The outlaws were eventually driven off but not before one of their horses left evidence of his presence directly in front of the platform of the business car. Those, who assisted in putting the bandits to rout, were invited aboard to complete the journey to Barrhead. Among them was the Honorable Joe Clark, then leader of the Progressive Conservative Party.[5]

In the early days, the train was rarely on time, but on this occasion it was right on time. Unfortunately, the Barrhead railway station was no longer there. It had been sold and removed in 1971. Instead a large shopping complex was in the process of construction on two acres of the station grounds, leased from the railway. From the train guests climbed aboard a democrat and a horse drawn hay wagon. As if on cue, a hitch broke on the wagon and the horses bolted. By pushing the wagon to the street and hitching it to the leading buckboard everyone arrived at the banquet hall to enjoy the ceremonies.

As employees were sleepily preparing for work or sipping on that first cup of coffee on 20 October 1977 the radio announcement of a fire at Dunvegan Yards jolted them wide awake. Shift Foreman John Bannink and the crew had returned from lunch about 4:25 a.m. to discover fire creeping up one wall of the locomotive shop. The men's attempt to extinguish the flames was unsuccessful and the tinder dry wooden structure, built in 1943, burned rapidly. The building was little more than a shell by the time the fire brigade arrived. The loss of the shop temporarily interrupted the overhaul and upgrading of

NAR locomotives.

Good news arrived with the spring of 1978. The Government of Canada announced that NAR would be a signatory to its Branch Line Rehabilitation Program.[6] When funds were made available to grain dependent lines in July 1977 NAR applied. The payment was the result of mountainous paper work produced by the railway's Comptroller D.N. Tinston and his staff. He recalls, "Everything we did related to the various departments. I had to know certain operating information. The cooperation between the departments helped the financial position of the company."[7] Thus began a collaboration between the audit office and general office that had never existed before in the history of the railway.

Financial Officers: retired auditors Charles Anderson and Fred Kavanagh with comptroller Doug Tinston
Photo: K.R. Perry

But a number of events lead up to NAR's inclusion in the federal government subsidy program. The McPherson Royal Commission on Transportation in 1959-1961 had made provision for losses on grain carrying lines through branch line loss subsidies to assist with keeping the lines operational. Branch line rehabilitation subsidies were also identified by the commission to assist railways with capital improvements. These were support programs which the Government of Canada acted on.[8]

In March 1967, the Canadian government had frozen certain unprofitable grain carrying lines in western Canada to prevent their abandonment and paid subsidies to their owners. Although the Canadian Transport Commission had notified NAR of its eligibility for subsidy payments, the memo was inadvertently filed away. There it lay until 1974 when some chance remarks by CPR and Canadian Transport officials alerted the general manager and comptroller to the fact that there were subsidies NAR should be pursuing.[9] With less than a year to go before the "freeze" expired on 1 January 1975, Comptroller Tinston wondered if his department could meet the deadline. His staff did not disappoint him.

Doug Tinston had become NAR's chief financial officer early in 1973, after the sudden death of Comptroller Tom Waite. A graduate from Queen's University, the chartered accountant worked in the private sector, the Department of National Revenue, and the Ford Motor Company, before joining CNR. At the time of his appointment to NAR, he was chief accountant, general, at CN Rail's headquarters in Montreal and an expert on taxation matters.

Tinston liked the NAR's size, "it allowed everyone to keep in touch with all aspects of the operation." His quiet, unaffected manner belied his penchant for figures. When he realized NAR was eligible for branch line subsidies, he proceeded delving into the losses of past years. He knew a small railway, such as NAR, could benefit from making application if it could document the losses it had incurred over the years. The preparation of the data was painstaking and monotonous work. A system was devised for the audit office staff so that the information could be obtained in the process of their normal daily routine. Tinston handled the legalities and the paperwork. It all culminated in NAR receiving monies to which it was entitled but had been denied prior to his arrival.

Traffic levels dropped in 1978, but persistent lobbying finally paid off and a lump sum payment was received in May 1978 from the Canadian Transport Commission for prior years' branch line losses. Although the amount received represented only a portion of the amount outstanding, it improved the railway's financial picture considerably and the railway accounts showed a positive balance from that time forward.[10]

September 1978 brought a little glamor to NAR when a special train was run to Smith from Dunvegan Yards and returned to accommodate Universal Productions Canada Inc. The film company was shooting a $8 million feature length motion picture based on Olive Fredericksen's book *Silence of the North*. Some of the scenes involved a train of that period in the Smith/Hondo area. The Alberta Pioneer Railway Association supplied a baggage car and a combination baggage coach car, painted in the green color scheme typical of the Alberta and Great Waterways Railway. The steam locomotive used was supplied by the government of British Columbia and was transported to Smith with the main rods removed. NAR's genial road foreman instructor and mechanical supervisor made his debut as an actor in these scenes.

Frank Dove took the train up the hill toward Hondo while cameramen filmed the "passengers" inside the moving cars. The following day he was at the throttle of the steam locomotive as it crossed the Athabasca River bridge at Smith. The train on the bridge acted as a backdrop for a scene being filmed down by the river. When the movie was released Dove attended the premiere. The 22 September 1981 morning edition of the Edmonton Journal carried a headline: "ENGINEER HIT THE BIG SCREEN WITH FULL HEAD OF STEAM." When Dove arrived at work that morning he found the article taped to his office door with a huge star and the caption "A star is born." All clues led to the culprit being Draftsman Randy Domstad.

While the film took a step back to the days of steam, a step forward was being taken in the area of train operation. Train orders were in the process of being phased out as the manual block system [MBS] of train operation was implemented. MBS eliminated superiority of trains on moderate traffic lines. An MBS Clearance was the only authority for movement. All trains were designated as Extra, added direction or "Work Extra."

Designed for lower density lines, the MBS system had proven to be more efficient and flexible than other nonmechanical systems. Chief Train Dispatcher John Kobylanski spent many hours studying the CNR's system, adapting it to NAR conditions and training operating personnel.[11] The system was first implemented on the Peace River subdivision. He knew that part of the province well. He had been raised on a homestead near Rycroft, Alberta, and joined the NAR as third assistant agent in the station at Peace River. From there he travelled the system until his promotion to assistant to the supervisor of transportation in 1969. That he took his job seriously and strove to be a bit better than good was noticed by management. By 1974 he was supervisor, car control and three years later chief train dispatcher, a job with stress built in. Kobylanski was determined that if the MBS system was unsuccessful it would not be his fault. But it was an unqualified success and by October 1978 was expanded to include all subdivisions west of Smith.[12]

Instruction in MBS extended to the locomotive engineer training program. Approximately 30 engineers were qualified during those years under the tutelage of

Back: *Retired Chief Train Dispatcher Sam Mickelson and Bill Donlevy with Senior* Clerk Car Control, Ed Bailey. Front: *Chief Train Dispatcher John Koblanski* Photo: J.H. Laurie

Instructor Frank Dove. He had 33 years of experience in the running trades to his credit and knew the pleasure of occupying the coveted right hand seat of a locomotive. Rules and Safety Instructor Harold Stepney handled the instruction in rules and MBS. He had 44 years of railway service, many of them as a locomotive engineer. As Rules Instructor, he was responsible for examining all staff required to be qualified in the Uniform Code of Operating Rules as well as the MBS. After completing instruction, the students were assigned to various experienced locomotive engineers whom they accompanied on regular tours of duty. The success of the training programs depended upon the veteran engineers who continued to train these young men in actual working conditions.

Class of student locomotive Engineers, February, 1980. Back: *Len Lindsay, Rob Dent, Rick Bayers, Tom Trzmiel Ward Beagan, Kim Golanowski and Jim Paras.* Front: *Mike kuziw, Sid Tanquay and Instructor Frank Dove.*

It was about this time that section crews found themselves with the new title of track maintenance forces. Training programs for these employees were initiated at the CNR training centre at Kamloops, British Columbia. Some of the older folk growled that "an old dog could not learn new tricks," but they all passed the examinations and younger ones benefitted from the instruction.

While all the studying was taking place, Peace River was celebrating the Diamond Jubilee of the opening of the Peace River Bridge built by J.D. McArthur. The aging span was still carrying rail traffic. In 1968 a highway bridge had been built by Alberta

Transportation to divert vehicular and pedestrian traffic from the railway bridge. Festivities began on 6 August 1978 with the crossing of the bridge by a golden coach pulled by three diesel locomotives with Norman Valiquette at the throttle. Pulling out of the station the train broke through a ceremonial ribbon at the south approach to the bridge.

The golden coach had no resemblance to Cinderella's. It was none other than rules instruction car 18001. A few gallons of paint and new curtains had done wonders for the old timer. Its refurbishing had been planned for the NAR's Golden Anniversary celebration in 1979, but was accelerated. Inside, early railway equipment was on display. Afterwards the coach was moved to Fairview, which celebrated its golden jubilee from 7-13 August. On 7 August, the regular north wayfreight was rescheduled to arrive at the town at 1200. Engineer Ivan Ivancin moved his train forward until it broke through a ceremonial ribbon to commemorate the arrival of the first passenger train. The coach did not go into storage afterwards. Instead as 1979 rolled around, NAR's celebration of its first half century gathered steam. An old section handcar was refurbished by the car department and mounted on a trailer. It appeared at parades and exhibits towed by a company car bearing NAR fiftieth anniversary banners.

For three days in early July, it was McLennan's turn to celebrate. A homecoming attracted thousands to the town's sixty-

Clerks Susan Small and Rita Bouwsema with NAR's float which won second prize in the Edmonton Klondike Days Parade, July, 1979.
Photo: E.G. Holtner

fifth anniversary, but engine No. 73 stole the show.[13] The last NAR steam locomotive still in existence was deadheaded to McLennan as part of the consist of a special train on 6 July.[14] A team of retired and active railroaders worked on the old engine for weeks prior to the trip. In spite of the tender care, the engine's boiler did not meet Canadian Transport Commission standards and the engine could not move by its own power. There were cheers and some misty eyes as the old workhorse received some assistance to break through the banner at McLennan.

As part of NAR's golden anniversary celebrations, General Manager Pitts named each locomotive in the fleet after a northern

historical figure, town or river and 100 new lumber boxcars came off the assembly line at National Steel Car in Hamilton, Ontario, in mid-May. The gold colored cars carried blue NAR markings and the slogan "From the land of the Mighty Peace." They were immediately placed in North American service. The new cars put an end to the hijacking of CNR lumber cars en route to the GSL Railway, when NAR was short of cars.[15]

Locomotive No. 73, NAR's only surviving steam locomotive outshines two diesels.
Photo: E.G. JHoltner

The railway chose its fiftieth anniversary year to honor "old rails." Timetable number 73, dated 29 April 1979, had two new mileage names in it and three more were added the following year. The junction with the Barrhead subdivision at Busby was named Carley Junction. Station Agent Ira Card, General Manager James M. MacArthur, Section Foreman Wm. "Banko" Bence and Locomotive Engineer Fred Crowell, whom we have already met, were posthumously honored. A private siding at Mile 135.41 Grande Prairie subdivision was named "Iracard." The trackage at Mile 8.0 on the Peace River subdivision became known as "Crowell."

Locomotive No. 403 "Athabasca River," No. 401 "Peace River," and No. 404 "Smoky River" on Heart Bridge.
Photo: E.G. Holtner

Train with some of NAR's fifty foot boxcars crossing Strugeon Bridge.
Photo: E.G. Holtner

The naming of Carley Junction honored more than one railroader. Conductor John "Jack" Carley, Sr. and his three sons were all railroaders. The senior Carley came to the ED & BC as a conductor from the Grand Trunk Railway in 1914 to spend the rest of his career with the NAR. Jack Carley, Jr. felt fortunate to get a job as a pump man at McLennan when work was scarce during the Depression years and soon became a trainman. He served with the RCAF during the war and returned to the NAR where he was a conductor until retirement. Percy Carley was a trucker on the railway in May 1940, but later transferred into agency work. He was the victim of a fire that destroyed the station when he was agent at Eaglesham in 1966. At age 15, Pat Carley worked for the NAR during the school holidays. By 1945, he was a permanent employee, and like his father and brother Jack, train service appealed to him.

Carley Junction had just begun to have a familiar ring about it when Pat Carley lost both legs below the knee joints and badly fractured his left shoulder in a railway accident. He was trainman on Mixed Extra 303 South on 30 October 1979, when the accident occurred during switching operations at Chard, 73 miles out of Fort McMurray. Difficulties in coupling cars caused him to fall between a flat car and a water car.[16] Conductor Jim Walsh radioed the dispatcher, who contacted the RCMP at Fort McMurray. The railway was the only means of land transportation in and out of Chard. A helicopter landing next to the train transported Carley to the hospital at Fort McMurray. Later that evening, he was airlifted to the General Hospital in Edmonton for surgery.

The Carley mettle came to the fore and in a little over three weeks Pat Carley was learning to walk with artificial limbs. To everyone's surprise, he was soon driving a car equipped with normal foot controls. By November 1980, he was back in the saddle, but riding a different horse. As training officer, he assisted Harold Stepney in the instruction of operating personnel in rules and operating procedures. When Stepney retired, Carley succeeded him as rules and safety instructor. His was an example of the type of railway accident that can happen and an inspiration in how to handle it. Walking on what amounts to stilts had its pitfalls for a man over six feet tall. No one laughed harder than Carley at the scrapes his artificial limbs got him into. Once he slipped on a marble floor in CNR's Montreal office; the rush to assist him was quickly arrested as his legs went flying. There was a lot more than his pride hurt in the fall, but he could laugh at the absurdity of the situation.

Mechanic B. John Kirtio was not so fortunate. He lost his life in a highway accident, while returning from a work assignment on 7 March 1979. The NAR half ton truck he was driving was in a collision with a semi-trailer near Gibbons, Alberta. Kirtio, who was born in Poland, had been with the railway from 1940. His death cast a shadow on the anniversary celebrations of the railway.

What was probably the most talked about event of the railway's fiftieth anniversary was an afternoon tea held on 16 September to honor the surviving 94 retirees who had been in its service the year NAR was incorporated. Accompanied by spouses and relatives, 45 "old rails" arrived for the celebration. There were some poignant moments as hesitant recognitions were followed by pumping handshakes between people who had not seen each other for over 30 years. Although he could not be in attendance, the general manager conveyed a personal message by the wizardry of electronics and the assistance of Alec Messum, the able Master of Ceremonies. Fred Kavanagh, at 94 years was the oldest retired NAR officer there. With a steady hand he cut a cake decorated with the blue and gold NAR logo. Among the older railroaders there was 91 year old Bert Viney, retired station agent. There were also two 86 year olds: William Ellstock, retired roadmaster, and Glen "Cy" Barker, whose hand had been at the throttle of the railway's locomotives since 1912.

As old friends renewed acquaintances, the chatter rose to such a crescendo that at times it drowned out the music of General Accountant Art Rowe on his trombone and his accompanist, Mr. Schollmeyer, on the accordion. For a short while these proud old-timers were strong young men again, as they regaled their audiences with stories of accomplishments. The hardship and deprivations of those early years and the sicknesses that had plagued some in their sunset years were completely forgotten in the pleasure of seeing colleagues and reliving with them the past of a railway that had been a changing, growing entity.

There was a justifiable pride in the railway these dignified men had helped to build, which extended to all departments. This inordinate pride developed from the necessity for thrift, and having at their disposal minimal resources and discarded equipment from other railways. Adversity had only encouraged them to use their ingenuity to tackle the insurmountable. These qualities the veterans attempted to pass on to younger NAR employees with some measure of success. Jim Pitts recalls "the typical NAR employee's quiet confidence in his ability and pride in the company were quite noticeable to an outsider and were traits that, I think, set them apart and placed them a cut above other railroaders."[17]

Roy Ellstock accompanies his father, retired Roadmaster William Ellstock.
Photo: Provincial Archives of Alberta, 86.587/73

Retired Auditor Fred Kavanagh cuts the cake at NAR's 50th Anniversary Tea, 16 September 1979.
Photo: Provincial Archives of Alberta, 86.587/52

Russ Craig, Harry Swift and Frank Darby tell some tall tales of their station agent days.
Photo: Provincial Archives of Alberta, 86.587/99

Bill Simmons and Jack Christie chat with Glen
"Cy" Barker whose railway service dates from 1912.
Photo: Provincial Archives of
Alberta, 86.587/104

Before retirement sectionmen Stan Kisielewicz
and John Netolicky kept the NAR track serviceable
Photo: ProvincialArchives of Alberta
86.587/16

Retired Section Foreman Fred Suchy and Anne Suchy
share a joke with Sectionman John Shanz and Mary Schanz.
Photo: Provincial Archives of
Alberta, 86.587/98

Retired conductors Dick Coulman and Wm.
"Buttons" Mair recall the days of passenger trains.
Photo: Provincial Archives of
Alberta, *86.357/19*

27

Sun Sets on NAR

Early in 1980, unsubstantiated rumors began circulating about NAR's fate. Rumors of unsuccessful offers for its purchase had become a fact of life for the railway's employees and most disregarded them.[1] By March it was common knowledge that CN Rail was negotiating with CP Rail for the acquisition of NAR. Back in April 1977, chief commissioner of the Grain Handling and Transportation Commission, Mr. Justice Emmett Hall, had suggested the integration of the NAR with CNR in his recommendations. Few at NAR had taken this suggestion seriously, but now it was a very real possibility. The fate of the railway was confirmed in June.[2]

On 29 June 1980, the NAR Board of Directors in Montreal ratified an agreement between the parent companies for the procurement by CN Rail of CP Rail's half share of NAR and approval was requested of the Canadian Transport Commission.[3] The sale at a negotiated price of $34.5 million and other considerations allowed the CPR to retain its right to solicit traffic to and from the former NAR system through Edmonton. A six month period of preparation for the amalgamation was allotted and negotiations began with the various unions involved.

Hearts skipped a beat at the thought of the proposed changes, but the pulse of the railway was comforting. As the final chapter in the NAR's history was drawing to a close, a goal the city of Grande Prairie had been aiming at for almost 15 years was realized in June 1980. For a year, the NAR had been involved in negotiations for the relocation of its yard tracks, office, freight shed and telecommunication facilities to the ARR yards operated by CNR. With the city's growth, the location of NAR's facilities in the downtown core had become a bone of contention. The tracks sliced the downtown area in two causing chronic traffic jams at the 100th Street crossing when switching operations were in progress. Once an agreement was reached with Grande Prairie and the ARR to provide the financing and property to which NAR facilities could be moved, the relocation became a reality.[4]

The relocation was the responsibility of Roadmaster Ernie Lindstrom, whose headquarters had been Grande Prairie since December 1975. But it was Track Maintenance Foreman Ed Heft, with 28 years of experience, and his trackmen who did the physical labor that made the project go smoothly. The move cleared 17 acres of prime downtown land for redevelopment and assisted in the consolidation of CNR and NAR operations. Communications equipment had to be moved to the new site. If having a backhoe cutting through a cable laid a few days earlier tested nerves, a half-ton truck hitting the corner of staff headquarters at 2:00 a.m. one morning was the absolute limit for communications personnel. The scrunching of metal woke up Equipment Inspector Jay Duhamel and Assistant Plant Supervisor Dennis Mahoney. But Travelling Repeater Attendant Ed Wirachowsky continued to sleep even though he slept in the bedroom that received the impact.

Meanwhile, NAR was attempting to find a use for Lynton yard near Fort McMurray. After Syncrude built an assembly yard in Edmonton, the amount of material NAR hauled north dwindled.[5] Prior to that, NAR had "added to [the] Lynton yard an extremely efficient and expensive sulphur loading pad, support tracks and track scale" to accommodate GCOS.[6] But the bottom had

fallen out of the sulphur market by 1976 and the facility stood idle. An offer by a sulphur forming operator to lease the yard in 1980 was snapped up and molten sulphur, a by-product of the oil sands, began to move by truck to Lynton. There it was converted to a coarse granular material and loaded into rail cars. Cars loaded to capacity with the yellow sulphur began moving over the railway to the west coast.

On the Barrhead subdivision, the upgrading program, which had begun in 1979, was in full swing. When Roadmaster Peter Semenchuk retired before completion of the project, Fred Kulynych succeeded him. In spite of technological advances in the industry, rail laying still required manpower. This was done by Gang 12 under the direction of Foreman John Zurkan. As they had done for many years, Zurkan and his wife, Sally, who was timekeeper, worked as a team on the gang.

While work out on the line continued without interruption, the Manpower Planning Committee, set up to ensure a smooth transition, sought to give surplus employees full consideration in filling positions on CNR. Although relations between the two railways and their staffs had usually been cordial and informal, it was a disquieting time for NAR personnel as they pondered their futures. Bolstered by their high standards and pride in their railway the close-knit family feeling among NAR railroaders surfaced. Many had spent their entire careers with NAR and did not welcome a change.

At a luncheon to honor Walter Arason on his retirement are left to right: *Jack King, Clarence Comrie, Bob Lloyd, Alec Messum, Jim Laurie, Frank Dove, Jim Pitts, Harold Stepney, Ena Schneider, Jim Rouse and Walter Arason.*
Photo: L.L. Halasa

Some eligible employees took advantage of the CN Rail Pension Plan permitting employees 55 years or older with 30 or more years of service to elect early retirement. There was empathy with those who chose to take early retirement rather than adjust to a new style of management, but the majority took the giant leap and reached for the new horizons offered by the larger organization. Soon some of them would be scattered across the country from British Columbia to Quebec in new positions.

CN Rail was bound by the collective agreements already in effect on NAR. Except for the running trades, unionized employees were sandwiched in with their CN Rail coun-

Locomotive No. 203, renumbered CN 4604,
pulls into the CN Yards in Edmonton.
Photo: E.G. Holtner

terparts. Agreements made with the running trades granted "homestead rights" to NAR members enabling trainmen and enginemen to work the same territory they had covered when it was NAR.

Regulatory approvals were received before Christmas 1980 to enable purchase arrangements to be completed by the year end. CN Rail's Mountain Region Vice-President Ross Walker was sympathetic to the disruption experienced by NAR's personnel, many of them second and third generation employees, and insisted that the integration be done gradually to minimize potential adverse effects during the adjustment period. On 1 January 1981 a new day dawned as NAR became the Peace River Division of the CN Rail's Mountain Region.[7]

Hitched to the CN Rail team, NAR would lose its identity and bring an era in railroading in northern Alberta to a close. Back in 1929 NAR had been the "giant" that was created from four smaller railways in a consolidation that transformed the pioneer-

ing railway into a highly successful operation both financially and in terms of its contribution to the quality of life in northern Alberta. But its frontier days were long gone and now NAR was part of a transcontinental railway. No longer would the familiar blue and gold diamond logo be seen as trains rolled by the towns the railway and its predecessors had brought into existence.

No amount of change can obliterate the fact that the NAR was the lifeline to northern Alberta before the advent of roads and airplanes. Alberta owes much to J.D. McArthur, whose vision opened up the north country to settlers, and to the railroaders under whose guidance the railway was transformed into a modern facility. The NAR played an intrinsic part in the development of the north, and while it may fade into history, the prosperity it brought Alberta will linger. Whenever its "old rails" meet they will recall the adventures, the challenges, the frustrations and the triumphs of the railway's glory days.

Locomotive No. 206 and train on the Athabasca Bridge at Smith
Photo: E.G. Holtner

Abbreviations

CEA   City of Edmonton Archives
GAI   Glenbow-Alberta Institute
PAA   Provincial Archives of Alberta
PAC   Public Archives of Canada

Notes for Chapter 1

[1] Trust Indenture, The Edmonton, Dunvegan and British Columbia Railway Company to National Trust Company Limited and His Majesty the King, representing the province of Alberta, securing 30 year, 4 percent Guaranteed Debenture Stock, 22 July 1912.

[2] Stanley H. McCuaig to Mrs. Betty McArthur, 5 March 1971.

[3] Mrs. Kay Baylis, telephone interview, 13 May 1987, Toronto, Ont.

[4] "J.D. McArthur Passes Away," *Province*, [Vancouver], 10 January 1927.

[5] Maurice Mahood, "Northern Alberta Railways," unpublished draft manuscript, chapter 4, p. 2.

[6] McCuaig to McArthur, 5 March 1971.

[7] R.G. MacBeth, *Peace River Letters*, (Vancouver: 1915), p.11.

[8] "Obituary," *Canadian Railway and Marine World*, February 1927, CPR Archives.

[9] John A. Eagle, "J.D. McArthur and the Peace River Railway," *Alberta History*, (Autumn 1981), p. 34.

[10] J.D. McArthur to M. Dailey, 7 February 1919.

[11] McCuaig to McArthur, 5 March 1971.

[12] J.W. Judge, "Early Railroading in Northern Alberta," *Alberta Historical Review*, (Summer 1958), p. 12.

[13] "Cousin Recalls Fabulous Builder," *Herald-Tribune*, [Grande Prairie], 23 September 1955, Charles MacDonell to author, 24 June 1986.

[14] Grant MacEwan, *The Battle for the Bay* (Saskatoon: Western Producer Book Service, 1975), p. 123.

[15] G.W.E. Smith interview, 4 March 1986.

[16] Hugh Macintyre, diary, 1912, Acc. 82.38/1, PAA.

[17] Declaration of Abandonment documents, Acc. #82.38/2, PAA.

[18] "Obituaries: J.D. McArthur, Veteran Builder of West, Dead," *Winnipeg Tribune*, 10 January 1927.

[19] Mrs. Kay Baylis telephone interview, 13 May 1987.

Notes for Chapter 2

[1] *Statutes of Canada*, 6-7, Edward VII, Chapter 85.

[2] Acc. 84.388, file 1100.140.1, PAA.

[3] Canada, Department of Transport, *Statutory History of the Steam and Electric Railways of Canada 1836-1937* (1938), p. 197.

[4] Mahood, "NAR," chapter 15, p.4A.

[5] Mahood, "NAR," chapter 15, p. 4A.

[6] J.D. McArthur, "A Brief History of the Edmonton, Dunvegan & British Columbia Railway, and of the Central Canada Railway," 12 April 1920, RG43, Vol. 556, #17773A Part II, PAC.

[7] J.W. Judge, "Early Railroading," *Alberta Historical Review*, (Summer, 1958), p.13.

[8] "Steel Rails are Hard to Secure," *Edmonton Bulletin*, 19 March 1912, p. 1.

[9]Evidence given by W.R. Smith before the Public Accounts Committee, 16 March 1916, Acc. 74.1, Item 309, PAA.

[10]"Agreement between His Majesty the King and the Edmonton, Dunvegan and British Columbia Railway Company," 9 June 1912, Acc. 70.414/48, PAA.

[11]Certificates of Ownership, 31 October 1892, 29 June 1908, 12 January 1912, Alberta Land Titles Office, Edmonton.

[12]Mahood, "NAR," chapter 3, p. 17.

[13]Mahood, "NAR," chapter 3, p. 18.

[14]G.E. Barker interview, 15 February 1988.

[15]City of Edmonton building permits October 1914, taken out under the name of the Alberta & Great Waterways Railway, which McArthur was also building, CEA.

[16]J.W. Judge, "Early Railroading," *Alberta Historical Review*, (Summer, 1958), p. 15.

[17]J.D. Williams, "A History of the Edmonton, Dunvegan & British Columbia Railway, 1907-1929," (unpublished M.A. thesis, University of Alberta, April 1956), p. 28.

[18]Williams, "History of ED & BC," p. 29.

[19]"Expert Engineers Here on Monday," *The Northern News*, [Athabasca], 18 June 1915.

[20]"To Complete 120 Miles of M'Arthur Line this Year," *Edmonton Bulletin*, 20 August 1912.

[21]Williams, "History of ED & BC," p. 30.

[22]"ED & BC Line Now At Morinville," *Edmonton Journal*, 14 January 1913; *Grouard News*, 25 January 1913.

[23]Waller B. Smith to author, 13 November 1986.

[24]Douglas R. Smith to author, 16 December 1986.

[25]Evidence before the Public Accounts Committee, 16 April 1915, pp. 41, 43, 52.

[26]Malcolm MacKinnon, "Northward Ho! or the Great Waterways Road," pp. 70, 114, M.766, GAI; Mrs. N. Prest interview, 21 March 1986.

[27]Mahood, "NAR," chapter 4, p. 10.

[28]G.E. Barker interview, 30 January 1986.

[29]Mahood, "NAR," chapter 6, p. 6.

[30]Mahood, "NAR," chapter 4, p. 12.

[31]Williams, "History of ED & BC," p. 32.

[32]Advertisement by Port Cornwall Board of Trade, *Grande Prairie Herald*, 30 December 1913.

[33]"Local News," *Grande Prairie Herald*, 27 January 1914, p. 1.

[34]History Book Committee, *Sodbusters* (Edmonton: Bulletin-Commercial Canada), pp. 33-34.

[35]Charles A. MacDonell to author, 24 June 1986. Ewen MacDonell was from Lancaster, Ontario.

[36]Miss Isabel M. Campbell, ed., *Pioneers of the Peace* (Grande Prairie and District Old Timers' Association, 1975), p. 322.

[37]*Henderson's Directory*, 1915, CEA.

[38]Neil Hyslop, notes, n.d.

Notes for Chapter 3

[1]Mahood, "NAR," chapter 5, p. 1A.

[2]McLennan History Book Committee, *Trails and Rails North – History of McLennan and District* (McLennan: McLennan History Book Committee, 1981), p. 172.

[3]Mahood, "NAR," chapter 5, p. 1A.

[4]RG 43, Volume 544, file 17277, PAC.

[5]Mahood, "NAR," chapter 5, p. 11A.

[6]Lee Halasa interview, 27 May 1986.

[7]"On the Northland, Limited," *Edmonton Bulletin*, 9 November 1914.

[8]John F. Gilpin, *Edmonton – Gateway to the North* (Canada: Windsor Publications, 1984), p. 75.

[9]*Henderson's Directory*, 1909, CEA.

[10]J.M. MacArthur to Miss Jane Godherson, 10 April 1950.

[11]Tracks forming the letter Y.

Notes for Chapter 4

[1]Kenneth S. McLennan to K.R. Perry, 21 November 1974.

[2]*San Francisco Theological Seminary Bulletin*, clipping, n.d.

[3]Rev. R.G. MacBeth, *Peace River Letters*, (Vancouver: 1915), p. 11.

[4]*San Francisco Theological Seminary Bulletin*, clipping, n.d.

[5]History Book Committee, *History of McLennan*, p. 1.

[6]History Book Committee, *History of McLennan*, p. 313.

[7]Mahood, "NAR," chapter 6, p. 3.

[8]K.R. Perry to Miss Joan Carley, 2 July 1973.

[9]W. Ellstock interview, 15 February 1988.

[10]RG 43, Vol.571, file 181898, PAC.

[11]McArthur, "History of ED & BC," p. 3.

[12]Holden Swift, "McLennan – a History in Capsule," n.d.

[13]W.J. Donlevy, notes, September 1988.

[14]G.W.E. Smith interview, 3 November 1985.

[15]History Book Committee, *Sodbusters*, p. 98.

[16]Myrtle Crowell interview, 27 October 1980.

[17]"Edmonton, Dunvegan and British Columbia Railway Schedule for Enginemen, effective 1 June 1916."

[18]G.W.E. Smith interview, 6 August 1986.

[19]V. Maurice, *Fifty Years in the Peace River Country and a Short Story of the Alaska Highway* (High Prairie: 1947), p. 71.

[20]J.G. MacGregor, *The Land of Twelve Foot Davis* (Edmonton: Applied Art Products Ltd., 1952), p. 349.

[21]Mrs. Lillian Donlevy, telephone interview, 16 February 1988.

[22]Mrs. Margaret Jones to Maurice Mahood, 28 October 1980.

[23]Mahood, "NAR," chapter 6, p. 9.

[24]Mahood, "NAR,", chapter 6, p. 10.

[25]History Book Committee, *History of McLennan*, p. 245.

[26]History Book Committee, *History of McLennan*, pp. 311-313.

[27]Mahood, "NAR," chapter 6, p. 15.

[28]Marie Cimon Beaupre, ed., *By the Peavine . . . in the Smoky . . . of the Peace* (Edmonton: Stuart Brandle Printing, 1980), p. 205.

[29]M. Mahood to C. McCombs, 3 September 1980. (8 June 1987), p. 26

[30]Mahood, "NAR," chapter 11, p. 7.

[31]Mrs. Myrtle Crowell interview, 27 October 1980.

[32]Margaret Jones to Maurice Mahood, 28 October 1980.

[33]Margaret Jones to Maurice Mahood, 28 October 1980.

[34]W.C. Kirkland interview, 24 June 1977, audio tape, Peace River Centennial Museum.

[35]"Town of McLennan," publicity booklet, revised November 1958.

Notes for Chapter 5

[1]"Railway News,"*Grande Prairie Herald*, 26 January 1915.

[2]Gertrude Bryan, *Land of the Spirit, History of Spirit River United Church*, (Menzies Printer: n.d.), p. 42.

[3]Mahood, "NAR," chapter 7, p. 5.

[4]Williams, "History of ED & BC," p. 70.

[5]G. Robinson, "Reminiscences of G. Robinson of life in Peace River 1915-1935," A.R661, GAI.

[6]Sheila Douglass, *A Candle in the Grub Box, A Struggle for Survival in the Northern Wilderness* (Victoria: Shires Books, 1977), p. 46.

[7]Harold Fryer, *Alberta – The Pioneer Years* (Langley, British Columbia: Stagecoach Publishing Co. Ltd., 1977), p. 157.

[8]Robinson, "Reminiscences."

[9]Mr. and Mrs. Karl Olson interview, 14 August 1987, Watino, Alberta.

[10]"Prudent's Crossing Growing,"*Grande Prairie Herald*, 9 March 1915.

[11]Robinson, "Reminiscences."

[12]Pioneer History Society of Hythe and Area, *Pioneer Round-up: A History of Albright, Demmitt, Goodfare, Hythe, Lymburn, Valhalla* (Calgary: Friesen & Sons Ltd., 1972), p. 209.

[13]Williams, "History of ED & BC," p. 71.

[14]"Spirit River Merchants Preparing For Rush of Winter Trade,"*Grande Prairie Herald*, 18 January 1916.

[15]Macintyre diary, p. 88.

[16]C.A. Dawson and R.W. Murchie, *The Settlement of the Peace River Country, A Study of a Pioneer Area* (Canada: The MacMillan Company of Canada Limited, 1934), p. 36.

[17]Margaret Loggie, "Dunvegan, Fort of the Past," p. 8, Acc. 971.231, L829, PAA.

[18]"Closing of H.B. Post at Dunvegan Marks Passing of Landmark,"*Peace River Record*, 24 May 1918.

[19]A bridge has long since replaced the ferry and the mission church has been restored and designated an historic resource by Alberta Historic Sites.

[20]"Press Telegraphic Service,"*Grande Prairie Herald*, 30 October 1914, p. 1.

[21]McArthur, "History of ED & BC and CC Railways."

[22]"Grade on ED & BC Completed One Third of Distance to Grande Prairie,"*Grande Prairie Herald*, 24 August 1915, p. 1.

[23]Sexsmith to the Smoky Historical Society, *Wagon Trails Grown Over - Sexsmith to the Smoky* (Edmonton: Friesen Printers, 1980), p. 930.

[24]"Grande Prairie Building News,"*Grande Prairie Herald*, 11 April 1916.

[25]"Large Crowd Assembles to Witness Driving of Last Spike,"*Grande Prairie Herald*, 28 March 1916.

[26]Campbell, *Pioneers of the Peace*, p. 14.

[27]"Large Crowd Assembles,"*Grande Prairie Herald*, 28 March 1916.

[28]"Big Excursion Party Leaves on ED & BC

for Grande Prairie,"*Edmonton Bulletin,* 30 June 1916.

²⁹"Streams Swollen by Recent Rains Do Considerable Damage,"*Grande Prairie Herald,* 11 July 1916.

³⁰Orville Willis interview, 2 September 1985.

Notes for Chapter 6

¹Walter Mueller, as told to Mrs. Gertrude Bryan, *Reminiscing with Walt* (Spirit River, 1964), p. 23.

²"Work to be Pushed on Line of ED & BC to Boundary,"*Edmonton Bulletin,* 14 June 1916.

³"Peace River to Get Improved Train Service,"*Grande Prairie Herald,* 19 September 1916, p. 1.

⁴"Cousin Recalls Fabulous Builder,"*Grande Prairie Herald-Tribune,* 23 September 1955; Mahood, "NAR," chapter 10, p. 4A.

⁵Mrs. Betty McArthur interview, 6 May 1981, Grande Prairie, Alberta.

⁶Mahood, "NAR," chapter 10, p. 6A.

⁷*Statutes of Canada,* 1916, 6-7 George V, chapter 1, Vote 110.

⁸RG43, Vol.555, file 17773, Part I, PAC.

⁹RG43, Vol. 555, file 17773, Part I, PAC.

¹⁰Mahood, "NAR," chapter 10, p. 6A.

¹¹Mulcahy v. Edmonton, Dunvegan and British Columbia Railway Company, *Western Weekly Reports,* 1919, p. 644, Law Courts Library, Edmonton, Alberta.

¹²Mulcahy v. ED & BC Ry., 1919, p. 585.

¹³Eunice E. Ferguson, "Guaranteed bonds –

A High Venture," 21 November 1983.

¹⁴RG43, Vol.555, file 17773, Part I, PAC.

¹⁵Williams, "History of ED & BC," p. 103.

¹⁶RG43, Vol.555, File 17773, Part I, PAC.

¹⁷Alex Ferguson, inspecting engineer, Department of Railway and Canals, Ottawa, to W.A. Bowden, chief engineer, RG43, Vol555, File 17773, Part I, PAC.

¹⁸"To Look After Interests of J.D. McArthur,"*Edmonton Bulletin,* 6 May 1919.

¹⁹Association of Professional Engineers of the provnce of Manitoba records.

²⁰Rea, J.E., *The Winnipeg General Strike* (Toronto/ Montreal: Holdt, Rinehart and Winston of Canada, 1973).

²¹"Sympathetic Strike is Called Off,"*Edmonton Bulletin,* 25 June 1919.

²²"Agreement between the Edmonton, Dunvegan and British Columbia Railway and Machinists, Boilermakers, Blacksmiths and Carmen, effective 1 July 1917 to 1 July 1918."

²³Carl Whiteman interview, 21 November 1984; Gerald Whiteman interview, 19 August 1985.

²⁴Fred Faust interview, 9 November 1987.

²⁵*Henderson's Directory,* 1919-1924.

²⁶"Peace River Country Has Bumper Crops,"*Edmonton Bulletin,* 28 August 1919.

²⁷Northern Alberta Railways,"Looking Back," *The Headlight,* June 1972.

²⁸Mahood, "NAR," chapter 12, p. 2.

²⁹"J.D. McArthur At Ottawa Regarding ED & BC Railway,"*Edmonton Bulletin,* 6 October 1919.

³⁰Williams, "History of ED & BC," p. 104.

³¹Alberta Professional Engineers, Geologists

and Geophysicists Association records.

[32]*Alberta Historical Review,* (Summer, 1958).

Notes for Chapter 7

[1]Robert Kroetsch, *Alberta* (Canada: Macmillan Company of Canada, 1968), p. 174.

[2]*Statutes of Alberta,* 4 George V, 1913, Chapter 46 (First Session).

[3]*Statutes of Alberta,* 4 George V, 1913, Chapter 7 (Second Session).

[4]A.R. Gibson to A. Chard, 3 April 1928.

[5]Mahood, "NAR," chapter 7, p. 4.

[6]"Reno, The Busy Burg At The Meeting Point of Steel and Trail,"*Peace River Record,* 29 April 1915.

[7]J.G. MacGregor, *The Land of Twelve Foot Davis,* (Edmonton: Applied Art Products, 1952), p. 349.

[8]"Railway Line Will Positively Come To Peace River Crossing," *Peace River Record,* 11 March 1915.

[9]Williams, "History of ED & BC," pp. 65-66.

[10]F.T. Judah interview, 13 January 1986.

[11]Mahood, "NAR", chapter 10, p. 7.

[12]"ED & BC Trains To Run Over GTP Tracks," *Edmonton Bulletin, 13 April 1918.*

[13]G.A. Walker to C.E. Stockdill, 11 May 1922.

[14]Mrs. N. Prest interview, 8 October 1986.

[15]W.J. Donlevy notes, September, 1988.

[16]Mahood, "NAR," chapter 7, p. 11.

[17]*Canadian Annual Review,* 1915, p.708.

[18]George France, "Sixty Years to the Peace 1916-1976," *Canadian Rail,* No. 314, March 1978, p. 75.

[19]Incorporated under Dominion Letters Patent, 21 October 1915.

[20]Mahood, "NAR," chapter 2, p. 11.

[21]Charles Dominy interview, 23 June 1985.

[22]60th anniversary of Peace River bridge celebrations, 6 August 1978, audio tape, Peace River Centennial Museum.

[23]Mahood, "NAR," chapter 2, p. 12.

[24]Mahood, "NAR," chapter 2, p. 12.

[25]W.R. Smith, Testimony before Public Accounts Committee, 16 April 1915, p. 28, Acc. No. 70.414/129, PAA.

[26]"ED & BC Make Important Arrangements," *Grande Prairie Herald,* 12 September 1916.

[27]"Memorandum of Agreement," 13 November 1917, between Grand Trunk Pacific Railway Company and the ED & BC, A & GW and CC railways.

[28]George de Mille, *Oil in Canada West, The Early Years* (Calgary: Northwest Printing and Lithographing Ltd., 1970) p. 214.

[29]"Railway To The McArthur Well," *Peace River Record,* 21 December 1917.

[30]"Wholesale Bribery Being Attempted By Liberal Heelers," *Peace River Record,* 27 June 1917.

[31]*Statutes of Canada,* 8-9 George V, 1918, chapter 52, Item 382.

[32]"Last Piers Being Completed For Bridge Across The Peace" *Peace River Record,* 15 February 1918.

[33]Katherine Hoskin, ed. *I Remember Peace River, Alberta and Adjacent Districts 1914-1916. Part II,* (Peace River: The Women's Institute of Peace River, 1975-1976) p. 92.

[34]McArthur, "Histroy of ED & BC," RG43, Vol. 556, No. 17773A, Part II.

[35]History Book Committee, *History of McLennan,* p. 218.

[36]Neil Hyslop, telephone interview, 10 March 1986.

[37]"Railway Construction Limited," *Peace River Record,* 12 April 1918.

[38]Tom Keenan, "Peace River," *Alberta Motorist,* (July/August 1979), p. 9.

[39]"Steel To Vanrena Within Twelve Months," *Peace River Record*, 2 November 1917.

[40]Hoskin, *I Remember Peace River*, p. 89.

[41]"Pasturage and Hay Along Dunvegan Line is Sufficient," *Edmonton Bulletin*, 14 July 1919.

Notes for Chapter 8

[1]*Statutes of Dominion of Canada*, 4-5 Edward VII, 1905, chapter 58.

[2]Alberta Recreation and Parks, "A History of Lesser Slave Lake," 3 December 1981, p. 47.

[3]John W. Chalmers et al, *The Land of Peter Pond*, Occasional Publication Number 12 (Edmonton: Boreal Institute for Northern Studies, 1974), p. 78.

[4]"Evidence taken at Royal Commission re: A & GW Railway Co.," 1910, p. 5, Acc. No. 74.1/322, PAA.

[5]"To Open North in Three Years," *Edmonton Bulletin*, 30 September 1909.

[6]The State Historical Society of Missouri, records.

[7]Morris Zaslow, "A History of Transportation and Development of the Mackenzie Basin from 1871 to 1921" (unpublished thesis, University of Toronto, 1948), p. 192, Ref: TC 17820, National Library of Canada.

[8]*Men of Affairs in Greater Kansas City, 1912* (Kansas City, Mo: Gate City Press, 1912), p. 116.

[9]Joint collection, University of Missouri, Western Historical Manuscript Collection.

[10]The State Historical Society of Missouri, Centennial History of Missouri, pp. 280-285.

[11]Centennial History of Missouri, pp. 280-285.

[12]"A & GW Royal Commission," 1910, p. 628.

[13]"A & GW Criticism Coming to a Head," *Edmonton Bulletin*, 22 February 1910.

[14]A & GW Royal Commission 1910, p. 634.

[15]*Statutes of Alberta*, 9 Edward VII, 1909, Chapter 46.

[16]*Statutes of Alberta*, 9 Edward VII, 1909, Chapter 16.

[17]"Manitoba Legislature Scrapbook," 30 April 1909.

[18]C.W. Parker, ed., *Who's Who in Western Canada*, (Toronto: Canadian Press Association, 1911 and 1912).

[19]"A GW Royal Commission," 1910, p. 1937.

[20]A & GW Royal Commission 1910, p. 1937.

[21]"Decision to Be Given Shortly," *Edmonton Bulletin*, 6 January 1912.

[22]Canadian Annual Review of Public Affairs, 1910.

[23]Zaslow, "Transportation and Development of the Mackenzie Basin," p. 189.

[24]L.G. Thomas, *The Liberal Party in Alberta, a History of Politics in the Province of Alberta 1905-1921* (Canada: University of Toronto Press, 1969), p. 70; Morris Zaslow, *The Opening of the Canadian North 1870-1914* (Toronto: McClelland and Stewart, c.1971), p. 213.

[25]"First Sod Was Turned Today," *Edmonton Bulletin*, 15 November 1909.

[26]John Blue, *Alberta Past and Present* (Chicago: Pioneer Historical Publishing, 1924), p. 125.

[27]"Climax Will Be Reached Today," *Edmonton Bulletin*, 25 February 1910.

[28]Journals of the Legislative Assembly of the province of Alberta, 10 February to 26 May 1910, p. 70.

[29]Thomas, *The Liberal Party in Alberta* (Toronto: University of Toronto Press, 1969), p. 82.

[30]Douglas R. Babcock, *A Gentleman of Strathcona: Alexander Cameron Rutherford*, Occasional Paper No. 8 (Edmonton: Historic Sites Service, 1980), p. 62.

[31]Blue, *Alberta Past and Present*, p. 127.

[32]Canadian Annual Review of Public Affairs,

1910.

[33]"Alberta, Royal Commission on the Alberta and Great Waterways Railway Company Report," Legislature Library, Edmonton, Alberta.

[34]*Henderson's Directory*, 1911.

[35]"Fugitive of Map of A & GW Turns Up,"*Edmonton Bulletin*, 10 December 1910.

[36]"Waterway's Clarke Has Another Bluff,"*Edmonton Bulletin*, 23 January 1912.

[37]Acc. 70.414, PAA.

Notes for Chapter 9

[1]"Agreement between The Edmonton Dunvegan & British Columbia Railway Company, and The Alberta and Great Waterways Railway Company," 3 May 1918.

[2]"McArthur Starts Work on A & GW," *Edmonton Bulletin*, 29 December 1913.

[3]"Opening Up North Country," *The Northern News*, 23 January 1914.

[4]A.W. (Tony) Cashman, *More Edmonton Stories* (Edmonton: The Institute of Applied Art, 1958), p. 219.

[5]Boyle & District Historical Society, *Forests, Furrows and Faith – A History of Boyle and Districts* (Winnipeg: Inter-Collegiate Press, 1982), p. 458.

[6]Historical Society, *A History of Boyle and Districts,*, p. 315.

[7]Jean Chubb and Hilde Milligan, *Leaves of Yesteryear – A History of the Bon Accord District and the Biographies of the Men and Women who Pioneered the Area* (Bon Accord F.W.U.A., Local 502, Edmonton: Co-op Press, 1969), p. 90.

[8]Chubb and Milligan, *Leaves of Yesteryear*, p. 54.

[9]Historical Society, *A History of Boyle and Districts*, p. 569-570.

[10]Historical Society, *A History of Boyle and Districts*, p. 16.

[11]Historical Society, *A History of Boyle and Districts,*., p. 27.

[12]Otto Michetti to author, 7 May 1985.

[13]"Evidence given before the Public Accounts Committee," 16 March 1916, p. 31, Acc. 74.1/309, PAA.

[14]Information from map drawn by retired NAR Roadmaster Otto Michetti.

[15]MacKinnon, "Northward Ho!," p.132, Acc.M.766, GAI; N Otto Michetti interview, 22 August 1986.

[16]"Evidence given before the Public Accounts Committee," 16 March 1916, p. 31.

[17]"Lac La Biche," *Edmonton Bulletin*, 17 May 1917.

[18]"No Extension Likely," *Edmonton Bulletin*, 2 March 1926.

[19]T.W. Pawlik, H. Grant, eds., *Lac La Biche – Oasis of the North* (Lac La Biche: The Golden Jubilee Historical Committee, 1969), p. 8.

[20]J.G. MacGregor, *Edmonton, A History* (Edmonton: Hurtig Publishers, 1967), p. 22.

[21]Mike Maccagno, *Rendezvous – Notre Dame des Victoires* (Lac La Biche: M. Maccago, 1987), section 1.3.

[22]Maccagno, *Rendezvous*, section 1.6.

[23]Acc. 67.100, PAA.

[24]"Ken Liddell's Column," *Calgary Herald*, 27 May 1975.

[25]Miss Mary Watson interview, 27 August 1987.

[26]Fire destroyed the Lac La Biche Inn in 1988.

[27]"Minutes of Meeting of Board of Directors, A & GW, 8 December 1921," Acc. 84.388/19, PAA.

[28]George Buck, "The McKeen Cars Mystery," *The Marker*, pp. 141-156.

[29]Robertson, Wm. E., *The Woodstock and Sycamore Traction Company* (Wisconsin: National

Bus Trader, 1985), p. 52.

[30]Mahood, "NAR," chapter 9, p. 10A.

[31]Glenn Kelly to M. Mahood, 14 October 1980.

[32]Mahood, "NAR," chapter 9, p. 7.

[33]Miss Mary Watson interview, 14 April 1983.

[34]Mahood, "NAR," chapter 9, p. 4.

[35]"Lac La Biche Claims Five Edmonton Victims," *Edmonton Bulletin*, 11 August 1916. Newspaper error – only 4 were drowned.

[36]Lac La Biche Heritage Society, *Lac La Biche Yesterday & Today* (Calgary: D.W. Friesen & Sons, 1975), p. 184.

[37]"Lac La Biche in Ashes," *Edmonton Bulletin*, 21 May 1919.

[38]Minutes Board of Directors' Meeting, A & GW, 4 August 1921.

[39]In 1920 those rails that could be salvaged were torn up and moved to McArthur's logging operation to Widewater on Lesser Slave Lake.

Notes for Chapter 10

[1]Mahood, "NAR," chapter 9, p. 6.

[2]J.G. MacGregor, *Paddle Wheels to Bucket-Wheels on the Athabasca* (Toronto: McClelland and Stewart, 1974), p. 152.

[3]Otto Michetti to author, 7 May 1985.

[4]Anna Barabash, telephone interview, 21 August 1983, .

[5]William Barabash, telephone interview, 21 August 1983, .

[6]James S. Walsh interview, 22 July 1987.

[7]"Public Accounts Committee 16 April 1915," Acc. 70.414, Box 5, Item 129, PAA.

[8]G.J. Tranter, *Link to the North*, (England: November 1946), p. 77.

[9]Otto Michetti to R.D.C. Comrie, 5 September 1986.

[10]Mahood, "NAR," chapter 11, p. 3.

[11]"People at House River Are Forced into Hills," *Edmonton Bulletin*, 22 April 1918.

[12]Papers of William Pearce 1848-1930, University of Alberta Archives.

[13]Papers of William Pearce 1848-1930.

[14]"A & GW Line is Being Extended," *Edmonton Bulletin*, 1 January 1919.

[15]"Weekly Service from Lac La Biche to McMurray," *Edmonton Bulletin*, 26 September 1919.

[16]Mahood, "NAR," chapter 11, p. 10.

[17]Donley vs Edmonton Dunvegan & British Columbia Railway, Supreme Court, Alberta, 1920, Law Courts Library, Edmonton.

[18]Tranter, *Link to the North*, p. 77.

[19]"Weekly Service from Lac La Biche to McMurray," *Edmonton Bulletin*, 26 September 1919.

[20]"Weekly Service . . . " *Edmonton Bulletin*, 26 September 1919.

[21]Otto Michetti to R.D.C. Comrie, 5 September 1986.

[22]"Will Assist in Moving Freight at McMurray," *Edmonton Bulletin*, 28 August 1919.

Notes for Chapter 11

[1]RG43, Vol.555, file 17773, Part I, PAC.

[2]Various accounts show the name spelled Dougherty, Docherty and Doherty.

[3]Mahood, "NAR," chapter 11, p. 14.

[4]Ed Buchanan, telephone interview, 19 July 1988, S/Sgt. Buchanan, RCMP, met the train in Edmonton. He recalls Mrs. Doherty escaped from Kingston Penitentiary and was found working as a cook in Alberta Hospital, Ponoka, one and a half years later.

[5]Lillian Donlevy interview, 11 October 1985.

[6]Holden Swift to M. Mahood, 26 October

1980.

[7]Glenn Kelly to M. Mahood, 29 October 1980.

[8]W.J. Donlevy notes, September 1988.

[9]George A. Walker, CPR chairman, address to CPR Officers' Association, Calgary, 1930; Mahood, "NAR," chapter 11, pp. 15-17.

[10]Mahood, "NAR," chapter 12, p. 10.

[11]Mrs. Marie Rose Dandurand interview, 12 May 1987. The hotel had at one time been the immigration hall.

[12]Mrs. Myrtle Crowell interview, 27 October 1980.

[13]J.D. McArthur to W.R. Smith, 23 March 1920.

[14]*Statutes of Alberta*, 10, George V, 1920, Chapter 6.

[15]"Man's Arm Amputated by Train Wheel," *Edmonton Bulletin*, 16 April 1920.

[16]Glen Barker interview, 30 September 1986.

[17]"Increase in Rates on ED & BC," *Edmonton Bulletin*, 1 May 1920.

[18]"Case Finished Against Boost in Rail Rates," *Edmonton Bulletin*, 23 June 1920.

[19]Canadian Railway and Marine World, October 1919, CPR Archives.

[20]"ED & BC Representatives Threaten to Throw up Sponge,"*Edmonton Bulletin*, 20 June 1920.

[21]Williams, "History of ED & BC," p. 109; Mahood, "NAR," chapter 12, pp. 15-16.

[22]Hoskins, ed. *I Remember Peace River*, p. 94.

[23]Williams, "History of ED & BC," p. 108.

[24]In 1918 the name was first used when the Government of Canada began taking over railways with financial difficulties.

[25]*Statutes of Alberta*, 10 George V, 1920, Chapter 6.

Notes for Chapter 12

[1]*Statutes of Alberta*, 11 George V, 1921, Chapter 56.

[2]"CPR Given 5 year Option on ED & BC," *Edmonton Bulletin*, 26 July 1920.

[3]"Settlement of North Railway Agreement Again Held Up," *Edmonton Journal*, 5 August 1925.

[4]Agreement between the Edmonton, Dunvegan & British Columbia and Central Canada railways, the province of Alberta, J.D. McArthur Company Limited and the Union Bank of Canada, Canadian Pacific Railway, and John D. McArthur, 21 July 1920.

[5]"Officials Named by General Manager Macgregor," *Edmonton Bulletin*, 23 July 1920.

[6]Mrs. N. Prest interview, 25 October 1984.

[7]Mrs. Margaret Nix to author, 24 March 1986.

[8]"Canadian Pacific Sets out to Vigorously Develop Northland," *Edmonton Journal*, 29 July 1920.

[9]"Canadian Pacific Sets Out . . ." *Edmonton Journal*, 29 July 1920.

[10]Mahood, "NAR," chapter 13, p. 1.

[11]John W. Macgregor interview, 23 May 1983.

[12]Alfred Price, *Rail Life – A book of Yarns* (Toronto: Thomas Allen, 1925), p. 196; Canadian Pacific Archives.

[13]Helen Hill to M. Mahood, 2 September 1983; Mahood, "NAR," chapter 13, p. 3.

[14]G.W.E. Smith interview, 4 November 1980.

[15]Mahood, "NAR," chapter 13, pp. 4-5.

[16]Helen Hill to M. Mahood, 2 September 1983.

[17]"New Stations Are Opened on the ED & BC," *Edmonton Bulletin*, 7 September 1920.

[18]Mahood, "NAR," chapter 13, p. 10.

[19]Roy Newnham to M. Mahood, 24 October 1980.

[20]Williams, "History of ED & BC," p. 118.

[21]Williams, "History of ED & BC," p. 119.

22F.J. Kavanagh interview, 16 May 1982.

23Mahood, "NAR," chapter 13, p. 13.

24Fred Kavanagh interview, 16 May 1982.

25Mahood, "NAR," chapter 13, p. 13.

26"Province Absolutely Protected On Agreement," *Edmonton Bulletin*, 1 April 1921.

27"R.E. Campbell's Motion...Defeated in Legislature," *Edmonton Bulletin*, 8 April 1921.

28"Pouce Coupe Oil Locations Turn in Big Revenue," *Edmonton Bulletin*, 28 January 1921.

29"We Get Letters," *The Headlight*, May 1974.

30Mrs. V.W.E. Smith interview, 12 April 1988.

31James R. Sheady to author, 15 July 1988.

32Association of Professional Engineers, Geologists, and Geophysicists of Alberta, records.

33Department of Railways, *Alberta Annual Report*, 1922.

34Mahood, "NAR," chapter 14, p. 12.

35Mahood, "NAR,

36The code OS, meaning "on sheet" was used by telegraph operators to report trains leaving their stations to the dispatcher.

37Mahood, "NAR," chapter 14, p. 13.

38D.C. Coleman to The Honorable V.W. Smith, 27 November 1922.

39D.C. Coleman to Premier Greenfield, 9 March 1923.

40Mrs. Audrey Whiteman interview, 21 November 1984.

41Glen Kirkland interview, 15 August 1985.

42*Statutes of Alberta*, 11 George V, 1921, Chapter 64.

43G.W.E. Smith interview, 22 October 1984.

44*Statutes of Alberta*, 11 George V, 1922, Chapter 41.

45Acc. No. 70.414/631, PAA.

46Ken Bolton, et al, *The Albertans* (Edmonton: Lone Pine Media Productions Ltd., 1981), p. 56.

47M. Mahood to H. Swift, 5 June 1977.

48M. Mahood to R.D.C. Comrie, 23 October 1984.

Notes for Chapter 13

1Ena Schneider, "The Peanut Road," *Canadian Rail*, No. 398, (May-June 1987).

2"Trains Will Be Running Directly Into Fort McMurray," *Edmonton Bulletin*, 10 September 1920.

3Acc.70.414, Box 5, Item 129, PAA.

4H.A. Warner, "The Alberta and Great Waterways Railway," *The Transmitter*, (November, 1921).

5"Trains Will Be Running Directly Into Fort McMurray," *Edmonton Bulletin*, 10 September 1920.

6"Memorandum of Agreement," 31 August 1920, Acc. No. 70.414/433, PAA.

7Northern Construction Company, "Brief History of Northern Construction Company Ltd.," n.d.

8Walter Hill, "Early Days of the Northern Alberta Railways, formerly the Alberta & Great Waterways R.R.," *The Headlight*, (November 1973).

9Princess Patricia Canadian Light Infantry Regimental Museum, records.

10Acc. 70.414, Item 388, Box 10, PAA.

11Tony Cashman, *Singing Wires* (Alberta: Alberta Government Telephones, 1972), p. 256.

12Pharmaceutical Association Archives, Edmonton.

13Walter Hill interview, 3 May 1986, Fort McMurray, Alberta.

14Mahood, "NAR," chapter 14, pp. 3-6.

15Mrs. V.W.E. Smith interview, 12 April 1988.

16Ena Schneider, "John Callaghan – a Legend," *The Headlight*, (July 1979), p. 8.

17Stan Morgan and Alec Messum interview, 8 November 1983.

18Stan Morgan interview, 12 September 1983.

19Mahood, "NAR," chapter 14, p. 18.

[20]Mahood, "NAR," chapter 14, p. 19.

[21]Warren Caragata, *Alberta Labour – a Heritage Untold* (Toronto: James Lorimer & Company, 1979) p. 61.

[22]"A & GW – List of Employees and their Salaries as at August 18th and October 31st, 1921," Acc. 84.388, File 1100.191.1, PAA.

[23]"A & GW - List of Employees and their Salaries,", Acc.84.388, File 1100.191.1, PAA.

[24]Northern Construction Company Ltd., records.

[25]"McMurray People Told That Railway Will Not Reach There Until . . ." *Edmonton Bulletin*, 28 October 1921; Mahood, "NAR," chapter 15, p. 3.

[26]"McMurray People Told . . ." *Edmonton Bulletin* 28 October 1921.

[27]"Bridge Across Creek is Only Obstacle," *Edmonton Bulletin*, 13 September 1921.

[28]Hill, "The NAR and A & GW," *The Headlight*, (November, 1973).

[29]Walter Hill to M. Mahood, 18 March 1981. Retired Superintendent of Communications Al Smith recalls that this phone service was never integrated with the Alberta Government Telephone system which took over the local telephone system in the late 1950s.

[30]Hill, "The NAR and A & GW," *The Headlight*, (November, 1973).

[31]Frank W. Anderson, *The Rum Runners*, (Frontier Book No. 11).

[32]Otto Michetti to author, 7 May 1985.

[33]Mahood, "NAR," chapter 15, p. 8.

[34]Department of Railways, Alberta Annual Report, 1925.

[35]H.V. Viney interview, 4 October 1980.

[36]H.V. Viney interview, 4 October 1980.

[37]"Express Messenger on Waterways is a Friend To All," *Edmonton Journal*, 25 July 1925.

[38]James G. MacGregor, *A History of Alberta* (Edmonton: Hurtig Publishers, 1977), p. 216-217.

[39]Jno. Callaghan to J.A. Macgregor, 9 February 1924.

Notes for Chapter 14

[1]"Denies ED & BC Has Deteriorated," *Edmonton Journal*, 17 August 1926.

[2]"Province To Operate ED & BC With CN," *Edmonton Bulletin*, 5 November 1926.

[3]J.H. Frechette interview, 20 November 1980.

[4]J.H. Frechette interview, 20 November 1980.

[5]J.H. Frechette interview, 20 November 1980.

[6]J.H. Frechette interview, 20 November 1980.

[7]Charles Anderson interview, 23 October 1984.

[8]Memorandum of Agreement between Canadian Northern and Grand Trunk Pacific and ED & BC, CC, and A & GW, 11 November 1926.

[9]A.S. Messum interview, 8 November 1983.

[10]Shirley McLennan to author, 20 December 1985.

[11]The running gear of locomotive No. 14 is believed to have been dumped in front of a bridge pier in the Smoky River.

[12]G.W.E. Smith interview, 4 November 1980.

[13]"Winnipeg Co. Gets Contract For Railways," *Edmonton Bulletin*, 14 May 1928.

[14]R. Craig interview, 3 May 1981.

[15]Logan Sherries interview, 24 June 1977, Nampa, Alberta, audio tape, Peace River Centennial Museum.

[16]Hec MacLean, ed., *Waterhole and Land North of the Peace* (Fairview: Waterhole Old Timers Association, 1970), p.163.

[17]Eldon Oliver interview, 6 June 1986; Gordon Waite, "Reminiscences," 15 September 1985.

[18]*Statutes of Canada*, 18-19 George V, 1928.

[19]H.K. Williams to author 16 October 1987. He later became an executive with Greyhound Lines of Canada.

[20]Fred Hajek interview, 4 October 1984, Westlock, Alberta.

[21]Stan and Mary Hryniuk interview, 6 June 1985.

[22]South Peace Centennial Museum, Beaverlodge.

[23]E.C. Stacey, *Beaverlodge to the Rockies* (Calgary: D.W. Friesen & Sons, 1976), p. 105.

[24]"Happy Birthday, Hythe," *Heritage,* (May-June 1978), p. 17; Pioneer History Society of Hythe and Area, *Pioneer Round-up* (Calgary: D.W. Friesen & Sons, 1973), pp. 296-297.

Notes for Chapter 15

[1]*Statutes of Alberta,* 2-3 George V, 1912, Chapter 31.

[2]J.A. Macgregor to D.C. Coleman, President, ED & BC, 15 December 1921.

[3]*Statutes of Alberta,* 16-17 George V, 1926, Chapter 62.

[4]Department of Railways, Alberta Annual Report, 1926.

[5]"Surveyors Locating Route For Extension ED & BC Railway," *Edmonton Journal,* 12 April 1926.

[6]H.K. Williams to author, November 1987.
[7]Williams to author, November 1987.

[8]Mrs. Doris Dalby telephone interview, 12 February 1986.

[9]Fiftieth Anniversary Book Committee, *The Golden Years* (Barrhead: Barrhead and District Chamber of Commerce, 1977), p. 11.

[10]Department of Railways, *Alberta Annual Report,* 1927.

[11]Pembina Valley Railway Timetable No. 18, 17 October 1927.

[12]Lorne Frizzell to author, 6 July 1987.

[13]Lorne Frizzell to author, 10 April 1987.

[14]T. Roberts interview, 20 November 1984.

[15]Anniversary Book Committee, *The Golden Years,* p. 396.

[16]G.E. Barker interview, 25 August 1985.

[17]Anniversary Book Committee, *The Golden Years,* p. 397.

[18]NAR Timetable No. 37, 27 September 1953.

Notes for Chapter 16

[1]Premier Brownlee to E.W. Beatty, 7 October 1927.

[2]Agreement between The Canadian Pacific Railway Company and The Canadian National Railway Company, 29 January 1929, and signed 6 February 1929.

[3]Report of Northern Alberta Railways Company for the six months ending 31 December 1929.

[4]Report of the Deputy Minister of Railways to The Honorable Vernor W Smith, 1 January 1930.

[5]*Statutes of Canada,* 19-20 George V, 1929, Chapter 48, Bill 71 passed by the House of Commons 15 May 1929 and assented to 14 June 1929.

[6]Minutes Annual General Meeting of Shareholders, 1 April 1930.

[7]*Canadian Annual Review,* 1928-29.

[8]J.H Frechette interview, 20 November 1980.

[9]Ken Liddell, "Ken Liddell's Column," *The Calgary Herald,* 12 February 1974.

[10]Gordon Waite, "ED & BC, CC, NAR, and PV Railways," unpublished, p. 3.

[11]H.W. Tye interview with Geo. Gooderham of the Riveredge Foundation, 10 June 1974, D920 G649A, GAI.

[12]Eric J. Holmgren and Patricia M. Holmgren, *Place Names of Alberta* (Saskatoon: Western Producer Prairie Books, 1976).

[13]E.D. Froome interview, 18 September 1985,

Kelowna, BC

[14]H.K. Williams to author, 16 October 1987.

[15]"Steel Laid to Swan Lake Siding," *Grande Prairie Herald*, 17 October 1930.

[16]Olav Aaberg to Walter Arason, 23 November 1979.

[17]"First Passenger Train," *Peace River Block News*, 15 January 1981.

[18]Lillian York, ed., *Lure of the South Peace* (Dawson Creek: South Peace Historical Book Committee, 1981), p. 783.

[19]Gordon Waite, Interview, 29 July 1985.

[20]W.J. Donlevy, notes, September 1988.

[21]Roy Martins interview, 17 July 1985.

[22]Gordon Waite, "Reminiscences," unpublished, 15 September 1985, p.6.

[23]Waite, "Reminiscences," unpublished, p. 9.

[24]Waite, "Reminiscences," unpublished. p. 7.

[25]Waite, "Reminiscences," unpublished. p. 7

[26]E.C. Stacey, ed., *Beaverlodge to the Rockies Supplement* (Calgary: D.W. Friesen & Sons, 1976), pp. 107-111.

[27]M. Mahood to F. Darby, 29 March 1984.

[28]Rory Graeme to M.E. Collins, 29 May 1930.

[29]Waite, "The Long Arm of a Lineman," unpublished.

[30]Waite, "Reminiscences," unpublished, pp. 4-5.

Notes for Chapter 17

[1]Olav Aaberg interview, 28 August 1985.

[2]NAR Timetable No.3, 3 July 1931.

[3]W.J. Donlevy, "The Depression Years, Bucking the Spare Board," *The Retired Railvets News*, (Spring-Summer 1981).

[4]The Buffalo Lake Community Society, *Buffalo Trails – Tales of the Pioneers* (Buffalo Lakes: The Buffalo Lake Community Society, p. 180.

[5]W.C. Kirkland interview, audio-tape, Centennial Museum Peace River.

[6]R.D.C. Comrie, Interview, 21 July 1983.

[7]Orville Willis interview, 2 September 1985.

[8]H.W. Tye to J.F. Cooper, 16 June 1953.

[9]A.M. Bezanson, *The Peace River Trail* (Edmonton: The Journal Co., 1907).

[10]Jno. Callaghan to Board of Railway Commissioners, Ottawa, 15 August 1935.

[11]N.E. Persson interview, 2 August 1985.

[12]Keith A. Parker, "Arthur Evans; Western Radical," *Alberta History*, (Spring 1978), p.21.

[13]"Floods Continue To Cause Damage In North Country," *Peace River Record*, 12 July 1935.

[14]Historical Book Committee, *History of McLennan*, p.185.

[15]H.W. Tye to J.F. Cooper, June 16, 1953.

[16]Jack Graham interview, 8 August 1985.

[17]Holden Swift, "That Flood," *The Headlight*, September 1971, p. 3.

[18]Roy Collins interview, 23 July 1986.

[19]C.G. Dominy interview, 23 June 1985.

[20]W.J. Donlevy interview, 30 June 1987.

[21]Harry Swift interview, 24 September 1985.

[22]W.R. Lawton, at Mile 172, to M.E. Collins, 24 August 1935.

[23]"Residents Abandon Slave Lake Town," *Peace River Record*, 5 July 1935.

[24]Mahood, "NAR," chapter 15, p. 16.

[25]Mahood, "NAR," chapter 15, p. 16.

[26]Karl Olson interview, 14 August 1987, Watino, Alberta.

[27]Karl Olson interview, 15 June 1986, Watino, Alberta.

[28]Mrs. E. Christoffel interview, 23 February 1987.

[29]James Rouse interview, 23 June 1985.

[30]Mrs. Hilda M. Blake to author, 25 May 1987.

[31]General Manager to Board of Railway Commissioners, Ottawa, 15 August 1935.

[32]Mahood, "NAR," chapter 6, p. 8.
[33]Mahood, "NAR," chapter 6, p.. 8-9.
[34]Nick Zinko interview, 11 November 1985.
[35]Stan Deakin to author, 8 November 1985.
[36]L.L. Halasa interview, 27 May 1986.
[37]Mahood, "NAR," chapter 2, p. 15.
[38]Walter Johnson interview, 26 June 1987.

Notes for Chapter 18

[1]Alec Messum interview, November 1983.
[2]Otto Michetti to author, 18 November 1985.
[3]Charles Anderson interview, 23 October 1984.
[4]Roy Collins interview, 23 July 1986.
[5]W.J. Donlevy, notes, September 1988.
[6]Omer Lavallee says, "The term 'butterflies' arose as a result of notes to track personnel which officers threw off the back of moving trains. The notes fluttered in the tail wind of the train, hence the term."
[7]Charles Dominy interview, 23 June 1985.
[8]Donlevy, "A Boss to be Remembered – J.M.M."
[9]A.S. Messum, interview, 8 November 1983.
[10]A.S. Messum, Interview, 8 November 1983.
[11]H.W. Tye interview, D920, GAI.
[12]W.H. Tye to author, 16 January 1987.
[13]H.W. Tye to J.M. MacArthur, 31 December 1950.
[14]Stan and Mary Hryniuk interview, 6 June 1985.
[15]Darlene J. Comfort, *The Abasand Fiasco* (Edmonton: Friesen Printers, 1980), p. 35.
[16]Roy Ellstock telephone interview, 28 September 1988.
[17]D.J. Comfort, *Pass the McMurray Salt Please!* (Fort McMurray: Fort McMurray Public Library, 1975), p. 19.

[18]Ed. John W. Chalmers and the Staff of the Boreal Institute for Northern Studies, *The Land of Peter Pond*, Occasional Publication Number 12 (1974), p. 102.
[19]Ray Price, *Yellowknife* (Toronto: Peter Martin Associates, 1967), p. 124.
[20]Mrs. Elise G. Turnbull to author, 8 May 1987.
[21]H.V. Viney interview, 4 October 1980.
[22]Gordon Waite, "Reminiscences," 15 September 1985, p. 17.
[23]Memo, "Gold Bullion, handling of on NAR," 22 February 1939.
[24]Elsie G. Turnbull, "A Great Mine's Beginnings," *Up Here*, (February/March 1987), p. 27.
[25]Gerald Whiteman interview, 19 August 1985.

Notes for Chapter 19

[1]*Merit Students Encyclopedia*, vol.I, (U.S: Crowell-Collier Educational Corp., 1969), p. 351.
[2]Stan Cohen, *The Trail of '42 – A Pictorial History of the Alaska Highway* (Missoula, Montana: Pictorial Histories Publishing, 1979), p. 4.
[3]Richard L. Neuberger, "The Northern Alberta Railway," *Railway Magazine*, (January, 1954).
[4]United States Army, *The U.S. Army in Alaska*, Pamphlet 360-5, July 1972.
[5]C.P. Stacey, *Arms, Men and Governments – The War Policies of Canada 1939-1945* (Ottawa: Queen's Printer, 1970), p. 348.
[6]Don Menzies, ed., *The Alaska Highway* (Edmonton: Stuart Douglas, n.d.).
[7]Neuberger, "The Northern Alberta Railway," *Railroad Magazine*, (January, 1954).
[8]J.M. MacArthur, memo to file written after discussion with G.R. Pearkes, 5 September 1939.

[9]Jim Christy, *Rough Road to the North, Travels Along the Alaska Highway* (Toronto: Doubleday Canada, 1980), p. 30.

[10]D. Baker to author, 30 August 1985.

[11]J.E. Deakin to railway union representatives, 27 November 1942.

[12]George Stephenson interview, 12 August 1986.

[13]Jack Graham interview, 8 August 1985.

[14]Jack Graham interview, 8 August 1985.

[15]Mrs. Irene Hardie to author, 20 November 1985.

[16]Bill Donlevy notes, Spetember 1988.

[17]Jack Graham interview, 8 August 1985.

[18]Otto Michetti to author 7 May 1985.

[19]Mel Hauer to author, 17 November 1985.

[20]C.G. Dominy interview, 23 June 1985.

[21]J.G. Wintermute interview, 1 October 1985.

[22]Mrs. Shirley Hunter, 16 January 1987.

[23]Mrs. Margaret Nix telephone interview, 12 April 1986, Toronto, Ontario,

[24]Miss Gwen Vigus interview, 28 January 1986.

[25]Charles & Lillian Dominy interview, 23 June 1985.

[26]Charles & Lillian Dominy interview, 23 June 1985.

[27]Charles & Lillian Dominy interview, 23 June 1985.

[28]History Book Committee, *History of McLennan*, p. 185.

[29]L. Pucci telephone interview, 14 January 1988.

[30]Joe Frechette to author, 26 July 1985.

[31]Olga Steele to author, 18 May 1987.

[32]Olga Steele to author, 18 May 1987.

[33]Richard L. Neuberger, "The Atomic Line," *Railway Progress*, July, 1950.

[34]Otto Michetti interview, 1 September 1988.

[35]G.W.E. Smith telephone interview, 18 August 1986.

[36]C.A.R. Passmore interview, 1 May 1981.

[37]*Echoes Along the Athabasca River* (Smith: Smith Half Century Plus Historical Book Committee, 1984), p. 46.

Notes for Chapter 20

[1]"Rapid Growth of Dawson Creek Brings Vital Problems," *Peace River Block News,* 7 January 1943.

[2]NAR booklet, "Highlights in the History of the Northern Alberta Railways," 1980.

[3]W.J. Donlevy interview, 11 October 1985.

[4]J.E.G. Potter to M. Mahood, 24 October 1980.

[5]Heather Menzies, "A Passage To Adventure," *Edmonton Journal,* 21 September 1974.

[6]Stan Morgan interview, 8 November 1983.

[7]Bill Donlevy notes, September, 1988.

[8]F.J. Kavanagh interview, 16 May 1982.

[9]Charles Anderson interview, 23 October 1984.

[10]Charles Anderson interview, 23 October 1984.

[11]Stan Cohen, *The Trail of '42,* p. 18.

[12]Dennis Mahoney interview, 7 August 1986.

[13]T. Sgt. Joseph Opperman, 843rd Signal Service Battalion, U.S. Army Corps., *Pole-Line to Alaska* (U.S.: Commercial Printers), p. 2.

[14]Allen E. Wharton, Office of the Chief Signal Officer, U.S. War Dept., Washington, to J.M. MacArthur, 6 August 1942.

[15]J. Holden interview, 10 July 1986.

[16]Harry Briggs, superintendent of communications, to the General Manager, 6 June 1946.

[17]W.J. Donlevy interview, 11 October 1985.

[18]W. Howe interview, 16 June 1986, McLennan, Alberta.

[19]"Miller Construction Company Exonerated," *Peace River Block News,* 6 January 1944.

[20]Nick Moskalyk interview, 21 August 1985.

[21]Mrs. Alta Wilton interview, 15 September 1985.

[22]W.J. Donlevy interview, 11 October 1985.

[23]Ida Sanderson, "Eddie Breault didn't come Home," *Western People*, 23 April 1987.

[24]"Explosion and Fire Takes Five Lives," *Peace River Block News*, 25 February 1943.

[25]Bill Thompson, "The Night Dawson Creek Burned Down," *Alaska Magazine*, (January, 1981).

[26]"Miller Construction Company Exonerated," *Peace River Block News*, 6 January 1944.

[27]"Alaska Highway Official Now," *Peace River Block News*, 12 August 1943.

[28]Nick Moskalyk interview, 21 August 1985.

[29]Orville Willis interview, 2 September 1985.

Notes for Chapter 21

[1]George de Mille, *Oil in Canada West* (Calgary: Northwest Printing and Lithographing, 1969), p. 199.

[2]Gilpin, *Edmonton Gateway to the North*, p. 178.

[3]Chalmers, *The Land of Peter Pond*, p. 103.

[4]Richard L. Neuberger, "The Northern Alberta Railway," *Railroad Magazine*, (January, 1954).

[5]Tranter, *Link to the North*, p. 244.

[6]Otto Michetti to author, 7 May 1985.

[7]Otto Michetti to author, 7 May 1985.

[8]Paul Sawin interview, 13 August 1987, Beaverlodge, Alberta.

[9]Otto Michetti to author, 18 November 1985.

[10]J.M. MacArthur to Operating Committee, 14 July 1942.

[11]Walter Hill, "The A & GW and NAR," *The Headlight*, (February, 1974), p. 2.

[12]Hill, "The A & GW and NAR," *The Headlight*, (February, 1974), p. 2.

[13]M.T. LaBrier to author, 16 February 1981.

[14]Stan and Mary Hryniuk interview, 6 June 1985.

[15]Paul Sawin interview, 13 August 1987.

[16]Paul Sawin interview, 13 August 1987.

[17]Otto Michetti to author, 18 November 1985.

[18]Bruce Hunter telephone interview with R.D.C. Comrie, 26 March 1987.

[19]de Mille, *Oil in Canada West*, p. 210.

[20]Richard L. Neuberger, "Gold, Oil and Pitchblende Lure of North's Fabulous Wilderness," *The Oregonian Sunday Magazine*, 28 August 1949.

[21]Robert Bothwell, *Eldorado - Canada's National Uranium Company* (Toronto: University of Toronto Press, 1984), p. 127.

[22]Neuberger, "The Atomic Line," *Railway Progress*, (July, 1950), p. 20.

[23]B. Carmichael Sumner, "Down North on the Mackenzie," *The Beaver*, (Spring, 1965), p. 33.

Notes for Chapter 22

[1]Annual Reports, 1945, 1946, 1947, covering Colonization and Land Settlement Activities in the Peace River area of Alberta and British Columbia.

[2]L.L. Halasa interview, 27 May 1986.

[3]Charles and Lillian Dominy interview, 23 June 1985.

[4]L.L. Halasa interview, 27 May 1986.

[5]G. Kirkland interview, 15 August 1985.

[6]C.J. Swanson, "The Runaway Caboose," unpublished, 23 July 1985.

[7]Ken Liddell, *I'll Take the Train* (Saskatoon: Western Producer Prairie Books, 1966), p. 108.

[8]Under the Brown system of discipline an accumulation of 60 demerit marks warranted dismissal. Demerit marks could be reduced at

the rate of 20 per demerit-free year. On the other hand, accumulated merit marks remained on an employee's record permanently. There was no provision for merit marks to cancel out demerit marks.

[9]Gordon Waite, "Reminiscences," 15 September 1985, p. 30.

[10]Stan and Mary Hryniuk interview, 6 June 1985.

[11]Stan and Mary Hryniuk interview, 6 June 1985.

[12]Otto Michetti interview, 1 September 1988.

[13]Acc. 86.587, p. 290, PAA.

[14]D.R.B. Macnaughton interview, 4 May 1981.

[15]Glen Kirkland interview, 15 August 1985.

[16]Orville Willis interview, 2 September 1985.

[17]"Inquest Rules Death of NAR Porter was Accidental," *The Fairview Post*, 2 October 1958.

[18]Jack Graham interview, 8 August 1985.

[19]Mrs. J. Bowden interview, 19 January 1988.

[20]Otto Michetti interview, 7 May 1985.

[21]Holden Swift, *The Retired Railvets News*, (Autumn, 1982), p. 3.

[22]R.D.C. Comrie to Geo. L. Brown, 23 November 1953.

[23]W.R. Gilchrist interview, 22 July 1985.

[24]W.R. Lawton's accident report, 17 November 1959.

[25]L.L. Halasa to J.H. Vollans, 17 November 1959.

[26]R. Craig interview, 3 May 1981.

[27]Mrs. E.M. Chausse to author, 16 April 1986.

[28]Stan Morgan interview, September 1983.

[29]Stan Morgan interview, September 1983.

[30]W.R. Lawton to General Manager, 11 November 1959.

[31]"Inquest Probes Train Collision," *Edmonton Journal*, 26 January 1960.

Notes for Chapter 23

[1]G.W.E. Smith interview, 3 November 1985.

[2]G.W.E. Smith interview, 4 November 1980.

[3]Boyle and District Historical Society, *Forests, Furrows and Faith*, p. 519.

[4]Lon Marsh, "End of an Era," *Canadian Rail*, No. 387, (July-August, 1985).

[5]Nick Moskalyk interview, 21 August 1985.

[6]M.T. LaBrier to author, 16 February 1981.

[7]CN Rail Public Relations, Edmonton, 18 January 1988; *Edmonton Journal*, 20 April 1964.

[8]"Highlights in the History of the Northern Alberta Railways," 1980.

[9]Ena Schneider, "The Peanut Line," *Canadian Rail*, (May-June, 1987).

[10]R.V. Storms to author, November 1984.

[11]W.J. Donlevy interview, 30 October 1985.

[12]Sam Rouleau interview, 23 September 1985.

[13]J.O. Pitts interview, 10 August 1987.

[14]Sam Rouleau interview, 23 September 1985.

[15]E. Bachand interview, 22 July 1985.

[16]E. Bachand interview, 22 July 1985.

[17]J.G. MacGregor, *Paddle Wheels to Bucket Wheels on the Athabasca* (Toronto: McClelland & Stewart, 1974), p.178.

[18]Gordon Waite, "Reminiscences," 15 September 1985, p.35.

[19]W. Johnson interview, 26 June 1987, Grande Prairie, Alberta.

[20]W.W. McNalley interview, 2 June 1987.

[21]G.A. Smith interview, 25 May 1988.

Notes for Chapter 24

[1]CN Rail Public Relations, Edmonton, 18 January 1988.

[2]John Munro, Canada's Minister of Labor, to

K.R. Perry, 22 January 1973.

[3]"The GM's Corner," *The Headlight*, (June, 1972), p. 2.

[4]C.J. Irwin, NAR's solicitor, to Canadian Transport Committee, 26 February 1969.

[5]C.J. Irwin, to Canadian Transport Committee, 26 February 1969.

[6]A.J. Dove interview, 8 July 1987.

[7]J.G. Rouse interview, 23 July 1985.

[8]A.J. Dove interview, 8 July 1987.

[9]A.J. Dove interview, 8 July 1987.

[10]"New Stores Building Open," *The Headlight*, December 1971.

[11]J.A. King, telephone interview , 28 February 1988, Winfield, B.C.

[12]"Rails North," *The Headlight*, March 1972, p. 1.

[13]"Headquarters To Move To Dunvegan Yards," *The Headlight*, March 1972, p. 1.

[14]"Track Hanging After Washout," *Edmonton Journal*, 17 June 1972.

[15]"The Smoky Does It Again," *The Headlight*, September 1972.

[16]"Santa Special," *The Headlight*, March 1973, p. 1.

[17]"From Dream To Reality," *The Headlight*, March 1973, p. 1.

[18]G.A. Smith interview, 25 May 1988.

Notes for Chapter 25

[1]Robert E. McRory, *Energy Heritage – Oil Sands and Heavy Oils of Alberta* (Edmonton: Alberta Energy and Natural Resources, 1982), p. 42.

[2]"Now Very Prominent in Fort McMurray," *The Headlight*, October 1974, p. 1.

[3]"The G.M.'s Corner," *The Headlight*, October 1974.

[4]"Bill Donlevy Can't Stay Away," *The Headlight*, October 1974, p. 4.

[5]Larry Pratt, *The Tar Sands* (Edmonton: Hurtig Publishers, 1976), pp. 149-178.

[6]J.S. Walsh, telephone interview, 4 March 1988.

[7]J.S. Walsh, telephone interview, 4 March 1988.

[8]Carl Whiteman interview, 21 November 1984.

[9]Gerald Whiteman interview, 19 August 1985.

[10]Gerald Whiteman interview, 19 August 1985.

[11]*Building and Working Together – a Study of the Thorhild Area* (Winnipeg: Intercollegiate Press), p. 30.

[12]"Donna Porada Named D.C. Telegraph Agent," *The Headlight*, November 1973, p. 1.

[13]"Vandalism," *The Headlight*, April 1975, p. 1.

[14]Gordon Waite, "Even Boxcars are Doing it," *The Headlight*, (May, 1974), p. 1.

[15]"Engineman Clark, Trainman Gauvreau Find Some . . ." *The Headlight*, May, 1974, p. 4. -" *The Headlight*, May 1974, p. 4.

[16]"The 207 Rebuilt and Back in Service," *The Headlight*, January 1975, p. 1.

[17]"The G.M.'s Corner," *The Headlight*, February 1976.

[18]J.H. Laurie interview, 20 July 1987.

Notes for Chapter 26

[1]N. Dziwenka telephone interview, 28 February 1988, Lac La Biche, Alberta.

[2]J.O. Pitts interview, 10 August 1987.

[3]N. Dziwenka interview, 28 February 1988.

[4]"Three Derailments in 24 Hours," *The*

Headlight, June 1977.

[5]"Barrhead is 50 Years Old," *The Headlight,* September 1977, p. 1.

[6]"The G.M.'s Corner," *The Headlight,* April 1978. p. 2.

[7]D.N. Tinston interview, 10 August 1987.

[8]J.O. Pitts interview, 10 August 1987.

[9]D.N. Tinston interview, 10 August 1987.

[10]"G.M.'s Corner," *The Headlight,* July 1978.

[11]J.O. Pitts interview, 10 August 1987.

[12]"MBS System Successful," *The Headlight,* October 1978, p. 1.

[13]Norm Corness, "A Valiant Effort to Help McLennan," *The Marker,* September 1979.

[14]Engine 73 was rescued from the scrap heap at Premier Steel, Edmonton, a division of Stelco Canada, by the Rocky Mountain Division of the Canadian Railroad Historical Association. The Alberta Pioneer Railway Association was formed shortly afterwards and the locomotive is maintained at their museum near Namao, Alberta.

[15]A.J. Dove interview, 8 July 1987.

[16]J.S. Walsh interview, 22 June 1987.

[17]J.O. Pitts, notes, August 1988.

Notes for Chapter 27

[1]Editorial, "Farewell NAR," *The Retired Rail-vets News,* (Winter, 1980-81).

[2]J.O. Pitts to all NAR employees, 26 June 1980.

[3]"NAR Joins The Fold," *Alberta Report,* 11 July 1980, pp. 16-17.

[4]"NAR Relocates In ARR Yard," *The Headlight,* July 1980, p. 1.

[5]J.O. Pitts interview, 10 August 1987.

[6]K.R. Perry to C.J. Irwin, 5 October 1976.

[7]Bill Palmer, "The North Beckons," *CN Rail*

Movin, 13,1 (January/February, 1981): pp. 9-12.

Index

About The Author

Ena Schneider, who was born in Wicklow, Republic of Ireland, lived in Africa and Australia and travelled through New Zealand, Indonesia, Malaysia and Thailand before immigrating to Canada in 1971. She worked for the Northern Alberta Railways for ten years as executive secretary and editorial assistant on the in-house staff newspaper, and is now archivist technician with the Edmonton Public Schools Archives-Museum. Ena is a member of the Historical Society of Alberta, the Writer's Guild of Alberta, the Canadian Railway Historical Association, the Alberta Museums Association and the Alberta Society of Archivists.

The idea for this book was the "brainchild" of Maurice Mahood and Clarence Comrie, both of whom worked for the Edmonton, Dunvegan and British Columbia Railway and its successor, the Northern Alberta Railways, for 45 years. Maurice began compiling and drafting a manuscript from research and interviews conducted by Clarence and Ena. Unfortunately, he passed away when the early chapters were still in the embryo stage.

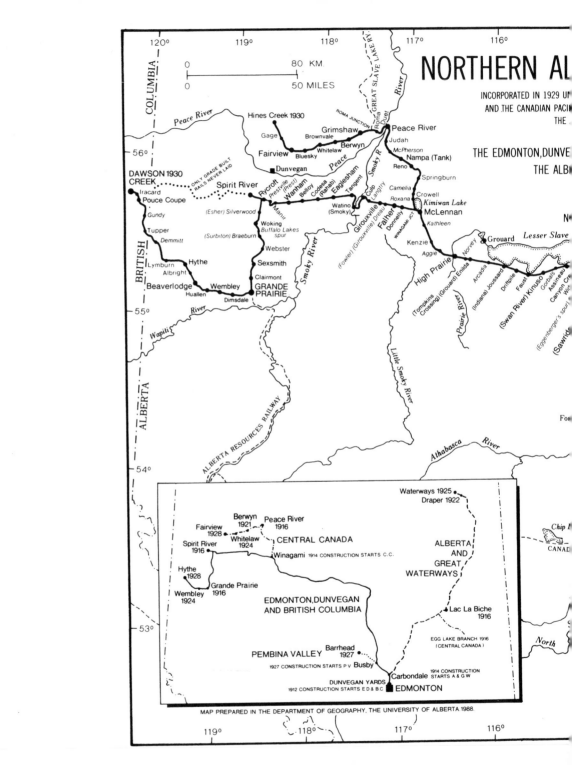

NORTHERN AL

INCORPORATED IN 1929 U
AND THE CANADIAN PACI
THE

THE EDMONTON, DUNVE

THE ALB

N

MAP PREPARED IN THE DEPARTMENT OF GEOGRAPHY, THE UNIVERSITY OF ALBERTA. 1988.